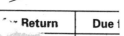

CW00538625

The Humours of
PLANXTY

Leagues O'Toole is a Dublin-born journalist and broadcaster. Graduating from the world of fanzine publishing, he became a well-known music writer and champion of leftfield artists. For three years, he presented and researched the *No Disco* music programme for RTÉ television, focusing on independent and innovative music and video production. As part of that series, he made a critically acclaimed documentary about Planxty. He is currently the editor of the *Foggy Notions* music magazine and regularly presents and produces programmes for Today FM. *The Humours of Planxty* is his first book.

The Humours of
PLANXTY

Leagues O'Toole

HODDER
HEADLINE
IRELAND

Copyright © 2006 Leagues O'Toole
Copyright © Discography, 2006 Kieran Kelly

First published in 2006 by Hodder Headline Ireland

1

The right of Leagues O'Toole to be identified as the Author of the Work has
been asserted by him in accordance with the Copyright,
Designs and Patents Act, 1988.

Every reasonable effort has been made to contact copyright holders. If
any images used in this book have been reproduced without permission we
would like to rectify this in future editions and encourage owners of copyright
not acknowledged to contact us.

A CIP catalogue record for this title is available from the British Library.

ISBN 978 0340 83797 9

Typeset in SabonMT by Hodder Headline Ireland
Cover design by Anú Design, Tara
Printed and bound in Great Britain by Clays Ltd, St Ives plc

Hodder Headline Ireland's policy is to use papers that are natural, renewable
and recyclable products and made from wood grown in sustainable forests.
The logging and manufacturing processes are expected to conform to the
environmental regulations of the country of origin.

Hodder Headline Ireland
8 Castlecourt Centre, Castleknock, Dublin 15
Ireland

A division of Hodder Headline, 338 Euston Road, London NW1 3BH,
England

Contents

To Laurence and Patricia O'Toole –
without whom there would be nothing

Introduction

The story of Planxty is an ongoing saga. It is far from clear-cut where the story of the band actually begins, and less obvious still where and when it will end. When Christy, Andy, Liam and Dónal formed the band in 1972, they were already seasoned and respected musicians whose individual careers had spawned albums and tours, myths and legends, fiascos and triumphs. Even at the embryonic stage of Planxty's formation, they had volumes of history behind them. Yet nothing they had experienced touched the pinnacle of musical achievement that would follow in the wake of Planxty.

Each individual journey that led to the formation of Planxty is integral to the almost-instant impact they had on the music world in 1972. From the very start, Christy Moore was undoubtedly the most well-known of the four members. Through years of hard work on the British folk circuit, he commanded great respect, carried a snowballing repertoire of songs and developed a uniquely tender singing voice.

Dónal Lunny had also accumulated a wealth of experience, enjoying fleeting fame with a dashing folk-pop trio called Emmet Spiceland, as well as years performing with ensembles on the

Dublin folk scene and a period of creative development at the National College of Art & Design in Dublin.

Liam O'Flynn had already evolved as a musician through a rites of passage relationship with that most demanding of traditional Irish instruments, the uilleann pipes. Subsequent to his tutoring, O'Flynn's musical knowledge was further enriched with all the other wonderful facets of traditional culture – the folklore, the lineage, the principal characters and the influence of the music in everyday life. He talks at length in this book about the importance of having complete respect for the material and traditional culture at large.

Equally colourful was the early career of London-born Andy Irvine. The child actor turned Woody-Guthrie-socialist-folk enthusiast was one of the young maverick figures of the burgeoning 1960s folk scene in Dublin. His band, Sweeney's Men, expanded the parameters of Irish music, blazing a trail and paving the way for the future explorations of Planxty.

When these four musicians did finally come together, the collective repertoire sizzled with originality and imagination. There are various occasions, outlined throughout this book, when the four core members of Planxty encountered each other and each other's music prior to the formation of the band. For Christy and Dónal, the relationship runs as far back as schooldays in Newbridge, County Kildare. Years later, they witnessed Liam O'Flynn playing his pipes in youthful reverie at the seminal sessions at Dowling's pub in Prosperous, County Kildare. And throughout the colourful folk circuits of the 1960s, the name Andy Irvine was becoming increasingly well known. A mutual respect was fast growing between each of the four future band-mates. At the risk of suggesting some 'mystical' forces were at play, it seems almost preordained that these four individuals would be somehow magnetised to each other.

But the timeline of events charting the band's journey from 1972 to the present day is fractured. Six studio albums are divided into two periods of activity, which begin at the start and the end of the 1970s respectively. The first period is defined by an exhila-rating momentum – a sense of innovation, youthful energy, a feeling of change, movement, with exciting cultural ramifi-cations. But with that comes all the trappings of a great rock 'n' roll story: the excess, the business calamities, the gruelling schedules and the personality clashes. Planxty (mark one) began to come apart in 1974, but it was restored four years later as a vehicle for more complex, decorative and perhaps exotic-sounding music. This second period was less intensive. Recordings and tours were more sporadic and the band under-went continual line-up changes until it practically drifted to an end in 1983. The band remained dormant for twenty-three years.

At times, their story reads like a manual of what *not* to do in the music industry. In many ways, it paints the classic picture of musicians so concerned with artistic achievement that they completely neglect their own business interests. It is no secret that this naïveté is a hallmark both of the era in question and of the nature of folk music and the people who make it and, through a thorny series of events, most of Planxty's back catalogue ended up in the control of other people. Yet to the ears of their audience, an audience that is expanding to this day, the music itself will always remain the sole domain of Planxty.

From the word go, Planxty never stuck to the rules. Unlike many other bands, being in Planxty did not mean an end to the members' individual musical journeys, or their collaborations with other musicians and groups. And, beyond the nucleus of the four core members, there is a busy periphery of secondary players. The impact of a long line of notable musicians who contributed to the Planxty canon is considerable: Johnny

Moynihan, Paul Brady, Matt Molloy and Bill Whelan, to name but a few.

Yet, at the end of the day, it is testament to their indisputable musical empathy that the four original members of Moore, Lunny, Irvine and O'Flynn have returned to each other time and again. It wasn't just a deep musical understanding that these men shared. Regardless of whatever crises and disasters the band has endured, an almost heroic sense of humour prevails. That humour came to fruition during the giddy ebullience of that first year in 1972 – a period Christy Moore describes as 'the zaniest year of my life'. And anyone who has had the pleasure of attending recent concerts will testify that the wit has certainly not left them. Indeed, Planxty concerts are renowned for momentary lapses into hilarity, before the next wave of music takes flight.

The concerts further emphasise the importance of understanding the roots and sources of the compositions they play. The songs and tunes are often preceded with in-depth introductions; whether it's something mined from the P.W. Joyce collection, or learned from the singing of John Reilly, a tune composed by the great, blind harper Turlough O'Carolan, or learned from the playing of Willie Clancy. The whole experience is thoroughly educational. Even in times of both scorn and acceptance at the hands of the traditional community, Planxty has remained true to this ideal.

However, it would probably be incorrect to class Planxty specifically as a 'traditional' group. It was obvious from the beginning that many of the younger members of the Planxty audience were hearing traditional music in a whole new context. For starters, the configuration of string instruments, such as bouzouki, mandolin and guitar, with traditional instruments, such as uilleann pipes, tin whistle and bodhrán, created a whole new sound. Furthermore, the combination of slow airs, dance tunes and folk songs offered exciting diversity. And the sheer gusto of the performances gave the music a whole new dynamic. Folk, traditional, experimental, hippie or world music, whatever you want to call it, it's probably best described simply as Planxty music.

The story of Planxty reveals a band of many humours, both musically and personally. In these pages, band members recall times of buoyancy and fervour, darker periods of inner conflict and bad behaviour, strange experiences and incidents of surreal back-of-the-van comedy. But, regardless of any sentiments of regret or resentment expressed, each individual's story is dominated by fond memories and artistic fulfilment.

As well as piecing together this frequently hazy history of events, these pages also document the glorious re-emergence of Planxty in recent years – 'The Third Coming', as it were. As events transpired, Planxty didn't simply return to greet old friends. Yes, there were moments of poignant nostalgia, but there was also a fresh generation of listeners waiting in anticipation. It has become exciting all over again. The future remains open and the saga continues…

Leagues O'Toole
July 2006

Prologue

Saturday, 11 October 2003. A sepia-coloured poster is tacked to the door of the Royal Spa Hotel in Lisdoonvarna, County Clare. The event is billed as 'The Mugs Gig' and lists the names of four musicians underneath.

For the outside world, it is like any other sunny but chilly Saturday evening on the west coast of Ireland but, for the two hundred of us tucked inside this small room, it's a night where many of our dreams come true. By 8 p.m., we are all ready: young and old, bearded and clean-shaven, first-timers and veterans. All eyes are on the stage and there isn't a murmur. The bar is closed and, for once, no one cares. The Mugs Gig – the name taken from the club Andy Irvine and Dónal Lunny ran in Slattery's Pub on Capel Street in Dublin in the early 1970s – is now in session.

The four musicians take their seats onstage before us to a deafening ovation, a clutter of bodhráns, bouzoukis, mandolins and guitars piled around their feet. These gentlemen accumulate well over two hundred years of experience between them, yet it's not weariness they carry on their faces tonight. If anything, they seem as excited and nervous about the significance of this event as we do. To say that the sense of occasion is palpable would be an understatement.

Lined up, as they always have been, from stage left to right: Dónal Lunny, Andy Irvine, Liam Óg O'Flynn and Christy Moore. Collectively we have known, loved and mythologised them as Planxty, the band that trailblazed the great revival of the 1970s and burned open a portal to the future for traditional and folk music.

Tonight, we fall in love all over again as they cascade through over two hours of songs and tunes: from the bright-eyed idealism of the 1960s, from the unstoppable cultural convergences of the 1970s, from as far back as famine days and further still, mining ancient compendiums of words and music and enlivening them with this amazing four-pronged personality.

It's been some twenty-three years since they last played together in this original line-up and it is reassuring to know that all the scraps, mishaps and hedonism endured through years on the road together – not to mention the music industry bloodsuckers they encountered along the way – haven't drained their enthusiasm for the music or dampened the magic of their chemistry.

County Clare is the idyllic scene for this happening. Apart from being one of Ireland's foremost mainstays of traditional music, it is a county where the members of Planxty have individually experienced musical epiphanies that would change the course of their lives.

Tonight, Andy will sing about summers spent further down the coast in Miltown Malbay 'worshipping at the feet of Willie Clancy' with his pals in Sweeney's Men, and gazing love-struck into the Atlantic Ocean at Spanish Point. Not far down the road is the traditional mecca of Doolin, once the bohemian playground of George Bernard Shaw and J.M. Synge, a place of music and dance and poetry. Doolin was where Paddy Doherty, the congenial owner of the Royal Spa Hotel, staged the world-famous Lisdoonvarna Festival in the late 1970s, an event where Planxty played several memorable sets.

Just below us is the town of Kilfenora and further inland is the town of Tulla, the homes of Ireland's first céilí bands, where a young Christy Moore held down a position in the bank by day and joined in sessions with the greats by night. Clare is also the home of Liam O'Flynn's late mother, and included amongst his clan is the wonderful Clare fiddler Junior Crehan, from whom he learned many fine tunes. These days, the heir apparent plays his tunes on Willie Clancy's pipes, a good indication of the standing he has earned as Ireland's most acclaimed piper.

Tonight is not purely a reunion, but rather a continuum, by their own definition. They've been described as The Beatles of traditional Irish music many times, and, indeed, there is something equally timeless about this music.

Planxty first exploded onto the Irish music scene in 1972, when headline acts shivered at the prospect of following them on stage, when Irish teenagers roared for encores and reacted wildly to traditional music like they never had before, when even staunch traditionalists had to hold their hands up and concede that here was something special.

It all seamlessly slides back into place tonight. The telepathic bouzouki-mandolin melodies of Lunny and Irvine weave in and out of each other like the threads of a Le Brocquy tapestry. Andy's voice is preciously fragile, pouring pathos into songs like 'As I Roved Out' and his own 'The West Coast of Clare' in a way no one else ever could. Christy's voice is pure soft-focus soul. He sings the epic 'Little Musgrave' and entrances the room for eleven minutes without falter. Liam Óg beside him duly comments, 'I think that's what you call a man on form.'

O'Flynn himself is what you might call a 'next-level' musician. His uilleann pipe solo piece was always a regular feature of the Planxty gig. Tonight, he chooses one of the most venerated and complex compositions from the traditional canon, 'The Foxhunt'. His three colleagues watch on in wonder as he takes us through each stage, vividly portraying the chase, the wails of the prey, the celebration of the hunt party and the closing lament for the fox. It leaves us breathless.

But it's when all four virtuosos are in full flow together that Planxty really displays the electricity of their union. 'The Raggle Taggle Gypsy', learned from the singing of Traveller John Reilly, is truly staggering. This is one of their live centrepieces from the 1970s, which segues into the seventeenth-century air 'Tabhair Dom Do Lámh'. When they make the bridge from the song to the tune, there's a roar of recognition from the audience. It's a beautiful moment. In fact, it's one of *the* moments in Irish music.

Between the songs and the reels and jigs there is, of course, another great dimension to the Planxty performance. The banter is shared out amongst all four members. Although Christy is recognised as the comic of the band, there's a collective wit at play. Tonight Dónal comes across as the joker in the pack, following up moments of hilarity with more one-liners, to the point of almost being unable to start up the next song, such is the uncontrollable laughter on stage. Equally enjoyable are the stories of the songs, portrayals of the singers, the situations they heard them in, the fables of the ancient tunes, and how they have tumbled through history, juggled from the lap of one generation to another. The Planxty experience is as educational as it is visceral.

They play a set of jigs near the end, Dónal strumming like there's no tomorrow, Christy pounding the bodhrán. 'Tear the arse out of it!' he cries from one end of the stage to the other.

They finish it off with 'Three Drunken Maidens', their debut release on manager Des Kelly's Ruby Records back in 1972. It was a hit back then and it's a hit tonight, loose and wild and raucous. We clap and cheer till our hands are sore and our throats are hoarse.

After the show, we're left to sit and reflect on what we've just witnessed. 'It was great for us for the first hour and then it fell apart,' says Christy, always the self-critic. 'The wheels came off halfway through,' agrees Dónal. Nonetheless, it was enough of a success to give them the thirst for more. Tonight, Planxty was officially resumed. There would be more high times to come, but there is also a story to tell: an adventure involving four men possessed with music and the characters and the experiences, the friends and foes that fuelled the journey.

For now in the Royal Spa, the bar is open again and little pockets of music are blossoming up from different corners. 'This guy has an amazing collection of tunes,' says Dónal, making his way over to a box player holding court in one corner. In this part of the world, the music never stops.

Chapter 1

The Rakes of Kildare

Across the black peat-wrapped Bog of Allen, past the flora and fauna of Ballinafagh and Pollardstown Fen, to the verdant plains of The Curragh over which the finest horses hurtle, the county of Kildare is a profusely lush spread of Ireland. It is the birthplace of both Christy Moore and Liam Óg O'Flynn, the home county of Dónal Lunny from the age of five, and the place where these three wide-eyed teenagers, in the throes of musical awakening, encountered each other for the first time. The 'thoroughbred county' has a special connection to the story of Planxty.

Christy Moore was born in 1945 in Newbridge, a former garrison town slap bang in the middle of the county, where his family lived in an ex-British army officer's house on Moorfield Terrace. Christy's father, Andy, who passed away when Christy was eleven years old, was well respected in the area, a one-time soldier, politician and grocer. In between school hours, Christy spent much of his time working in his father's shop. His mother Nancy (maiden name Power, hailing from Armulcan, Navan) was a prominent figure in Navan music circles before she moved to Kildare and she carried her love of music and singing to her children.

Christy was the oldest of six children, and both his sister, Eilish, and brother, Barry (Luka Bloom), are avid singers like his mother. 'My mother was always playing the piano and singing pop songs and Percy French-style songs. I remember her singing 'Seán Ó'Duibhir a' Ghleanna', 'The Foggy Dew', 'Kevin Barry', 'The Garden Where the Praties Grow' and 'The Mountains of Mourne',' recalls Christy, delving into his earliest memories. 'She used to stage little concerts in the house. We'd appear from behind the curtain and sing these songs. So I kind of grew up where performing was a normal thing to do.'

Christy's childhood activities weren't much different from most energetic Irish teenagers of the day. He played GAA football, took piano lessons, sang solo in the choir, served as an altar boy and joined the FCA. 'I started doing piano lessons when I was about seven or eight, but that never engaged me even though I did the exams. I used to learn the things off by heart and let on I was kind of sight-reading them. I could never actually read music properly. I studied the piano for a good number of years with different people, with a nun called Sister Michael, with a woman called Marie Slowey, and a man called Dr Josef Cuypers in Newbridge College. I think I went up to about grade seven or eight on the piano. But I was always more interested in busking, jamming on the piano, early rock 'n' roll, Jerry Lee Lewis and Elvis Presley.'

Similar to Christy, it was the pop airwaves that bewitched Dónal Lunny from a young age, rather than anything from the traditional canon. He was born into a large family in Tullamore,

County Offaly, in 1947 and lived there until the age of five. 'It left me with a nice little pocket of memories from Tullamore, which didn't get confused with the rest of my childhood, which I sort of like,' he reflects. 'My dad was with Bord na Móna. Before that, he'd been with the ESB and various others. He was an engineer. When he took up with Bord na Móna, he commuted for a brief while, but it just made sense to move to Newbridge where he was based workwise. It was a huge change for us all, but it was fine.'

Dónal describes an idyllic childhood immersed in the joys of the outdoors, roaming the fertile farmland around Newbridge. 'We lived on the very outskirts of town and I spent a lot of time trespassing on farmers' property out in the fields. It was wonderful.' His father, Frank, came from Enniskillen and his mother, Mary Rogers, came from Rannafast in the Donegal Gaeltacht, and together they raised four boys and five girls. There was a history of music in his family too, though it wasn't always obvious to Dónal just how prominent that was.

'For years, I would say, "Well there wasn't much music around." I was blind to it. It's like the things you grow up with that you don't see. My mother used to sing songs. My father used to sing as well. In his youth, he was part of a "barbershop quartet" kind of a thing – they actually sang on radio yonks ago. My mother, being from Rannafast in Donegal, her language was Irish. I always said she thought in Irish and she'd sort of translate it into English. And if she got emotional about anything, out would come the Irish. So our first language was Irish, it was what we all spoke in the house until we started school. By that stage, we'd absorbed English anyway. So there was kind of a connection there with Irish music because the songs my mother knew were all songs in Irish from Donegal. My father had met my mother in Rannafast, where he was learning Irish at the time. He was living in Enniskillen at the summer colleges. He became really good at the language and he was very much interested in Irish music. Our family would go to Donegal on holidays. We'd spend anything up to two months in Rannafast. I was absolutely fluent in Irish at that time, at the age of twelve.'

Dónal remembers an Estonian woman, Mrs Hangelaid, who lived down the road from them in Newbridge and taught five of the Lunny children to play piano. 'I was five years old at the time and I was the youngest being taught and naturally the one who tested her patience the most because I had the concentration span of a fly. Even though I can remember the pieces she taught *still*, and I understood the music very well at the time, I wanted to be outside playing. It became terrible. Because of my restlessness, it began to feed back and she would lose her patience. It all started losing its charm for me and eventually I cried off, I begged to be allowed stop.

'It was a pity in one way because I think I would have progressed if I'd actually managed to take off. I didn't get back to playing piano until I was about twelve or thirteen. My sisters Eveleen and Máire had pursued piano in school and they were well up on the grades. I used to really like some of the pieces they played and I learned them by ear just hanging around and listening. Because I could pick it up by ear, I used to kind of tease them!'

Despite Dónal's lack of concentration, his aptitude for music, art and language was developing at a young age, almost prodigiously so. He was lucky in that he had a series of positive influential role models in his young school life that literally steered him on the right track. 'When I was at Newbridge College secondary school I was doing very badly. It was partly because of Irish. I was very good at Irish so I didn't have to work at it. I was good at English because I had started reading aged two and a half or something, before we had left Tullamore.

I read avidly. I was also good at art. They were three things I didn't have to work at, so my other subjects suffered. I was actually doing nothing. It was a bit disastrous, the three years that I spent at Newbridge College.' In his third year there, Fr Flanagan, who Dónal remembers as 'a great man altogether, a wonderful artist and a musician,' came around the classes doing auditions for a choral recital. The college used to put on a Gilbert and Sullivan operetta every year and, in this particular year, they decided to do a choral recital and Fr Flanagan was presiding over it. 'I had been kept back for a year, for good reason,' recalls Dónal with guilty laughter. 'I wasn't fit to go on. So Fr Flanagan auditioned lots of people and discovered that I was very musical. He was brilliant. He just brought me on. He encouraged me wonderfully. It was too late in terms of my disaster in college, but it was a ray of sunshine and hope for me. It restored my morale.'

Dónal left Newbridge College in the summer of 1963 and joined the Patrician Brothers' school for the Intermediate Certificate year and so his educational rehabilitation began. 'It was like getting out of prison. It was fantastic what happened. They rescued me, put me back together. There were some great teachers there. There was the late Brother Sylvarius, who was the head of the Patrician Brothers in Ballyfin for some time. And Brother Maurice, who taught science and English, a wonderful teacher. I'm eternally grateful to them both for more or less saving me. You know, various religious orders have gots lots of bad press in recent times, but I have to say, my time with the Patrician Brothers was mostly very happy. There were a few cowboys in the primary school who seemed to enjoy inflicting pain, but there was no trace of anything like that in secondary. These were good people, very fair-minded. That was something that really affected me.'

The lure of the music was never far from Dónal's mind, however. He recalls a class mate, Joey O'Shea, who owned an electric guitar. 'Joey decided to form a band from people in our class. Everybody knew everybody and it was "Let's start a band!" There was wild excitement. The pop scene wasn't as cut and dried as it is now. There was "trad" jazz and "mainstream" jazz and all these things got into the charts during the early 1960s, you know. And indeed the things that caught my ears most were jazz things, because I didn't understand them; they were full of mystery and I loved it.

'There were fellas in the class who were going to get a trombone or a clarinet or a trumpet. And there were loads of people who wanted to get guitars. Eventually, when the dust settled, Joey was the lead guitarist, and then we had Andy Moroney on rhythm guitar, Mick Casey on electric bass and me on drums. I bought a second-hand kit of drums, which later I realised was a sort of céilí band set of drums, and they were in bits. The front skin was torn on the bass drum and there was a puncture in the skin underneath the snare and there was a cymbal with a crack in it. I think I had a tom as well. But it did fine. We actually performed a few times. We called ourselves The Cyclones, although I think there was a famous band called The Cyclones around that time.

'I drifted onto the guitar. I was trying to learn it, but I was left-handed and I knew I was at a disadvantage on a right-handed guitar. So I was trying to play it on my lap, and trying to play it the other side around, eventually it occurred to me to reverse the strings. I'd never heard of a left-handed guitar. This was a revelation to me. After I did that, I learned very quickly. I discovered the chords for myself. It was a lovely time, a time of discovery.'

In the late 1950s, a new musical whirlwind swept across Ireland. The Clancy Brothers from Carrick-on-Suir featured brothers Tom, Paddy and Liam Clancy, along with their friend,

Tommy Makem from Keady, County Armagh. They initially travelled to New York to pursue acting careers, but music took prominence and they became pivotal features of the Greenwich Village folk scene and favourites of a young troubadour called Bob Dylan. They sang boisterous Irish folk songs, which became singalong anthems. Their white woollen sweaters, sailor caps and hearty beards ensured their status as recognisable icons.

'That was a revolution,' recalls Dónal. 'A whole new world opened up for people around the country. People went wild about it. Suddenly, there were ballad sessions being held everywhere. You'd get very little music in the same night – you'd get a night of singing. The bands were carbon copies of The Clancy Brothers, dressed in bainín sweaters and singing all the Clancy Brothers' songs. I took up with a band called The Liffeysiders in Newbridge, who were led by a guy called Seán Reilly. We played a lot of Clancy Brothers' songs and other stuff and there were a few tunes in there as well. We had a great time.'

It was at this point in his life that young Dónal Lunny befriended another devout Clancy Brothers fan and make the first solid connection amongst the future Planxty players. 'I had met Christy for the first time in primary school. Each year had two classes. There were two fifth classes. He was in one and I was in the other and we didn't really meet very much. I hardly knew him before this time. The two classes converged when I was about ten years old, and became one big class with about seventy of us under the formidable Brother Lazarian. He was very tough and he ruled with an iron fist but, then again, imagine having seventy ten- and eleven-year-olds to deal with! When he left the room, there'd be uproar, the place would turn into a complete frenzy. Someone would be at the door. "He's comin', he's comin', he's comin'," and everybody would dive back behind their desks. Demented stuff. That was when I met Christy first.

We were both in the same class for one year. Then we both went to Newbridge College the same year, but Christy was in a different class so I hardly saw him for several years.'

As soon as he was old enough, Christy began making trips to England during his summer holidays. He made his first trip in 1961, aged sixteen, and worked for ten weeks before returning to Newbridge College.

Dónal's elder brother, Frank, also has vivid memories of school days in Newbridge. 'There was a guy who I had no love for at all. He was what you called "The Biffer", the guy who would punish people. Your name would be put on a list and it was his job to cane you. Outside this guy's room there might be thirty or forty fellas queuing up to get their hands slapped. I remember one day, it might have been fifth or sixth year at the time, and I heard this tremendous racket, roaring and shouting. It turns out all of the contents of Christy's desk had been thrown up into the air by Fr Flanagan and there were comics flying everywhere – *Billy the Kid Rides Again* and all this sort of stuff. Flanagan lost it. Christy had seemingly been studying the Wild West!'

'I would've been aware of Dónal because we didn't live very far away from each other and I would've been aware of the Lunny family,' recalls Christy. 'I would've known him as just another fella at school until the music thing started. Then I was kind of drawn towards him. My memory of it was that I was into The Clancy Brothers and heard that this other guy, Dónal Lunny, was also into The Clancy Brothers and that he had a guitar and could actually play Clancy Brothers tunes.'

'There was a good bond between our families,' confirms Dónal. 'It was the Lunnys and the Moores, you know. Several of us would go over to their house and spend the evening there and have the craic together. Christy got a guitar, and

I had a head start on him. He used to come around to me and go through chords and stuff like that.'

Christy and Dónal's mutual exploration of music continued on after their schooling and teenage years as they gradually began to take their respective talents more seriously.

'The Rakes of Kildare was an occasional trio with myself, Dónal and his brother Frank,' remembers Christy. 'We even did a few gigs. There was one night in the Town Hall in Newbridge, the annual Fianna Fáil dance. We did a guest spot at that. I remember B.P. Fallon was the compere, because B.P. was a bit of a television star in the black and white. I think our fee was three quid and a crate of stout and we came off and the fuckin' crate of stout was all gone. The repertoire would've included songs like 'Follow Me Up to Carlow' and 'The Curragh of Kildare'.'

'Christy started delving into books around this time,' explains Dónal. 'Some of them were current at the time, like Colm O'Loughlin's *Irish Street Ballads* – there's some great songs in that. And old books from libraries like *The Joyce Collection*, because you'd have songs, sometimes with only the words, sometimes with the words *and* the music. Christy dug up all sorts of things. I remember we worked out 'The Curragh of Kildare' and he put the chorus into it. Christy made a refrain out of it and that's how it became popular as well.'

'The Rakes of Kildare were probably formed in our sitting room in Athgarvan Road in Newbridge sometime in 1966,' recalls Frank Lunny. 'I played tin whistle. Mostly, we played in pub sessions. I think we only had two proper gigs together. The first one was booked for Easter Monday in 1966 in Hugh Neeson's pub in Newbridge. This was the fifty-year celebration of the Easter Rising. We went along, The Proclamation was read, and we played. What I knew was pretty basic. I would've sung a few songs. I knew a couple of jigs, and any amount of slow airs and maybe a couple of reels. That was it, and we had a good afternoon. Because it was the fifty-year celebration, the patrons of Neeson's had been saving for six months beforehand in a club. I think they put in two and sixpence each a week so they wouldn't be digging into their pockets on Easter Monday after the weekend. Anything up to a hundred people had contributed, so the booze was free. All our birthdays had come at once! After we played, they passed around the hat and it was filled with two-shilling pieces and half-crowns. At about seven o'clock, we went out to the backyard and Christy threw the money on the ground and divided it out. I think we had eight or nine pounds each. It was more money than I ever had! I always remember being very disappointed that day though because Christy had to go back to work in the bank. He was very responsible. I wanted to go on drinking all night, which I did, without him. I can't really remember the rest of the day.

'The repertoire was really Christy's,' continues Frank. 'One of my favourite songs was 'The Limerick Rake'. It used to knock me out when Christy sang that. He used to do lullabies, standard songs learned from his mother. There was also 'The Cliffs of Dooneen' and 'Spancill Hill', they were his, and a couple of well-known ballads, republican stuff. A lot of the songs were sung in schools at the time, but he actually transformed them and put his own stamp on them. Most kids sang these songs in national school and they would be forgotten, but he didn't forget them. He sung them. He gave them a whole new dimension with the guitar.'

Compared to the great ensembles that Christy Moore and Dónal Lunny would go on to contribute to, from Planxty to The Bothy Band to Moving Hearts, The Rakes of Kildare is an obscure yet formative footnote to the story. It was very much a time of discovery, young men exploring the intricate properties of the acoustic guitar and dipping into the deep well of clandestine words and music of the great Irish songbooks. 'I suppose The

Rakes of Kildare was only a blip in the whole story,' explains Dónal. 'It didn't last long and we did very little, but at the same time it was at a very intense moment so it was important in its way. I certainly didn't have ambitions to perform, although we did perform on occasions. It was purely for the fun of it.'

'It would've been at a time when I was starting to take the whole thing quite seriously,' explains Christy. 'I was starting to discover songs, songs that weren't known, songs that weren't in the national repertoire as I knew it. There was great kudos attached to turning up with a song that nobody had heard before. Everybody would be saying, "Where'd you fuckin' get that?" I can remember showing up with songs like 'Mary from Dungloe', 'The Rambler from Clare', 'The Enniskillen Dragoon' and the buzz off that was inspiring. It inspired me to go on and look farther afield. I suppose that's when it was all starting to come together. And you began to dream, "Jaysus, wouldn't it be great to be able to do that all the time?"'

That dream was just around the corner. There was a piper from the nearby town of Kill and a beatnik troubadour from London, both going through a similar process of musical discovery. If The Rakes of Kildare was the tentative, embryonic vehicle for Dónal and Christy's first forays into repertoire and accompaniment, then the sessions held at Dowling's pub and Downings house in Prosperous were something more akin to the thick of the action. Prosperous is a small town that stands above the damp peat of the Bog of Allen. It was christened in a long-passed era of industrial optimism, but it was a buzzing hotbed of musical activity in the 1960s.

Since Irish musicians first revelled in the concept of playing music in public houses in England in the 1940s, the session has been an intrinsic element of the culture. It eventually caught on in Ireland in the 1960s through the petitions of musicians returning home from years abroad. Christy Moore and Dónal Lunny had the privilege to be immersed in one of the most vibrant pub sessions in Ireland, courtesy of the magnanimous patronage of the late and much-loved landlord, Pat Dowling, who kept accordions, bodhráns, banjos and flutes all on standby in case a musician popped in and felt like joining in the session.

'Some of the other people in The Liffeysiders used to go out to Prosperous where there was a weekly or even twice-weekly session in Pat Dowling's pub,' remembers Dónal. 'We'd all pile into Mick Curran's van and we'd spend the night out there and just play music for hours and hours. It'd be traditional music and just the odd song, so it was the other way around to the ballad sessions. It was a great stomping ground for me because I was playing guitar and I was the only one. That left me at a great advantage as I could try anything I wanted, and probably no one noticed anyway. I could just hack away along with the players.

'I learned hundreds of tunes at that time. I also started picking up the bodhrán. Sometimes the bodhrán was just lovely with the music because, if it was a bit slack, the sort of fundamental note of the bodhrán might be in tune with the music. I noticed this very early on and then I started applying pressure to the skin to get it in tune with the music. So I've taken that on now, playing it in a way that – I don't know if it gets on people's nerves or not, to play it like a bass, you know, moving with the music. I think it has a nice quality. And it doesn't take up half as much room as a proper bass!'

'Dónal had great musicality,' claims Frank Lunny proudly. 'I was musically dyslexic. He'd pick up a mouth organ and could play it in five minutes. He was on another plane and was having a great time. They used to play in Derby House, a hotel in Kildare. It was there one night that the Rynnes – Andy and Davoc – came over. Andy played tin whistle, Davoc played flute.

It was these guys who said, "Look, why don't you come back to Prosperous?" And that's how that happened. I think next week or the week after, we were over in Prosperous. The real traditional influence came from that direction.'

'Ned Farrell played bodhrán and sometimes assumed the Master of Ceremonies role and would call upon people to sing songs or play tunes,' recalls Dónal. 'It was very nice, lovely. It was highly civilised. And Pat Dowling himself was such a hospitable man, such a generous man. He was fantastic. He used to have a raffle at Christmas and anyone who bought a ticket got a prize. You know the seventy-fifth prize was like a hamper with a bottle of whiskey and a bottle of brandy. He looked after everybody. He was absolutely brilliant. I never knew anybody like him.'

Davoc Rynne came from a renowned Prosperous family of music enthusiasts and was another key figure in the music sessions. He would keep the music going into the early hours by bringing the session from Dowling's down the road and into the basement kitchen of his wonderful Georgian family house, Downings. Davoc was very much immersed in the traditional sphere of Irish music. He was involved in Comhaltas Ceoltóirí Éireann, an institution founded in the early 1950s to preserve and promote traditional Irish music and dancing, to encourage the practice of the Irish language and to co-operate with all bodies dedicated to the restoration of the Irish culture at large. Comhaltas branches were established all over the country and abroad, with the purpose of forging bonds between communities involved in attaining these goals.

'Around 1965, myself and Nan McCormack started a branch of Comhaltas in Prosperous,' explains Davoc. 'Meetings were held in the local school and then adjourned to Pat Dowling's pub, where the real music began. Musicians such as Frank Burke, Ned Farrell, Micky and Mary Maguire, Gerry Mahony, Micky

Carroll and Mick Crehan all took part regularly. These sessions were casual and progressed into a weekly Wednesday night session, all of this with huge support and encouragement from the great Pat Dowling. They were fairly lively sessions with up to half a dozen musicians playing and local singers and characters giving their all. Pat always sent out huge trays of thick sandwiches with lots of ham and Branston pickle and mugs of tea. He was a most generous man. He'd sometimes give out freebies – Wellingtons, overalls, pens, and so on. He also drove musicians to fleadh cheoils all over the country.'

After hours, Davoc recalls that they would all retire to the basement in Downings with large bottles and play all night. 'The first sessions in Downings started with Ciaran Bourke [The Dubliners] *circa* 1961. He came to work as a tradesman on a job we had in Downings for a period of a couple of months. He spent a lot of his spare time sourcing musicians and singers in the area. He'd sit in and have a drink with them and exchange tunes. Whoever was playing in Pat Dowling's was always invited back to the house, people like Ted Furey, Johnny Moynihan, Barney McKenna, The Grehan Sisters, Peggy Jordan and her daughter Mary.'

Downings was built in 1802; the original building had been burned down by rebels of the 1798 Rising during an event known as The Battle of Prosperous. Davoc's brother Andrew, who currently owns the house, describes scenes of late-night craic and music in his biography, *The Vasectomy Doctor*.

The basement had a stone-flagged floor, which lent the room fantastic natural acoustics and resonance. The uilleann piping of, say, Liam Óg O'Flynn or the mandolin playing of Francy Grehan were all greatly enhanced by this feature. Heat of a winter's night was provided for by

way of an enormous open fire onto which old furniture
was usually thrown – benches or old chests of drawers or
anything that came to hand. Davoc was in the antique
business at this stage, so burning furniture was not quite
as bizarre as [it] may first appear. And in any case it was
always good for a laugh. There was a pair of hob-nailed
boots kept on a shelf. If anyone was in the mood for it
they could put these on and batter to the music. At times
the whole place took on a surreal quality, an out-of-world
aura to it.

Dónal Lunny chuckles at these memories of the Downings sessions. 'We had great nights there, sometimes twice a week, which went on at the weekend until five in the morning. On a few occasions, perfectly good sugan chairs went into the fire. It was brilliant. There was a great sense of freedom and abandon about the sessions there.'

Davoc, who would marry Christy's sister Anne in 1968 ('Christy led the gorgeous bride up the aisle!'), has vivid memories of the Moore and Lunny clans in those heady days. 'The Lunnys and the Moores came regularly on Wednesday nights. Every member of these outstanding families would participate – including parents. Remember, these were "noble call" sessions and no one got away without performing! The Moores' and Lunnys' contribution to the basement-party era, for craic, music and yarns, can never be overstated. They were absolutely fabulous. From old Frank Lunny singing 'The Flower of Sweet Strabane' to Nancy Moore singing 'The Four Green Fields'. What was wonderful for the times that were in it was the way all the old folk came as well and all performed. And that was across the board, like the recently deceased Mick Crehan playing the whistle and his old landlady playing the spoons!

'My first impression of Christy had been at a fleadh cheoil in Boyle,' continues Davoc. 'He had just come back from a trip to England. I had gone to the fleadh with Mick Curran and Christy walked into Grehan's and they all knew him. I asked, "Who's he?" The first song I heard him sing was 'Whiskey in the Jar'. He had a very strong voice and I was very impressed by him and wondered why I hadn't heard him before. Mick put me right telling me, "He's one of our own." Dónal was a young, dedicated guitarist – too young for me to pal around with. I was very impressed with his musical ability, but not so much for the instrument because I was a bit of a "purist" in those days. Ridiculous Comhaltas rules!'

Since the first fleadh cheoil was staged in Mullingar in 1951, the whole concept of traditional musicians from all over the country (and indeed the world) descending on one town for a weekend of music competitions, dancing, drinking, parades, pageants and general craic had blossomed with massive popularity. For some, the fleadh cheoil was a serious competitive event, with honour and reputations at stake. For others, it was purely a social event. Either way, it was a real celebration of music.

'The Dowling's sessions provided an opportunity to play and that was what drew me most,' explains Dónal. 'But there was the social aspect of it as well. We'd go off to the fleadhs together after that. I think I went to my first fleadh around 1965. It was in Boyle over a rainy Easter weekend. It was bitter cold and we were camped in a railway carriage, unbeknownst to the authorities, which was quite cool. There was no vandalism or anything. It was brilliant. Three days and nights we spent playing music. I'd go home and my head would be ringing with tunes for the next week. It would be like bells ringing in your head.'

In *The Vasectomy Doctor*, Andrew Rynne relives the magic of trips around the country without a care in the world, but he also relives the pitfalls of this free 'n' easy life.

> *Another hazard about going to a Fleadh was the weather. We never brought sleeping bags or tents or anything like that with us. We didn't own such luxuries in the first place and, in any case, we didn't see any need for them. 'Accommodation' at a Fleadh was the first hay barn you could find outside the town. You had to scout for these in the daylight and before you got too drunk. In theory, the whole thing sounds lovely, romantic even – sleeping snuggled up in the sweet new-mown hay and the farmer's wife bringing you out a cup of tea in the morning and the cuckoo calling in the background. The reality, of course, was something totally different.*
>
> *In a hay barn just outside Clones, it is pissing rain outside and it is 8.30 in the morning. Most of us are nursing moderate to severe hangovers and are having a bit of a lie-in. Christy Moore, Frank and Dónal Lunny, Peter Sheehy, Mick Bulfin and a whole lot more of us are holed up in this shed. The next thing and all of a sudden don't we hear this madman of a farmer and he's ranting and raving down on the floor under us. Then he grabs up a hayfork and starts lunging at the haystack to see if he can dislodge a few bodies. 'Get to fuck out of my hay barn,' he roars. I never saw a group of fellows leave a hay barn so quickly in all my life, rain or no rain.*

'Fleadhs were a very different story in those days because there wasn't the same infrastructure in place in Ireland,' explains Dónal. 'A fleadh would be held in a small town and 30,000 people would descend on the town for the weekend. Within four hours, there'd be no toilet paper, no bread, no milk! It just all started running out. There was a time when the drink ran out, in Thurles I think. It was either that or the publicans decided to shut their doors when the pubs were full, rather than allow them to get completely demented, which they used to be. They used to be madness. You'd kind of fight your way in the door and there'd be a session going on around the corner and you'd be barely able to hear it, let alone see it. That time in Thurles there was a bit of a riot and there was about 10,000 pint glasses broken on Main Street.'

The sessions in Dowling's pub and Downings house involved numerous young musicians flush with the joys of Irish music. 'Definitely the sessions at Prosperous were very important to me,' says Christy. 'I was interested in the songs, and the music was secondary. It was only later when I was in London that I began to appreciate Irish music. But the most significant aspect of those sessions was it was where I first heard Liam O'Flynn. And I was just blown away by what I heard, from the sound of the instrument. I didn't realise when I heard him that he was such a wonderful musician. It was only as time went on that I realised he was a macstro. He was the first piper I ever heard, and to this day, he remains the greatest.'

Chapter 2

The Piper from Kill

Séamus Ennis, one of Liam O'Flynn's primary piping mentors, once said that it took twenty-one years to become a piper – seven years learning, seven years practising and seven years playing. The great man wasn't exaggerating. Those who have travelled the long and arduous journey with the uilleann pipes will verify his claim. Coming to terms with the complex mechanics, the in-built accompaniment and multifarious layers of sound has proven quite a task for even the most dextrous of musicians. Unlike any other instrument in the traditional field, it is not immediately obvious how to hold this strange jumble of reeds, pipes, buttons and straps dangling from an inflatable bag. Yet the rewards for those who have overcome the intricate workings of the pipes are enormous. This is an instrument that bores deep into history, enlivening ancient sounds and images, jigs, reels, polkas and hornpipes for the dancing sets, and the most solemnly beautiful slow airs for the rapt romantics.

Liam Óg O'Flynn's own journey has seen him evolve from an eager ten-year-old tackling a set of practice pipes into a musician of international veneration. He has brought traditional music from the folk clubs to the concert halls, from sessions in Prosperous to nights at The Proms. His innovation with the music has afforded him collaborations with classical composers, symphony orchestras, rock stars, avant-garde figureheads and even poet laureates. He has now stepped into that great lineage of master preservers, a figure of sizeable cultural stature. But it was with the roguish assembly of beatnik folk musicians known and loved as Planxty that O'Flynn's prodigious repertoire of tunes reached an audience beyond the parameters of the traditional milieu.

Liam was exposed to the heart and soul of traditional culture from an early age. He was born in the town of Kill, County Kildare, in 1945 to Masie, his Clare mother, and Liam, his father from Kerry, both of whom he describes as immensely musical people. 'I see myself as related to the Clare tradition through my mother,' explains Liam. 'She was a first cousin of the great fiddler Junior Crehan. That family tie was very strong, not just on a musical level but on a friendship level, between my mother and Junior and his family. So, for me, it was about both the music and the people. I got drawn into the way of life. As children, Clare was one of the places we were brought to on holidays. My mother was from just outside Miltown Malbay. She played the piano and was a good singer. She was a hugely musical person. Myself and my brother and sister, Micheál and Maureen, were always encouraged to play, without any pressure being put on us.

'My father is still alive. He comes from County Kerry

originally, outside Tralee, with strong family connections in Dingle. So I also found myself visiting that part of the country an awful lot as a kid growing up. I consequently got to know not just Dingle, but places west of Dingle, and the traditions associated with those places. My father is a good fiddle player. And his father played the fiddle too. I remember that one year we entered the Oireachtas fiddle and pipes competition together and we won it, which was special.'

Liam's father's family moved to Naas, County Kildare, when he was young teenager. 'My grandfather was a travelling school-teacher, *timire taisteal*, as they were known – he must have been one of the first of them. He came up to Naas, I guess, by 1920.' Liam's father also became a national schoolteacher and made it his business to meet as many musicians as possible. He got to know people like Tommy Potts, the Dublin fiddler, and Sean Dempsey, the Kildare piper. There was a whole circle of musicians who met up for weekly sessions.

'My earliest memories are of sessions in the house with people like Junior Crehan's brother Vincey, who lived in Dublin and played tin whistle. He was a very good musician. And my mother's sister Josey also lived in Dublin and she was a terrific piano player. I remember gatherings and various friends calling in. I would be lying in bed at nine o'clock and the music would be going on below and my bedroom door would be left open. Soon after, I gradually made my way into the music physically, and was asked to do my little piece at these gatherings.'

No different to his as yet unacquainted young kindred spirits across the county, Liam was susceptible to the popular sounds of the radio. 'Like every other kid, I went through my pop music phase as well and I recall being in the sitting room on my own listening to Radio Luxembourg. I knew exactly what was going on in that world.' In spite of this, traditional music stole his allegiance.

He became an accomplished tin whistle player, and he admittedly 'scraped' away at the fiddle for a brief period. 'The tin whistle was my first instrument. I've a funny feeling I bought it at the Dingle Races. I think I was about six or seven years of age.'

It was the uilleann pipes, however, that became Liam's primary vehicle of expression. 'My father's first teaching job was in Newbridge, and my first contact with the pipes was through a friend of his, Tom Armstrong, who was a sergeant in the gardaí in Newbridge at the time. They used to meet up after school and, when my father was finished his day's work, they'd go down to the barracks and play in the big kitchen there for their own enjoyment. So a lifelong friendship grew up and, naturally, that family came to visit our house and we went to visit their house over the years.'

Liam was aged ten or eleven when he received his first set of practice pipes, made up of bellows, bag and chanter. A full set of uilleann pipes also includes drones and regulators for further accompaniment. To play the pipes, the musician must be seated, as the pipes are strapped around his or her waist and the bag part of the instrument is positioned under the left arm. Using a bellows, which is attached to the right elbow by a strap, air is pumped into the bag and subsequently through a wooden tube with a conical bore with seven holes at the front and one at the back. This is the chanter, the most important part of the instrument. The piper produces musical notes by covering and uncovering the holes on the chanter while applying pressure to the bag. The three drones lie across the piper's lap, offering a constant bed of accompaniment to the melody of the chanter. Finally, the regulators are three pipes with fitted keys, which overlay the drones and provide simple chordal accompaniment. It's a lot for a young novice to take in the complexity of the instrument and has frightened off many aspiring pipers.

Though some, such as Liam O'Flynn, embraced the endless possibilities of this labyrinthine instrument.

The great Johnny Doran, who died in 1950, was one such itinerant piper of renown. Although he wasn't aware of it at the time, Liam O'Flynn was directly exposed to Doran's whirlwind piping at a young age. 'I have no memory of it because I was a baby, but, apparently, Johnny Doran called to the house where I was born and reared in Kill. He had called to Tom Armstrong in Newbridge. Tom said to him, "When you're travelling on to Dublin, call into this man in Kill, he's a fiddle player." So he did. I was in the cradle when Doran came in and played a few tunes. One of the tunes, my father tells me, was a popular reel at the time, 'The Sligo Maid'. It's certainly nice to know that Doran passed through.'

Liam O'Flynn has drawn inspiration from all facets of the tradition and all manner of musicians that have gone before him, but there are three monoliths of uilleann piping that are most associated with his development as a piper: Leo Rowsome, Willie Clancy and Séamus Ennis. Leo Rowsome was a Dublin-born piper from a family well known in the Wexford piping tradition. His grandfather, Samuel Rowsome, a prominent farmer of Ballintore Ferns, County Wexford, was a highly respected player, as were his three sons, Thomas, John and Leo's father, William. Tapping into the family tradition, young Leo excelled in feis cheoil competitions in the early 1920s. He went on to become not just a great player, but also a tutor, broadcaster and a highly regarded pipe-maker.

'Leo Rowsome was, I believe, the greatest maker of uilleann pipes during the twentieth century,' states Liam confidently. 'And you could argue that maybe he was the greatest of all time. He came from a family of uilleann pipers, generations of them, so he was like the embodiment of the uilleann pipes.

History of the Uilleann Pipes

Through the ages the uilleann pipes have flourished in all walks of Irish life. The word 'uilleann' comes from the Irish word *uille*, meaning elbow, and clearly distinguishes the fact that the pipes are elbow-driven as opposed to the many varieties of mouth-blown bagpipes. Prior to that, they were known as 'union' pipes, in reference to the union of sound between the chanter, drones and regulators. Further back in history, we can trace the origins of the uilleann pipes back to the *Chuisleannach* pipes of mediaeval times and the ancient Irish war pipes or *Piob Mór*, which were similar to the Highland bagpipes of Scotland. The uilleann pipes were first heard in the late seventeenth century, and came to prominence, it is believed, in the eighteenth century – although the concert-pitch incarnation of the instrument that we hear today was developed in the late nineteenth century in Philadelphia by the Taylor brothers, who were originally from Drogheda.

The uilleann pipes have had a presence in practically all tiers of Irish society. Travelling or 'itinerant' pipers toured the country and beyond, performing at local fairs, and luring onlookers with their wild and exhilarating styles. 'It was a flamboyant style of playing,' explains Liam. 'I suppose partly because they played in outdoor situations like fairs and country gatherings and they had to attract attention.'

Uilleann piping was also popular in the farming communities with players such as Leo Rowsome's grandfather, Samuel, and the hugely influential blind piper Garrett Barry of Inagh, County Clare, who suffered permanent loss of sight from malnutrition and famine sickness, yet still managed to support himself through music. Many noted Anglo-Irish aristocrats also expressed a love for the instrument. The Big Houses of the early nineteenth century employed pipers, and numerous men of station have been accomplished players throughout Irish history. Noted 'gentlemen pipers' include

Lord Edward Fitzgerald, the fifth son of the Duke of Leinster, the celebrated eighteenth-century composer Walter 'Piper' Jackson, 'Sporting' Captain William Kelly of the Curragh of Kildare, and Lord Rossmore, who owned some 15,000 acres in County Monaghan. Indeed, there is something perhaps noble, and definitely illustrious about the sound of the uilleann pipes. One theory suggests that the idea of pumping air into the bag rather than blowing directly into the pipes was to maintain the dignity of the gentleman piper who wanted to avoid puffing out his face. One thing's for sure, these instruments were extravagantly crafted, made with silver, ivory and rare and exotic wood, all of which augmented their refinement and no doubt appealed to those doyens of wealth.

There were many musicians among the emigrating masses who left Ireland during the Great Famine seeking a new life in America. Subsequently, Irish music flourished in certain parts of the US. One such hotbed was Chicago, where police captain Francis O'Neill, originally from Tralibane, County Cork, employed immigrant Irish musicians on the force. The general superintendent sought out the finest players and offered them the security of a respectable job as well as adequate leisure time to continue their musical activities. Captain O'Neill collected and published eight books of some 3,500 traditional Irish tunes and historical references. Many of these books have been reprinted and remain in circulation as the bedrock of reference for traditional musicians the world over.

In traditional terms, O'Neill is a heroic figure, compiling and disseminating vast amounts of music at a time when it teetered on the brink of extinction. In Ireland, Irish music was being muffled and suppressed by the combined forces of imperialism and piety. In 1936, the State and clergy ensured the banning of house dances under the Dance Hall Act. This act of dire cultural impediment resulted in many of Ireland's best musicians emigrating to England and the United States. The mellifluous sound of music was dampened until the emergence of Comhaltas Ceoltóirí Éireann some years later.

He was completely in love with the instrument. My father was Leo's friend, so when I showed an interest in playing the pipes he went to Leo and asked would he make a practice set for me as a Christmas present. Following on from that, my father set up lessons for me with Leo. He taught in what was then the School of Music on Chatham Row, off Grafton Street, which is now the College of Music. Looking back on it, it's wonderful that traditional music was taught in what was a classical music institution at the time.'

The young apprentice piper spent many years evolving under Leo Rowsome's tutorage. He began aged eleven and continued until he was fifteen, and for about two more years from the age of seventeen. From Liam's accounts of this time, Rowsome was the perfect tutor. It was by fortuitous coincidence, or maybe the result of good old-fashioned destiny, that Liam should receive an opportunity like this, and it is something he has never taken for granted. 'I was really, really fortunate in that respect because my first teacher was a wonderful uilleann piper; he was a very good teacher and, of course, he was an absolute expert uilleann pipe-maker. He was an expert reed-maker as well. And, for an instrument as complex as this, that was a wonderful start because if things went wrong with the instrument, Leo Rowsome was there to fix them. It was no problem.'

Liam acknowledges that, like any instrument, it's difficult enough to learn to play the pipes. 'On top of that, you're faced with all sorts of problems to do with reeds and tuning and all sorts of things. I think that puts off a lot of young people from learning the instrument. It's the sort of instrument you need to have a special intuitive feel for and to be really dedicated to. It's not the sort of instrument you can walk away from for a couple of months and come back to and expect everything to be grand. It just doesn't work that way. And because I was so madly interested in music and particularly in the pipes, Leo cottoned on to that immediately ... and he just *gave* in every sense of the word. He really looked after me.'

The uilleann piping tradition has always been largely about the relationship of master and apprentice. The act of passing down the knowledge from one generation to the next relates to the very essence of oral tradition itself. 'Even though it was a teacher-pupil relationship, there was nothing formal about it, unlike having my piano lessons. This was almost more like a father-son relationship. I was so excited to have him as my teacher, and he was so excited to have a young lad who showed promise, as they say, and who was obviously keen. When I was sent off with my couple of tunes after a lesson I came back the next time and I really knew them because I wanted to show off these new tunes and play them well for Leo.

'Lessons took place on a Friday between six and seven in the evening. Frequently, Leo would be recording radio broadcasts, in which case he'd have a full set of pipes instead of the usual practice set. It was just a huge high for me to play with Leo, with him playing the full set of pipes. I absolutely loved going to those lessons. And I have to give huge thanks to my parents for that. Without my father driving me in and out of Dublin, that would never have happened.'

When other young 1960s kids were dreaming of rock 'n' roll and fumbling through elementary guitar chords, young Liam O'Flynn was wide-eyed with fascination for the pipes. All his spare time was spent practising and mastering whatever new tunes occupied his mind. 'At this time, my father was the local schoolmaster in Kill. Very often after school was finished, I'd get the keys of the school and get my bag and chanter and go into one of the classrooms and just sit and play there on my own. The sound was so amplified in the classroom I got a great sense of performance. I'd try and perfect each tune that I played. No one ever suggested that I should do that, but it's just something I was naturally drawn to do.'

One can't help but wonder why this ornate, if potentially perplexing, instrument that demands ambidextrous skill and tremendous powers of concentration would bewitch a young boy of Liam's age. 'I *desperately* wanted to play the pipes. You know, why is a fiddle player drawn to the fiddle? Or why is a singer drawn to sing? You just know within yourself that you have that talent and that you're drawn to a particular instrument. I'm instinctively drawn towards wind instruments, I suppose, even though I had been learning piano when I was about five or six and I did the piano exams and I did very well apparently, but I just didn't have the natural capability or whatever it is at the piano that I did have on the tin whistle and the pipes.'

When not practising or taking lessons, Liam was entering competitions at Oireachtas and fleadh cheoil events. He got an early taste of exposure thanks to the support of broadcaster Ciarán MacMathúna, whose Radio Éireann programmes *Ceolta Tíre* and *A Job of Journeywork* documented musical happenings around the country, featuring everyone from elder legends to ardent young apprentices. 'I remember Gareth Browne, the man who started Claddagh Records, was mad for the uilleann pipes and he was with Ciarán MacMathúna at a fleadh cheoil. I was probably eleven or twelve years of age and I was playing in this room. Gareth came in and then ran out and called Ciarán, saying, "Listen to this! Listen to this!" So Ciarán recorded me and that was the first time I was on the radio. That was a milestone. I remember listening to the radio the following Sunday and hearing myself introduced by Ciarán and being so excited. It was the start of a wonderful friendship, which continues still. You couldn't estimate what he's done for the tradition. When I think he was one who introduced all of us musicians to each other on his programmes. The lovely thing about him was he had no agenda about anything. He wasn't trying to push his idea about who was the best fiddle player or the best singer or whatever. They were all part of the tradition. He didn't use the programme to try and turn himself into a star.'

Relations in County Clare led Liam to the attention of the second great piper in his triumvirate of mentors, Willie Clancy. Clancy was not just a Clare piping legend, his influence has spread around the globe as a true icon of traditional Irish culture. His presence in Liam's life goes further back than even Liam himself can clearly remember. 'He was there from going way back to those childhood visits to Clare. I'm sure I must've met him – I must've been in the same room as him or heard him playing somewhere. I can't remember when I finally actually met Willie Clancy and struck up a rapport. It would've been in the mid-1960s, once I got my own transport and I would head off down to Clare for a weekend.

'He wasn't just a great musician, there was a lovely, lovely man behind the music. He was a very gentle and thoughtful person. He had an awareness of the value of his music and the tradition and just a great sense of respect and sensitivity – all bound up in enjoyment I must add – towards his tradition. He was a man with a real roguish sense of humour, and that all came out in the playing as well. People had great warmth towards him. I don't think I ever heard anyone say anything derogatory about him, and I've known an awful lot of people who knew him very well and not so well. It's always been positive things people have said.'

Willie Clancy wasn't just in love with the uilleann pipes as an instrument, he was completely captivated by the whole culture: the music, the dancing, the folklore and the language. In an interview for the *Dál gCais* magazine (which documents the

Willie Clancy

Willie Clancy was born in Miltown Malbay on Christmas Eve, 1918. As a young boy, he was enthralled by the stories his father, Gilbert, a concertina and flute player himself, told him of the great Garrett Barry. Clancy didn't begin playing the uilleann pipes until he was twenty. His first teacher was Johnny Doran, the piper who is said to have had the greatest influence over him.

Clancy became a great ambassador of the pipes, taking his music to London, Brittany, Warsaw – all over the world. Many of those close to him have commented that he was even more accomplished on the tin whistle and the flute than he was on the pipes. He recorded many broadcasts for RTÉ, but it is reckoned that he was never entirely comfortable with publicity. A master carpenter by trade, he later settled in Miltown Malbay with his wife, Doreen, to concentrate on the art of pipe- and reed-making. He died in January 1973 at the young age of fifty-four.

traditional culture of County Clare), he said, 'The Irish language is the greatest music of all.'

Every year, nearly a thousand students from all over the world attend the Willie Clancy Summer School in Miltown Malbay, where they are engaged in the full gamut of traditional culture practices. The rich programme of activities includes old-style step and traditional dance classes, seminars and lectures on traditional song and folklore, master classes in instruments such as pipes, accordion, concertina, whistle, flute and fiddle from some of the greatest living players and, of course, plenty of rip-roaring céilithe. Mere weeks after his death in January 1973, plans were in motion to set up the Willie Clancy Foundation and the summer school and two of Willie's closest friends and peers,

Junior Crehan and Martin Talty, were integral in its formation. By July, Scoil Samhraidh Willie Clancy was up and running. The school would both serve to preserve the memory of one of Clare's greatest sons and cultivate the music, lore and dancing that so enraptured him. Today, this priceless institution continues to flourish and there isn't a more apt guiding spirit for the young enthusiasts who attend the summer school, Miltown Malbay.

Liam O'Flynn was among the throng of great musicians from several generations who stood by the graveside and mourned the loss of this huge personality upon his untimely death in 1973. 'It was a wet day,' remembers Liam. 'It added to the sense of loss. I got to know the man pretty well, but like so many situations like that there was a strong sense of wishing I'd spent more time with him or that he was going to be around for longer. He was one of these people that you didn't just get tunes from, it was so much more about really what the tradition is all about, the essence of that old way of life.

'He was a very philosophical sort of man in his own way. He was all the time interested in finding out more and more background and meeting more people involved. One of the most memorable times I ever spent with him was in Friel's pub in Miltown Malbay. There was nothing in particular going on at the time, I just happened to be down visiting. I met Willie in the street and we went up to Friel's during the afternoon. There was this old woman there who was around ninety something years of age. Willie was absolutely delighted to meet her because he hadn't seen her for years. It was fascinating to sit there and listen to Willie Clancy and Masie Friel talking to this old lady. They were completely fascinated. She had memories going way back about people and places that they knew. It's part of the business of the absorption of not just musical notes, but that kind of experience. It's such an important part of becoming a traditional musician. It's not just what you hear on tape or off a record, you have to meet those people. But there's very few of them left now.'

By the age of seventeen, Liam had generated enough confidence and earned enough recognition to sit in on sessions with elder musicians. Like Dónal Lunny and Christy Moore, he benefited from the vibrant sessions scattered around the town of Prosperous in Pat Dowling's pub and the legendary basement sessions in Downings house. 'The elder Rynnes, the people of the house – Stephen Rynne and his wife, the well-known writer Alice Curtayne, and their children Davoc, Andrew, Bríd and Catherine – all had a terrific interest in Irish music,' explains Liam. 'They played music and they were big into the ballad boom of the time. I remember being invited to sessions, which took place in the basement of their house.' Davoc and his wife Anne (also a sister of Christy Moore), the householders of Downings at the time, both retain vivid memories of the impressive young piper. 'Liam Óg would have started to play in Pat Dowling's early on and would sometimes come down to the basement afterwards. He was a serious student of the pipes at the time rather than a craic musician,' recalls Davoc. Anne Rynne first saw Liam in 1958. 'He was playing at some event in the Grand Hotel in Newbridge. He was wearing short pants, which I thought were hilarious, and it was the first time I ever saw uilleann pipes.'

Like everyone else who encountered Pat Dowling, Liam acknowledges the landlord's generosity and spirit. 'Pat Dowling was a great friend of the music and the people who were into it. Pat himself didn't play anything but he loved people coming into the pub and playing. He was very kind to people as well, not just musicians, but people in the community. Those sessions were hugely enjoyable. It was the first time I'd been introduced to traditional music being accompanied in the Dónal Lunny manner, if you like. I'd been well used to the standard piano accompaniment in traditional music, but this was a different thing and I was absolutely fascinated with it. It was so musical.'

Dowling's of Prosperous was also integral to Liam's development for another very significant reason. It was the setting for his formal introduction to his third great piping influence, the late Séamus Ennis. Undoubtedly another giant of Irish music culture, Ennis was a piper, folklorist, archivist, broadcaster and raconteur.

'It was in Prosperous when I was introduced to him face-to-face. It was one of the Wednesday evening sessions in Dowling's. We heard a couple of days before that Séamus Ennis was coming down and I made sure I was in Dowling's that night. I was really looking forward to it and very much in awe. I'd come across him before, but had never met him properly. It was a wonderful meeting because he was well aware of who I was, that I was "up and coming" as it where. So he was fascinated to hear me play as well – I remember his first words: "You're very good, but you've an awful lot to learn and I'll teach you as much as I can." He put me in my place, but he also told me that he'd teach me all he knew. And I took him up on it.'

Indeed he did. Liam's time with Ennis offered further enlightenment, particularly the older piper's incredible marriage of styles and uniquely innovative touches. 'He would rearrange the odd note in a tune and just transform the tune. He evolved a new style of piping in a way. There are two extreme approaches to piping,' explains Liam. 'One is what they call a "close" style of piping, very staccato. It's an instrument that lends itself to staccato playing. And there's a more open style or legato style of playing. Ennis would've leaned towards the "close" style, but he wasn't bound down. Depending on the tune he was playing, and so on, he would mix the two extremes. As he said himself, his style was a synthesis of the styles of the old pipers.'

Séamus Ennis was born in Jamestown, north County Dublin, in 1919 and reared to the sound of his father James Ennis's piping. As a young man, he became a truly skilled player in his own right. When Colm Ó Lochlainn, editor of *Irish Street Ballads* and a friend of the Ennis family, heard of Séamus' intention to move to England to join the British army, he offered the young piper a position at Three Candles Press. Here Séamus mastered all aspects of the publishing business, including writing out slow airs for printed scores, a skill that would prove crucial to his future work.

Séamus was later recommended to Professor Séamus O'Duilearge of the Irish Folklore Commission, for whom he collected nearly 2,000 songs and dance tunes from various regions, including Connemara, the Aran Islands, Mayo, Donegal, west Cork and Kerry. In the Western Isles of Scotland, Ennis collected the Scots-Gaelic songs of John Lorne Campbell of Canna. He had an uncanny instinct for unearthing great music and performers, and the fact that he was able to communicate with people of different areas in a variety of dialects garnered him great respect and response from those whom he visited and documented.

He began work in Radio Éireann in August 1947 as an Outside Broadcast Officer and earned himself a reputation as a presenter of authority with the programmes *Music Stand* and *Folk Songs from the West* as he introduced great singers and musicians, such as Micho Russell, Martin Talty, Bobby Casey and Willie Clancy, as well as introducing music of different regional styles to a wider audience. Ennis also famously assisted the great American folk and field-recording archivist Alan Lomax with the Irish collection in his *World Library of Folk and*

Primitive Music series in 1951. In his diary, Lomax described his new colleague as 'lanky, pucked-faced, tall Séamus Ennis, the best pipe-player in Ireland'. In 1951, Ennis joined the BBC in London, where he worked as one of the presenters of the pioneering and massively popular folk music radio programme *As I Roved Out* with Brian George and, again, with Lomax. The programme provided an essential digest of the surviving folk cultures of Ireland, England, Wales and Scotland. For thousands of British listeners, it was their first taste of Irish music.

'He was this incredible musician,' says Liam O'Flynn, 'but most incredible musicians like that don't tend to go into the background of things in any sort of academic or structured way, like making radio programmes and collecting music. Ennis combined the two. Apparently, he has the largest single collection made by anyone in the Irish Folklore Commission. He did all that during the 1940s and 1950s. Because he was such a wonderful musician in his own right, when he went into places to collect music, he had the respect and the confidence of those people so they gave him their best stuff. That was very important.'

It's been a rocky road for the uilleann pipes, often replaced by the cheaper and more accessible instruments such as the concertina and melodeon. 'From the 1930s to the 1950s, the instrument almost became extinct, but it was thanks to figureheads such as Ennis, Clancy and Rowsome that it somehow stayed alive. In 1968, the uilleann pipers formed their own organisation, Na Píobairí Uilleann (the Society of Irish, Uilleann, or Union Pipers), which was very important to its survival. 'It was the brainchild of Breandán Breathnach [the great collector, piper, publisher and writer, 1912–1985],' explains Liam. 'He felt that, in order to preserve the instrument, there should be an organi-sation that would be run by uilleann pipers rather than the whole thing

be run by a larger organisation, such as Comhaltas Ceoltóirí
Éireann, for example, that would have other agendas. If you've
one organisation formed and run solely by uilleann pipers, it's
very straightforward, you've no agenda. I think he was absolutely
right. It was the best thing for the preservation of the instrument
and the music and the styles of playing.'

In 1958, Ennis returned home to work for the newly
established television station, Radio Telefís Éireann. With his
trusty and treasured set of pipes made by Morris Coyne of
Thomas Street, Dublin (*c*.1830), originally purchased by his
father, Jimmy, in a second-hand shop in London, Séamus Ennis
continued to make recordings and perform solo concerts and
with piping ensembles. Back on the roads of Ireland, he had now
upgraded his trusty pushbike to the legendary Ford Zephyr car
as he continued his collecting and vital documentation of Irish
music. In 1968, he attended the first meeting of Na Píobairí
Uilleann in Bettystown, County Meath.

That evening is the stuff of legend as pipers young and old
communed to inaugurate this new entity. Séamus Ennis sat back
as his younger colleagues displayed their talents, and, after a
couple of hours, he prepared his famous 130-year-old Coyne
pipes, reportedly testing the patience of onlookers as he spent
some twenty minutes tuning the drones. Of course, once he was
up and running, he soon had Ireland's finest assemblage of pipers
mesmerised by his unique flair. He finished his set with 'The
Bucks of Oranmore' and, in an unusual gesture, passed the pipes
to a surprised and reluctant Willie Clancy. After a couple of
tunes, Clancy attempted to pass the pipes back to Ennis but was
instructed to pass them on to Liam O'Flynn, their esteemed pupil
of the next generation.

'I remember being handed the pipes to play and being
absolutely gobsmacked,' admits Liam. 'I also knew the pipes

were extremely difficult to blow because the bellows weren't completely airtight. I used to watch Séamus playing them and the physical effort involved. It was a major business to just keep air in the thing. I remember Clancy's remark: "Séamus," he says, "the bellows, they wouldn't hold hay!"'

Séamus would later leave the Coyne pipes to Liam in his will. Liam's relationship with Séamus was another example of passing on the tradition from one generation to the next, sustaining it as a living organism. 'Séamus was so willing to part with all the information he had, whether it was tunes or techniques or whatever. There's that desire to pass it on. The notion of picking somebody who they feel is the right person in the sense that they're able to play well and they also have the appreciation and the interest.'

Séamus Ennis and Liam O'Flynn would go on to play music together, and even share a home together. In fact, the older piper's incomparable wisdom and support would prove invaluable until his death in 1982. Meanwhile, the Prosperous sessions continued into the 1970s. Liam O'Flynn was unaware of it during those early visits, but he would later return to the basement of Downings house to record a ground-breaking album with the musicians that would become Planxty.

Chapter 3

The Child Actor

The path of fascinating adventures and twists of fate that led Andy Irvine to great musical heights with Planxty can be traced back to his early childhood in London when, as a 'sensitive' young three-and-a-half-year-old, he was packed off to boarding school. 'I lived most of my early life in boarding schools. Nobody ever explained why to me, and I was always very tearful at the end of summer holidays,' reflects Andy.

'But the trauma of my early years in boarding school has made me very self-sufficient and I'm grateful for that at least.' This early experience provided Andy with the confidence to embark on a truly remarkable life that would see him tread the boards with theatre legends, plunge himself into the bohemian hinterland of the Irish folk world, hitch-hike his way around Eastern Europe and go on to perform all over the world with a long line of inspiring artists.

Andrew Kennedy Irvine was born in St John's Wood, north London, in 1942 to an Irish mother from Lisburn, County Antrim, and a Scottish father from Glasgow. Long before music took prominence in his life, he was conscripted into the family profession. 'My mother was an actress, as is my sister, and it always seemed to be in the runes that I would become an actor. My mother's name was Felice, and her stage name was Felice Lascelles. She was a musical-comedy actress and she had a great collection of 78s, songs from long-forgotten musical comedies that I listened to on a wind-up gramophone. She was wonderful. Regretfully, I didn't listen enough to all the stories she had when she was alive. She always had to be the centre of attention. As I always say about her, she may have given up the stage, but she never stopped acting! My father was a chartered accountant from Glasgow. He was a very withdrawn kind of a person, a closet saxophone player, but I never heard him play. He never spoke about his background and I had difficulty with him for most of my early life.'

During the summer holidays of 1950, Irvine received his first significant break as an actor at the tender age of nine. He landed a small yet key part in a film called *A Tale of Five Cities* starring Canadian actors Bonar Colleano and Barbara Kelly, and the glamorous Italian actress Gina Lollobrigida. 'Sadly, I never actually got to meet her because her scenes were filmed in Italy. But I somehow landed that role and it set me up to be an actor. At this point, I was good at my studies too and I was expecting to complete a good education but, when I was thirteen, I was offered a job in an ITV children's soap opera called *Round at the Redways*. There was a lot of debate about whether I should start my acting career at this point, or fulfil my educational studies. Eventually, it was decided that I would take the job, so I left the school that I was at, and started at this crappy school full of child actors where I learned nothing whatsoever, except maybe social interaction with the opposite sex, which I'd not had before and which frightened the shite out of me at first. But I quickly fell in love at the age of fourteen.'

Andy excelled on both stage and screen. He made his stage debut in the Grand Theatre in Wolverhampton, where his mother had made her farewell appearance. He received rave reviews for his performance in the TV drama *The Magpies*. Yet, despite his prodigious start in acting, music was gradually weaving its way further into his life. He started playing guitar at the age of thirteen, studying briefly under the renowned English classical guitarist Julian Bream, and later under one of Bream's pupils. 'Julian was the first person I ever heard close up playing a musical instrument, other than the piano. I was reduced to tears.'

In 1958, aged sixteen, he appeared in *Brouhaha* with Peter Sellers at the Aldwych Theatre in London's West End. 'He [Sellers] was a fascinating man,' remembers Andy. 'He was a little bit frightening because you couldn't tell what kind of humour he would be in. He seemed to suffer from depression. One of the stories I can remember is an actor came into our dressing room before the show one evening and said, "I just met Peter, he wants to see you." I thought, "My God, what's this?" So I went down and he said, "Oh, I got this guitar in a Spanish restaurant last night and I wonder what you think of it." So I played one of my classical pieces on it and he said, "That's very nice, it's yours with my compliments." So I had a guitar given to me by Peter Sellers. The show ran from August 1958 to March the following year. When we knew we were going to close, I decided I'd like to take a picture of Peter Sellers in his make-up in his dressing room, so I went in and asked him humbly whether I could. He was really into photography, and I had this cheap little camera. The flash didn't go off on the first attempt. Then it didn't go off on the second attempt. And finally it did on the third attempt. So there are three pictures, two of them pretty dark and one of them illuminated. The first black photograph is a big smile. In the second photograph his mouth is beginning to turn down. And by the time the flash went off his expression is like "For fuck's sake!'"

Around the same time, Andy had also acted in the feature film *Room at the Top* playing opposite the Oscar-nominated Lithuanian-born heart-throb Laurence Harvey. His mother insisted on arriving at the Leicester Square Odeon for the glitzy film première in a limousine, only to discover during the course of the screening that Andy's scene had been cut. They left by the back door and travelled home by bus. This blow, coupled with the oncoming hormonal changes of a young teenager, saw Andy's transition from the perfect child star to an altogether more awkward and self-conscious young thespian. Nonetheless, having sacrificed his education for acting, he felt duty-bound to pursue the profession. Once he left his 'awful' school at the age of sixteen, he became a full-time actor.

At this stage, Andy realised that his heart wasn't really in classical guitar and, along with most impressionable teenagers of the day, he became invigorated by the skiffle boom. The roots of the skiffle sound date as far back as the 1890s' American jug bands that played traditional jazz using jugs as rhythm instruments. Skiffle sketched a do-it-yourself blueprint that would be later mirrored by the late-1970s punk-rock movement. Washboards and tubs supplied the percussion, and home-made instruments were made out of tea chests, broom-handles and string with ukuleles and kazoos replacing guitars. Anyone could form a skiffle band, and almost everyone did. It became a peculiarly English phenomenon during the 1950s, a craze that would influence future stars such as The Beatles, Van Morrison,

The Shadows and The Rolling Stones, and subsequently become the precursor of the rock 'n' roll movement that exploded at the end of the decade.

Skiffle's big star was Lonnie Donegan, a Glasgow-born guitarist, who was highly literate in the American blues and who worked his way through a variety of Dixeland jazz outfits before breaking through with his own skiffle style and sending British teenagers into a frenzy with his infectious rhythms and rebellious demeanour. 'I'd become enraptured with the skiffle boom and two early Lonnie Donegan EPs in particular, *Backstairs Session* and *Skiffle Session*. When I heard skiffle, I gave up classical guitar, much to my father's horror. Two of my acting friends and I formed the A1 Skiffle Group. It wasn't till the name had been beautifully painted on the front of the Tea Chest Bass that someone read it as AI Skiffle Group – Andy Irvine Skiffle Group! It wasn't a great success.'

Skiffle was soon to be surpassed by a far greater inspiration in Andy's mind, though the clandestine clue came courtesy of Lonnie Donegan. 'On the back of one of the EPs, I found the name Woody Guthrie. I had never imagined anyone could be called Woody. I was determined to find out more about this mysterious man. I started by sending a letter to Mr Woody Guthrie, USA. After six weeks, it came back!'

Weeks later that same odd name would eerily reappear on the sleeve of an LP on display in the window of a record shop, *More Songs by Woody Guthrie and Cisco Houston*. 'Hearing Woody for the first time, yes, I remember that moment really well. I'd no idea who he was, whether he was famous or not, and I put this record on one of those automatic turntables – it sort of clicked – and I sat down and I waited and the very first da-da-da, the very first beat I thought, "Yes, this is it! Discovered it at last!" I had finally found my inspiration and mentor.'

Woody Guthrie

Woody Guthrie was the Oklahoma-born son of a cowboy who had travelled with the migrating Dust-Bowl refugees known as the 'Okies' in the mid-1930s. Penniless and hungry, Woody kept on the move and fell in love with the open road. His songs were influenced by alienation, social tension and political idealism. Numbers such as 'I Ain't Got No Home', 'Tom Joad' and 'Talking Dust Bowl Blues' became uplifting mantras for the working people, the unions and the socialist thinkers. He was also an acclaimed broadcaster, novelist and patron of leftist organisations. He served as a Marine and a soldier during the Second World War. His allies and collaborators included Leadbelly, Cisco Houston, Burl Ives, Pete Seeger, Derroll Adams and archivist Alan Lomax. Woody Guthrie was the great American protest singer: authentic, potent and prolific. He died in Creedmore State Hospital in Queens, New York, on 3 October 1967, aged fifty-five.

Andy Irvine's fascination with Woody Guthrie was all-encompassing. He wasn't just enthralled by the songs, the unbridled honesty of his voice and the earthy milieu of the American folk underbelly, he was equally motivated by the political ideas and sentiments that permeated almost everything Guthrie sang. His providence connected directly with Andy's own blooming ethos. Furthermore, the circle of folk singers, socialist icons and movements that rippled from the core of Guthrie's work were names that Andy would become diligently familiar with, even personally so in some instances.

One such luminary was Ramblin' Jack Elliot, a true legend of the road who had travelled as Guthrie's protégé in the early 1950s.

Andy went to see Ramblin' Jack play a hootenanny at The
Ballads and Blues Club in Soho, where he was mesmerised by the
songs and stories of Woody that Ramblin' Jack told. He followed
Jack and his wife, June, back to their lodgings, took note of the
address and promptly sent a letter. Andy soon befriended the
couple and became a constant fixture in their lives, arriving every
morning at 10 a.m. and waiting at the end of their bed until they
got up. Another young student of the guitar, and future legend,
Davy Graham, was also a frequent visitor. During this period,
Andy also befriended Derroll Adams, an old sparring partner of
Jack's, and he met the great Cisco Houston himself, who told
him to look him up in California whenever he was coming to the
States.

Woody Guthrie influenced the way Andy sang, the type of
song he wanted to sing and the instruments he played. Andy even
went so far as to mimic his idol's reverse harmonica style. 'It was
just guitar at first, and then when I got interested in Woody I
bought a mandolin and a bit of a fiddle and a harmonica,
because these were the instruments Woody played. When I met
Jack, I couldn't play any of these instruments. I made a little bit
of headway on the mandolin, I never had much success with the
fiddle and Jack showed me how to play the harmonica the way
Woody played it, upside down and back to front.'

This period of Andy's youth reads almost like some sort of
divine quest to meet his hero, Woody Guthrie. Alas, distance was
his enemy and it simply wasn't to be. His ambition to meet
Guthrie mirrored that of another budding young folk singer, Bob
Dylan. In his *Chronicles – Volume One*, Dylan talks in detail
about trips out of Manhattan's folk hotbed to visit Guthrie at
Greystone Hospital in Morristown, New Jersey, where he was
stricken with the genetic wasting disease Huntingdon's Chorea.
Dylan brought him Raleigh cigarettes and sat by his bedside

singing Guthrie his own songs of heart and courage for the ordinary man. Andy Irvine never had such a privilege. Despite his intentions, the timing of his discovery of Guthrie not long before the onslaught of ill health and mental deterioration, and the geographical gulf that separated them, prohibited Andy from ever meeting Guthrie in person. Nonetheless, communication was established.

As it turned out, Andy's initial, hopeful attempt at correspondence with 'Mr Woody Guthrie' was the first of many letters he wrote to the Oklahoma legend. He finally located Woody sometime around 1959 at the same New Jersey hospital where Bob Dylan had visited him. With great excitement, he received his first reply from a woman called Sid Gleason. Sid and her husband, Bob, would take Guthrie out of hospital and entertain him at weekends. Andy continued sending letters, sometimes twice a week and, without ever meeting her in person, he got very close to Sid Gleason. He even had plans to go to the US and live with the family.

Back home in England, he proudly recalls himself and Jack Elliot recording a tape for Woody. 'After we recorded one of Woody's songs, Jack said, "Andy, you sound more like Woody than I do!" Just as Guthrie had once said to Jack, "Jack, you sound more like me than I do!"' Andy still beams with pride at the memory of that moment. He also remembers another treasured moment – his moment of recognition. 'One morning the *Woody Guthrie Newsletter* arrived. It was an occasional mimeographed sheet or two saying how he was doing and what was going on with his records, and so on. It wasn't all that interesting, but this particular day it had this huge "thank you" list of names like Pete Seeger, Alan Lomax, Ralph Rinzler, Oscar Brand, Lionel Kilberg, Jack and June Elliot and all these famous people. I suppose I was kind of hoping my name might pop up in there somewhere.

And at the bottom it read *"and to Andy, from Woody, personally"*.
I never met him, but the fact that he knew who I was is quite a coup
because most of the people who knew Woody, or who Woody knew
of, are dead. And he really was the reason I got started.'

Woody Guthrie died in Creedmore State Hospital in Queens,
New York on 3 October 1967. The illuminating resonance of
Woody Guthrie's work will forever thrive, not just with the kids
of the 1950s, but each succeeding generation of new folk
mavericks, poets and Everyman champions. Andy Irvine's whole
course had now changed and he would soon find himself
impressing young folkies across the Irish Sea with his Oklahoma
croon and wheezing harmonica style. His independence also
began to take shape. He never did make that trip to New Jersey,
and then London was the place for him to be for a couple more
years. 'When I was eighteen years old, I was offered a spot on the
BBC repertory company, which meant that I was half an actor
and half a civil servant for the next two years, drawing a weekly
wage. My mother had died two years before that, in 1961, and I
didn't get on that well with my father. To my delight, he decided
to marry again, which gave me the out.'

At the BBC, Andy was enlisted into another world of fascinating characters, including the celebrated Belfast-born poet
Louis MacNeice who worked as writer in the BBC for over
twenty years. 'There was a pub quite near the BBC called The
George. They used to call it The Gluepot because it was very
hard to get out of, and all these intellectual people would drink
in there and I would hang out with them. Louis would be talking
to other famous poets and playwrights and I wouldn't really
understand a lot of the conversation, but I'd be hanging on every
word. I was much taken with Louis' secretary, Jenny Sheppard. I
used to go and visit her in the afternoons in Louis' office because
he spent the afternoons in the British Museum reading room.

I remember we were playing this game with a tennis ball one afternoon in his office when he came in unexpectedly and I had to beat a hasty retreat!'

In 1962, when his two-year contract with the Rep ended, Andy moved to Dublin. 'I very quickly met people who I really felt were coming from the same place as me. A lot of people really liked what I was doing. I was singing Woody Guthrie songs in an Oklahoma accent. And I liked what they were doing, which were mostly Clancy Brothers songs, although they didn't do it like the Clancy Brothers. "Strokey" was the word we used back then to describe The Clancys. All this manly stuff didn't sit very well with us, but a lot of the songs were good. I wasn't aware of The Clancys when I lived in England. I had only just discovered Séamus Ennis on the BBC on a programme called *As I Roved Out*, which was really my introduction to Irish music.'

In Dublin, a fresh new musical environment sprouted in front of Andy's eyes. 'I was living out in Templeogue with some friends whom I'd met through an actor friend called Billy Quinn. Billy and I went into the Brazen Head one Friday evening. There was a session there with Gerry Kearns, Derek Monks and Pierce McAuliffe. I sang and they sang and this is the moment that I realised there was something going on here which really interested me. I left Templeogue under a bit of a cloud, though. I suddenly became a "night person" and I didn't see them at all. I'd come home at three o'clock in the morning and I'd be in bed when they got up, and so on. And, quite rightly, they left me a note one day saying, "Maybe you should move out. You've obviously found your feet." So I did.'

Andy soon realised his move to Dublin was a case of being in the right place at the right time. A new breed of folk singer was emerging and a whole new musical landscape was unfolding. The acting world, in which Andy was still professionally involved, soon paled in comparison to the potential depth of expression, not to mention fun social activities, that music offered. So, as music began to take precedence, he got the last of his acting impulses out of his system. 'I played in The Olympia, The Gate, The Eblana and The Pike Theatre, which was a tiny little forty-nine-seater. The Pike had closed after the debacle of a production of *The Rose Tattoo*, the Tennessee Williams play, which was deemed a little bit outrageous for Dublin in 1957. The show was closed and the theatre with it, and it had been "dark" until these three girls took it over, one of whom was Deirdre McCartan, who later became Ronnie Drew's wife. The first show they put on was two one-act plays, one of which was *The Zoo Story* by Edward Albee. It lasted about forty-five minutes, but there were only two actors in it, and about fifteen pages of speech for me! Anyway, it went quite well.'

Andy also acted in a play by Padhraic Collum during the Dublin Theatre Festival in 1963. 'The last thing I did was a dreadful, dreadful musical. I couldn't dance, but there I was trying to do all these moves in a thing called *Sir Buccaneer*, which was hoping to go to the West End of London but didn't get within an ass's roar of it because it was fucking dreadful. I think after that I more or less packed it in.' He also worked in television drama, featuring for a while in *Tolka Row*, a popular RTÉ soap. 'I was playing the boyfriend of Laurie Morton, who was old enough to be my mother. I looked about half my age so I don't know how I got away with that. I also appeared in *Down at Flannery's*, a sort of forerunner for *Tolka Row*.'

Musically, the focus was firmly on O'Donoghue's pub on Merrion Row. The proprietors, Paddy and Maureen O'Dono-ghue, kept their busy and largely penniless musicians fed with bowls of soup and pints of stout. Some of the finest players and singers in Ireland, young and old, swapped songs and tunes, from the new generation of curious souls such as Luke Kelly, Ronnie Drew, Barney McKenna, Johnny Moynihan and Andy himself, to senior authorities such as Séamus Ennis, Joe Heaney and John Kelly.

'I remember someone pointing across the street and telling me, "That's Ronnie Drew and Barney McKenna," and I thought, "Um, good, yeah, they look interesting." And I got to meet them within minutes because O'Donoghue's was where everybody went. As soon as I found my feet there, I thought, "That's it, goodbye acting!" I kept it up for a while, though, to keep myself in pennies.' O'Donoghue's became Andy's second home. 'I used to sing long ballads in the very early morning in the men's toilet, which smelled of disinfectant. There was something wrong with the cistern and a drone emanated from it all the years I frequented the place. Singing against a drone is something I love to this day.'

Andrew Rynne, another regular frequenter of O'Donoghue's, affectionately describes Paddy and Maureen O'Donoghue in *The Vasectomy Doctor*:

> Maureen was a stout lady with a big heart. She administered to her minions from the tiny kitchen that opened into the space behind the bar. Here at lunch-time she presided over an enormous pot of home-made soup and she made up sandwiches to go with this – cheese and tomato, ham or chicken with lots of mustard. From this vantage point, she could see everything that was going on, which was usually quite a lot. Maureen never missed a trick ... Many is the time she would discreetly look after people by way of not charging them for soup and sandwiches or indeed the odd pint of Guinness. These might be men who may have fallen on hard times or perhaps who may have been the worst for the drink. Alcoholism and ballads are frequent bedfellows.

> *Paddy O'Donoghue too was a decent kind of a man*
> *with old-fashioned good manners and graciousness. He*
> *was bald, wore black-rimmed glasses and smoked St*
> *Bernard's plug-tobacco in a twisted pipe. He kept an eye*
> *on everything and made sure nobody got out of hand. He*
> *worked behind the bar and always had a good word for*
> *everyone.*

At this time, it seemed like the Baggot Street–Merrion quarter of Dublin's city centre was the nucleus of this burgeoning folk scene. 'I moved into 4 Mackey's Place, which is just off Pembroke Street. I was delighted there was a room there free because it was where Ronnie Drew lived. If O'Donoghue's was the centre of the world during opening hours, then Mackey's Place was definitely the place to be during the holy hour and after hours. I wasn't there very long. Ronnie and June got married when I'd been there about a month. Their wedding party wound up in mayhem and the police were called. I left early in the next morning to go to a fleadh in Kilrush. When I got back, I found all my stuff had been thrown out, not that I had very much, and it was all behind the bar in O'Donoghue's, so that was the end of Mackey's Place. Another good friend of mine, Liam Miller, a printer and a man of the arts, put me up in his house in 94 Baggot Street. I stayed there for a while until an actress friend of mine called Rosemary Crowson, who lived at 8 Lower Baggot Street, told me there was a room in 9 Baggot Street right opposite her window.'

It wasn't all just pubs and parties, of course. Andy had an almost studious interest in music. He scoured old songbooks like *The Child Collection* and Sam Henry's *Songs of the People* and Bert Lloyd's *Penguin Book of English Folk Songs* in the National Library. He, and the rest of Dublin's young beatnik generation, drew inspiration from the BBC *Radio Ballads* of Ewan McColl, Peggy Seeger and Charles Parker, the exhilarating Irish music collected and presented by broadcasters like Ciarán MacMathúna on Radio Éireann, and songs from the endless store of American old-time music. They would travel all over Ireland and mingle with the traditionalists at fleadh cheoil events, playing, listening, drinking and sleeping in hay barns.

'We were beatniks, really. People down the country would look at us very strangely. People wore suits. That's what men wore in the country. And we wore tatty old jeans with holes and patches. We had long hair and beards and people thought we were dirty. The great unwashed! We took the blame for a lot of things. If there was trouble at fleadh cheoils in the early 1960s, we were blamed. But we were mad into the music. Okay, we might have had too much to drink sometimes, but we would never have made a holy show of ourselves. It was the local young lads who did that, who suddenly had the excuse to go out drinking. I always felt angry about that.

'For the average bourgeois small-town shopkeeper citizen, we were the obvious people to blame. But we looked blameworthy. We looked like we should be drunk and disorderly or whatever, and perhaps they didn't want to blame their own sons. On the other hand, we got on very well with most traditional musicians at that time. There was no conflict there. They looked at us a little bit warily at first, and our music was not quite coming out of the same tradition as theirs. It was already mixed up with other music we'd heard.'

Prior to the 1960s folk boom, O'Donoghue's, like most pubs in Dublin, didn't allow music and singing. Legend has it that Dublin-born Johnny Moynihan, who would turn out to be a great musical ally and kindred spirit of Andy Irvine, was the first musician to play a note of music in O'Donoghue's, surreptitiously playing his tin whistle under the collar of his coat. 'Dublin pubs were deeply conservative and most of them had signs up saying "No Singing",' recalls Moynihan. 'I did hear afterwards that the reason for that was if you allowed singing, people would start singing rebel songs and that could end up in a row. It was an unspoken taboo, I suppose. There were signing sessions in places outside of the city centre like The Tap in Chapelizod, which I think was run by Frank Harte's father at the time, The Strawberry Beds, and a little country pub called The Dead Man Murray's. Maureen O'Donoghue told Gay Byrne in an interview that I played tin whistle from behind the lapel of my coat, which is quite possible. If you did want to convey a tune to somebody, to ask them or tell them about it, that would be one way to do it.'

Johnny Moynihan studied Architecture in UCD, where he met Eamonn O'Doherty, 'the single most expeditious member of our coterie as regards starting O'Donoghue's on the road to ruin'. O'Doherty was an artist and sculptor as well as an architectural student, and he was also a great socialiser. 'He would be knocking about with people from the art college. The architectural students used to go down to the College of Science, which is now part of Dáil Éireann. We used to go down there for physics and chemistry and, of course, on the way back then we'd call into O'Donoghue's.'

Moynihan discovered that there had been a folk music club in UCD, but that it was dormant because there were no officers left. The Folk Music Society started up again in college in 1958 or 1959, with Ronnie Drew as the first guest. 'Ronnie, who had a huge influence on us all, had been singing and playing guitar. He was a flamenco enthusiast and had been to Andalucia, where he'd actually worked there teaching English. Eamonn O'Doherty

was a real party animal. He had a flat in Stephen's Green where
Rice's pub used to be. We went back to his place for a session
after the gig that Ronnie did in the Folk Club and Ronnie regaled
us with stories and songs and had us absolutely spellbound. He
was great at observation, little human details. He was also very
funny.'

Andy vividly remembers meeting Johnny for the first time.
'Pierce McAuliffe was my big mate at that time. He played the
harmonica and guitar and we used to do a great version of
'Handsome Molly' with two harmonicas. I had a motorbike and
we went down to a fleadh in Newcastle West in County Limerick.
I think it was really a bodhrán competition, but it might as well
have been a fleadh because there was a lot of music in the town.
Late on Sunday night, we had to leave because Pierce had to get
back to his job on Monday morning to open the warehouse. We
were just about to leave when we bumped into Johnny
Moynihan. Pierce knew Johnny and he introduced us and we had
a brief conversation. I said, "I'll have to drive through the night
to get Pierce back to Dublin, will we see you there?" And Johnny
said, "Well, you haven't got any gloves?" I said, "No, it's gonna
be a bit cold." So he took a pair of socks out of his rucksack and
he gave them to me. I drove with the socks on my hands, but we
didn't get very far. We got as far as Birdhill and I couldn't go any
further because of the cold. Eventually, we found a hay barn and
we didn't wake up in time to get Pierce back to open up the
warehouse. So when he did get back some time around two
o'clock in the afternoon he was fired on the spot, and he left the
country for the Isle of Man.'

'I don't really remember that meeting with Andy,' admits
Moynihan. 'I'd heard he was about because the likes of us were
thin on the ground in those days. The first time he really
impinged on me was at a session up in the Phoenix Park, possibly

The Hole in the Wall pub, and afterwards we went to this guy's house, I think he was one of the mountaineering crew. At that time, traditional singing of a certain type and mountaineers seemed to go hand-in-hand for some reason. So we bought some bottles of Guinness and Andy bought a half bottle of whiskey and that really impressed me.

'We had a link in the sense that we were both fans of old-timey music. He was a huge fan of Woody Guthrie. I didn't know too much about Woody Guthrie myself and I didn't associate him with real old-timey music, more with Pete Seeger at the political protest end of the scale rather than the purely old-fashioned traditional music, the stuff I liked. We used to play stuff together, Andy and myself. He was fairly intense. He was a great man for the craic. He was always more of a raver than a rocker. He was sort of steeped in *The Goon Show* sense of humour and attitude and, of course, he was very theatrical. There were a lot of laughs to be had in a social situation and he would very easily get into a gag-cracking frame of mind. And he was also a great musician. He had a certain angst, shall we say, about maybe fitting into the scene, in a general sense, relating to the plain people of Ireland rather than relating to the acting scene in Dublin. That was something I wouldn't have found too strange anyway because I was a little bit that way myself, having had a sheltered upbringing. I got on very well with Andy.'

Other venues that welcomed scruffy young folk mavericks included The Coffee Kitchen on Molesworth Street, with sessions run by another rock climber, Dave Smythe, and which later moved to The Green Lounge, the pub next to the Green Cinema by St Stephen's Green. 'People scarcely got paid for it,' remembers Andy. 'You might meet Dave on a Friday and he'd say "Coming down to the Coffee Kitchen?" "No, I'm not sure." "I'll give you ten bob." "Oh, okay!"

Andy also remembers this time for the parties in Peggy Jordan's house in Kenilworth Square. 'Apart from the fact that we loved being in her company, it would probably mean free drink. She was a great matriarch of the arts at the time. She ran concerts in the Green Cinema and later in the Grafton Cinema and they were dreadful things. They were on Friday nights I think, and you'd really be taking your life in your hands because they didn't start until after closing time and the audience would be drunk and stroppy and noisy. There was one night I was on and I finished off with an unaccompanied ballad called 'Edward' and the audience was getting more and more restless while I was doing this and I got more and more angry and I remember saying at the end of it, "And if there were another ten verses of it I'd sing them to you," and I stormed off the stage. Joe Heaney stood up and clasped my hand and said, "Good man yourself, great stuff!" So I didn't feel too bad. If it wasn't good enough for late-night Dublin, it was good enough for Joe Heaney!'

Peggy Jordan also organised gigs in Howth. Andy remembers her ringing up O'Donoghue's to ask if they could get a few musicians together to replace a group who were unable to appear at The Abbey Tavern. Johnny and myself went up with somebody else and the audience was, once again, underwhelmed. 'I remember singing this really long ballad, a version of what they call 'The House Carpenter' in America. I took a little break in the middle on the guitar and Johnny leaned over and said, "Andy, I hate to tell you this" – he could barely suppress his hysterics – "there isn't one person in the whole place listening to you!" I looked up and I thought, "Fuck, he's right."'

In recent years, Andy concisely and poetically documented his early 1960s revelry in Dublin with a witty new autobiographical number titled 'O'Donoghue's Song'. It offers a

mouth-watering, fly-on-the-wall view of the music, antics and
characters of one of Ireland's most famous 1960s music pubs.

It was August 1962,
When I first set foot in O'Donoghue's
A world of music, friends and booze
Opened up before me
I never could have guessed as I walked through the door
Just what the future had in store
A blueprint for my life I saw
Lying there before me

I was an actor, I played straight
I played in the Gaiety, played at the Gate,
My mother in 1928,
Trod those boards before me
I was getting tired of the company, an actor's life was not
    for me
I said goodbye you'll never see
Me back here in Neary's
Johnny Moynihan in his fusty coat was the first to play
    there in Merrion Row
And he brought the Bouzouki to Ireland, you know
'Way storm along John.
Paddy and Maureen O'Donoghue,
Ciaran Bourke, Luke Kelly, Ronnie Drew,
Barney McKenna and me and you in the early 1960s

Paddy and Maureen very, very sound
Though she liked to camp on the moral high ground
If you had long hair you were outward bound
Go down you blood red roses.
Ronnie Drew in his fine suit of blue
And a voice like gravel that would cut you in two
We thought he was Dublin through and through

But he blew in from Dun Laoghaire

Joe Ryan and John Kelly in the front bar, their fiddles are
    from the County Clare
Joe Heaney sings in the cold night air
In the laneway after closing
Sea Shanties in perfect tune
And Séamus Ennis in the afternoon
It was all over much too soon
Days of wine and roses

Banjo Barney calling the tune, Mary Jordan's a whizz on
    the spoons
Up the Swannee and Down the Broom
Barney's rising to it
They carry him bodily out to the jacks
He empties his bladder and they carry him back
He lowers a pint and he's right back on track
How the fuck does he do it?

In the afternoon you might find there
Luke Kelly and his banjo and his red hair
O what a time what an atmosphere
What more could a young man wish for?
How I'd spend my time was never in doubt
This is what life was all about
A bowl of soup and a pint of stout
Agus fáigamíd siúid mar a tá sé

Dave Smythe never short of a witty phrase
Sonny Brogan love the way he plays
Ted McKenna, God bless the days of Italian Mandolinos
At closing time we didn't go far
Just down the road to the Pike Coffee Bar

Ah! the usual suspects, there you are
Have yez no homes to go to?
Putting up a note on the message board, Sweeney's Men
    have a gig, O Lord
We have to meet at 12 o'clock
For the journey down to Galway
But the Sweeney van broke down at the door
And we didn't get going till a quarter past four
To the merry tune of the Dolan snore,
Haul away me Rosie!

It all came to an end in 68 the rest of the world was lying
    in wait
And I started out for a new landscape set sail for the Pirin
    Mountains
From the old North Wall sailed away
All me friends were there on the quay
Won't be back for many's the day
But it was bloody great while it lasted!

It was August 1962
When I first set foot in O'Donoghue's
A world of music, friends and booze
Hastening towards me
I never could have guessed as I walked through the door
Just what the future had in store
A blueprint for my life I saw
Lying there before me.

Chapter 4

Art College, Albums and Treble Vodkas

Outside the sheltered circle of family, friends and neighbours in Newbridge and Prosperous, and those formative music sessions in Dowling's and Downings, a wide-open space was unfurling for Christy Moore and Dónal Lunny. Christy, in particular, began straying from home at a relatively early age. 'As I look back on it, I really left Newbridge when I was about fifteen or sixteen,' he explains. 'I started to spend holidays in England for the summers of 1961, 1962 and 1963. When I got my Leaving Cert, I went to work in the National Bank in Clonmel at the age of eighteen. Even as I started my life as bank clerk, I was already longing for something else. I was in Clonmel for a year and then I was transferred onto what was known as the relief staff, where you go around the country. My first posting was to Tulla, County Clare. I did a lot of work in Clare, travelling to different branches and filling in. In my three years in the bank, I was always dreaming of playing music.'

Through the years, there have been several conflicting accounts of Christy Moore's first paid performance, but as far as he is concerned it was during his days in Clonmel. 'I remember it was in the Collins Hall in Clonmel. A man called Paddy Fitzgerald promoted the gig. The reason I can remember it so clearly is because Frank Patterson was coming back from Rome, where he was studying, and he was giving a concert in his hometown. I was asked to play support. I remember I got a fiver for it, and it took me years and years and years before I ever got a fiver again!'

Of all places for a permeable young folk singer to be stationed, Christy Moore couldn't have asked for a more musically vibrant locale than the County Clare. While he was there, he encountered some of the country's finest musicians and singers, not to mention convivial pubs and salubrious landscapes. He took trips to the Mecca of Miltown Malbay to witness Willie Clancy in full flow. He rubbed shoulders with renowned east Clare fiddlers Paddy Canny and Vincent Griffin of the Tulla Céilí Band. In fact, it was in Tulla in 1964 that Christy saw a tape recorder for the first time in Joe McGrath's kitchen. Miracu-lously, McGrath's recording of the fledgling singer re-emerged some forty years later and a crackling version of 'Enniskillen Dragoon' was included on Christy's retrospective box set.

It was almost a double-identity lifestyle for Christy. He went through the motions of his administrative position by day and came alive with the zeal of a young man discovering his vocation by night. He was a wide-eyed aspirant amongst these giants of traditional music, but he didn't shy away from sitting in on the sessions. 'Oh absolutely. Because I could sing, you see. And I had a guitar. In those days, having a guitar would be a rarity.

There would be nobody else around singing Irish songs *and* playing guitar. You'd get invited, brought along. And some of the old musicians would love you to come in and give them a vamp, even though your chords mightn't always be right. A lot of the old musicians liked guitar accompaniment. That was a great time for me.'

Dónal Lunny had also moved away from his home in Kildare. His prodigious creative streak was to find fruition at the National College of Art & Design in Dublin in 1965. Life in college saw Dónal juggling music and artistic studies in a whir of activity. 'I was sixteen or seventeen. My brother Frank was in UCD doing Engineering and he was involved in the traditional scene in Dublin by then,' explains Dónal. 'He had teamed up with a bunch of musicians who played in pubs and who were generally immersed in music, people like Mick Moloney, Sean Corcoran, Johnny Morrissey, who were part of a wider circle of musicians. Then, prior to me moving to Dublin, Frank told me somebody had gone away to England for the summer and they needed someone to play guitar. So off to Dublin I did go with the guitar and dived in, playing with Mick Moloney and the aforementioned. Dan Maher was another man. He worked in An Post and played whistle, accordion and harmonica, and Tony Butler played banjo. We were a band called The Parnell Folk and I rapidly became a part of this band. People joined and left quite frequently so there was quite a turnover of musicians.'

After that, Dónal joined a band called The Emmet Folk, which also included Mick Moloney and Brian Bolgor. 'The material that we had was very good. At that time, we'd reached a stage were we had our own repertoire and once you start having your own repertoire, you start developing your own identity rather than just singing everybody's songs. We were taken quite seriously. We started a club at 95 Harcourt Street called

The 95 Club. It was quite successful, but also quite informal. One or two of us would be there every week and there would be various guests. There was a plethora of folk clubs in Dublin at that time. There was The Universal in Parnell Square, The Auld Triangle and the Coffee Kitchen in Molesworth Street. You weren't paid for performing there. Actually, we were; there was a main performer, but they wouldn't be paid very much. It'd be just a few quid. Everybody else would go along to play or sing or whatever. It was a great sort of platform for people. It was lovely. An awful lot of people sort of emerged from that. Some of the performers were not good, and some of them were great. But there was a tolerance there as well. Eventually, we split with Mick Moloney and amalgamated with Brian and Mick Byrne, who called their group The Spiceland Folk. We became The Emmet Spiceland. Eventually, Brian Bolger dropped out and we pressed on and became a professional trio.'

At the same time, Dónal was attempting to complete a course in the art college. 'I was interested in sculpture, but there was quite a push on getting a good School of Design formed, so I was kind of hustled into the design school. I didn't mind, really. I think Kilkenny Design came into being soon after that. But it was realised that there were very few Irish designers around – in graphic design, industrial design, whatever – it all came from outside, like most other things in Ireland at the time. So it was Basic Design for two years and Graphic Design for the last three years. I loved it, but being involved with performance with Mick and Brian really put a strain on what I was doing in the college because it just took up so much time physically. We'd travel around the country and come back the same night.' He began to miss morning classes. Performing as part of a band was a huge distraction and his two scholarships were constantly under threat from his erratic attendance.

However, Art College taught Dónal a great deal about the creative process that still stands to him today. 'I believe that being engaged in the visual arts actually helped my musical development, as there are so many parallels between the various disciplines. I developed a kind of mental visualisation of music, which is difficult to describe, but which has been with me ever since.' College life took an aberration towards the end of his tenure at NCAD in the form of student strike. 'The student strike happened in my final year. It was triggered by the realisation that the Diploma from NCAD had little or no currency outside Ireland at that time, academically or professionally. The strike took the form of boycotting scheduled classes and barricading part of the premises against anybody except students. I took to using the metalwork room every day, and through this, found my way into making jewellery.'

While at college, Dónal also caught up with Christy Moore, who had relocated to Dublin. As Dónal recalls, Christy's appearance never quite corresponded to his day job. 'Christy and I shared a flat in Pearse Street for a year. It was my second year in college and Christy was in the bank. He was an unlikely candidate for a bank. There was a certain dress code, which Christy barely adhered to. I mean, to walk into a bank on a Monday morning and see Christy there behind the counter staring at you…'

Christy found it difficult to get a foothold on the Dublin folk circuit in the mid-1960s. He remembers Peggy Jordan giving him a gig in The Embankment in 1964. 'It was the only gig I got around that time. I also got an audition out in Howth in The Abbey Tavern. But they never came back to me. That was a famous kind of place and I remember going out and being really nervous. There was a scene going on in those days, but I just couldn't get a look in. Dónal was making quite a name for himself, and I used to tag along with him, but I never got any gigs or supports or anything, even though I was keen. I remember one night in UCD in Earlsfort Terrace there was a big folk concert on and everyone was on the bill. I had been promised that I would get to sing and the fucking gig went on and on and on – in those days everybody got up and did two or three songs – and just as I was about to start there was a fire. So I never got to play. I was so upset. The fucking place went on fire.'

Christy had had enough. Summer trips to England had whetted his appetite for the folk scene across the water and the National Bank Strike of 1966 was the perfect excuse to make the break. So he took the boat to England with Frank Lunny. 'I think it was just to get the fuck out of here,' admits Christy. 'I worked one year in EMI in Hayes in Middlesex pressing records. I pressed 'Good Vibrations' by The Beach Boys for weeks on end, every night. I did a lot of different jobs in England – bar work, site work, factory work.'

Frank remembers the pair of them heading to Bury on the train to stay with Christy's aunt, who had a pub there. 'We sank a dozen Guinnesses and sang a couple of songs, and we made it there quite early in the morning. We settled into more music and drinking. Christy seemed to know a good few people in this pub. It was a place were the local nouveau riche frequented, I reckon. I do remember around two o'clock they took us out for dinner to a restaurant. We drank more whiskey and got pissed. I remember climbing up into an attic onto a bed and falling asleep at about three o'clock in the afternoon. I was woken up again at seven or eight o'clock and proceeded to get myself drunk again and by twelve o'clock I was drunk twice in the same day!'

They both ended up working in a pea factory. 'Christy probably put quality control back fifty years,' laughs Frank. 'We found a local and we started playing jigs and reels and

Christy was going down a bomb at this stage. He really was a fabulous singer. He only had to start singing and the bottles of stout started coming. I think it was The Fox and Hound pub. The sales of Guinness in The Fox and Hound were two dozen a week, but in about two weeks it went up to about forty-four dozen. They actually sent a sales rep up from head office to see what the hell was going on. It was a really great time, typical student stuff. Christy made a couple of contacts there. All that stuff would have passed over my head. I was on my next bottle of stout. But Christy was reasonably focused. I remember at lunch-time we'd go down to the subsidised canteen and a game of cards would start up. Christy was big into the cards at the time, but he didn't always do well and I remember there were days he lived on a bowl of soup and bread for one and thruppence. Thankfully you were allowed as much bread as you like. He lived.'

When that came to an end, Frank and Christy hitched their way to Norfolk to work on the oil rigs. Frank remembers getting a lift from a guy who had given up horology when he discovered that there was much more money to be made in roofing. 'He was also a mountain climber. He didn't mind that one of his apprentices had fallen fifty metres to his death the year before. It *was* dangerous. He liked us. He offered us a job. I was on for this, but I remember Christy said, "Fuck it. I'm not going down. It's better to be safe than dead", or something like that. He wasn't into heights and there was no way he was getting up on any roofs. So we went down and applied for a job on the rigs. Much to my fucking disgust, Christy got a job and I didn't. I always reckoned I could do ten times as much work as Moore, but he was a burly fella and I was only about ten stone. Christy was on the rigs for a number of months. I didn't contact him that much after that. I heard he had been sacked, that some English foreman came up to him and said, "Hey Paddy, get your finger out, you're not doing this job properly." There was a difference of opinion. He insulted Christy a little bit more, taking on his Irish heritage, and Christy clocked him. He was off the rig in half an hour. I think that was really the beginning of his career in music. He headed off to the clubs in Norfolk, down to London and he was on his way.

'He was just a marvellous singer. It was a lovely situation where you'd come in, you wouldn't talk or clatter around when Christy sang. No, you listened. Christy never took to people talking in the background, because he was used to attention and respect. I remember I was up in Dungloe in Donegal. He was singing a song and he threw the guitar down and rushed up the back and shouted, "Who is whistling?" It might have been me, actually. But he didn't like it!'

Meanwhile, back in Ireland, life for Dónal Lunny had become hectic as he contended with college demands and the rising profile of Emmet Spiceland. They had got off to a good start by winning a ballad-singing contest in 1967 in Wexford and, by February 1968, they'd topped the Irish charts with the single 'Mary from Dungloe'. 'We recorded that in Eamonn Andrews Studios on Henry Street in Dublin,' remembers Dónal. 'Eamonn Andrews Studios was the only place that one recorded at at the time. In fact, I think at the time it was the only studio in the country. I became instantly interested in recording. People didn't know what a producer was then. I didn't know what a producer was. Bill Sommerville-Large was the engineer, and, if truth be known, the actual producer as well because Bill would say things like "second string on the guitar is out of tune there". Bill was very proper, a wonderful engineer with perfect pitch, which is a rarity.'

Emmet Spiceland has been described as the equivalent of a boy band for the 1960s Irish folk generation. Their dashing good looks and seductive harmonies brought a touch of glamour and a hint of pop mania to the folk world. As Christy Moore said when asked to describe them, 'There wasn't a dry seat in the house.'

With the success of 'Mary from Dungloe', Emmet Spiceland developed a sort of fan base, which Dónal describes as 'brilliant and exhilarating at the time'. However, he concedes that 'it turned into a bit of a monster after a while because the same twenty-five girls turned up and collected an autograph from us at every gig'. 'That became the thing. We recorded 'Báidín Fheidhlimidh' and that I think that also did well. It was an interesting thing because neither Mick nor Brian spoke Irish. I taught them the Irish phonetically. So it was like they could've been speaking in Swahili. Some of the music was traditional but in the treatment of it, it was kind of poppy. We sang close harmonies and we sang them very well. We had a great blend between our three voices. We were as pop-conscious as trad conscious. "Trad" was a word that wasn't used very much back then. "Folk music" or "ballads" would've been the description more commonly used.'

Their first (and only) album, *The First*, was released in 1968 by Page One Records, who offered them a recording contract. Dónal acknowledges that he didn't read it very closely. 'Our manager at the time was a solicitor by the name of Joe Colgan. Joe was responsible for a lot of the success of Emmet Spiceland simply because he had no idea how to manage – he didn't know any of the conventional strategies of management – so he'd come up with these highly original ideas and that was part of the reason we became noticed and why we became popular. I think it was Joe's idea to perform in Croke Park and to sing at half-time at an All-Ireland. It was the first time in twenty-five years anybody had sung there. And then, three months later, someone

else did it and it kind of took off for a while. We went to London
to make the album, but we hadn't received the contract. When
the contract arrived, Joe said, "Don't sign that." But we said,
"We want to do this." It was the absolutely typical situation – a
young band who would do anything to make an album. It was a
rotten contract.

'Irony of ironies, the album was produced by [future Planxty
producer] Phil Coulter,' continues Dónal. 'There were some
things about that I still think back on and I'm slightly mystified.
Phil did arrangements for the songs. We never heard the arrangements. We walked into Delane Lea Studios in London where we
had maybe one or two days to record the album and there were
sixteen musicians. It was like, "Wow, what's this?" There was a
string section and a flute player. There was no consultation
involved and no negotiation. We had a layer of arrangement put
on our music, which we had no control over. So we were kind of
processed. Even though at the time I was very conscious of the
fact that it wasn't a fair reflection of Emmet Spiceland, I wasn't
passionate enough about what had happened. It was just a kind
of inevitability and we sort of accepted it in a way.

'There was another aspect of that as well. This idea origi-
nated from Phil as well, and that was to have dialogue in between
the tracks. I can't remember it exactly because I could never bear
to listen to the album afterwards. It was basically us talking to
each other and an imaginary character called Flan. This would
sort of illustrate the kind of teeny-bop aspect of the band. When
I think about it, it would probably relate to The Monkees or
something like that. Even though the music was serious, this was
pop territory. Flan was meant to be a kind of a leprechaun or
something like that. I distinctly remember the end of the album
there was a kind of a flourish played … rat-a-tat-dum-dum …
and then footsteps and then a door closing. And one of us says

to the other, "Who was that?" and then the other saying, "That was Phil Coulter, he produced the LP." That was like his signature on the album, you know. It was so embarrassing. It really did spoil the music. I listened to the album once and could never bear listening to it again. But we were talked into it, so … When the album was re-released, I managed to have the bits of talk taken out because it was excruciatingly embarrassing to listen back to.'

Dónal is surprised to hear people say they really like the album. 'I've begun to accept that there are some good things about it. But Brian had lost his voice, he physically couldn't sing. He was in a state of panic. He was devouring a jar of honey all day, taking hot showers, all this kind of stuff, to get his voice functioning again. Mick was the same, his voice went too, and that could've been psychosomatic, I don't know. So there was not even a hint of what the band really was. It was a disaster as far as we were concerned.'

Emmet Spiceland was Dónal's first real tutorial in the pitfalls of the music business. It seems this new world of managers, producers and record companies, not to mention imaginary leprechauns, could very quickly negate all the fun and satisfaction of making music professionally. 'I withdrew from the band. There was a personality thing, you know? It was difficult. I've lost touch with Brian and Mick. It began to stress me out. I don't remember exactly. I called it a day at a certain point. It was strange though, the course of the band and our interests musically really started to go in all kinds of directions. We were singing Leonard Cohen songs. We sang Beatles songs. We did lots of stuff like this, which was acceptable in certain circles and not in others. Some of the folk clubs liked this, but there were people that really didn't.'

Across the Irish Sea, a brawny troubadour was beginning to

make his presence felt. Christy Moore sang his songs up and down Britain. His first professional gig in England was at The Wellgreen Folk Club, Manchester, on 4 May 1966, where he was paid £6. Along the road, Christy was befriended by many renowned folk singers rotating the circuit. One such character was the rotund and boisterous Scottish singer Hamish Imlach, who offered Christy the low-down on sourcing good gigs, finding accommodation and avoiding dodgy promoters. He also schooled him in the art of tackling raucous audiences. Christy's repertoire was also quickly expanding as he picked up new British songs that were yet to be heard back home. He played key folk clubs such as Ian Campbell's Jug O'Punch in Digbeth, Birmingham, and Ewan McColl's legendary Singers Club in King's Cross, London. News filtered back to Ireland that Christy was making waves and, soon enough, offers of gigs slowly started to come in, as did invitations to record radio broadcasts for RTÉ and the BBC.

Christy's main focus turned towards recording an album to propel him into the higher echelons of the folk world. He auditioned unsuccessfully for Transatlantic, Nat Joseph's seminal folk label that recorded the likes of Pentangle, The Dubliners, Bert Jansch and Ralph McTell. But that was merely a setback. He met Dominic Behan, the Dublin-born playwright and songwriter, and younger brother of Brendan, in Shepherd's Bush in London in 1968 at a benefit gig. Dominic offered to help Christy fulfil his dream to make an album. And he did.

Paddy on the Road, Christy Moore's debut album, was recorded in Sound Techniques studio in Chelsea in 1969. The track listing drew from Christy's live repertoire of the time, songs such as 'The Curragh of Kildare', 'Cúnla', 'James Larkin' and four songs penned by Behan, who also produced the album. The instrumentation was supplied by a band of session musicians put together by a well-known English guitarist, Steve Benbow. The resulting record captured a raspy-voiced Irish folk singer with a sort of a sprightly easy-listening accompaniment, not dissimilar to incidental television music. It was an album of incongruous parts, limited to 500 copies, and was released on the Mercury label. It was a start, albeit an inauspicious one. 'I'd no control over it,' explains Christy. 'I didn't really know what I was trying to do. I was completely at sea. I'd never been in a recording studio before. I didn't know anything about the process. I soon realised that the people with whom I was working had no empathy with the songs I was singing.'

Christy needed a fresh approach. He needed musicians he admired and trusted. It would soon dawn on him that the musicians he sought lay closer to home, including Andy Irvine. Since his arrival in Dublin, Irvine had immersed himself completely in the folk scene. It was inevitable that he would chance upon the redoubtable Christy Moore at a club or a party or a session somewhere along the road.

'I remember meeting him at one of Peggy Jordan's parties,' says Andy. 'You'd hear about these parties in O'Donoghue's, "Peggy's having a party on Friday." Johnny would be there, Luke Kelly would be there, Liam Clancy might be there, if he was home from America, Séamus Ennis might be there. It was a social event that one wouldn't miss and it was free drink too, which was quite important at the time. I remember meeting Christy there one time he was back from England. He sang a few songs and that's the first time we actually played together. My impression of him was that he was a brash character, which is how he was then. Playing with him was good. It was easy to play along with. That's one of Christy's great assets. Playing with him allows you a lot of room, whereas playing with Andy allows you no room!

'I also have a memory that I met Christy when he came to a

gig of mine somewhere in Yorkshire,' continues Andy. 'He told
me he was playing with Hamish Imlach and I looked in my diary
and I had the day off and I went to wherever they were playing. I
met up with them and we drank all afternoon. I remember
noting from his performance that if you're too drunk to play, you
should stick to slow songs. He played a whole programme of
really slow songs and the audience loved it. We got a train to
Glasgow to the big folk club, The Scotia. We were all really hung
over. They knew the barman and, without asking, Hamish said,
"Jock (or whatever his name was), give us three treble vodkas." I
thought, "Yeah, that's probably about the right medicine." They
were put down on the counter and I picked mine up and was
about to drink it and savour the joy of the relief when I heard
Christy saying, "Jock, give us three more there." So I threw it
back because I knew that within twenty-five seconds I was going
to have to say, "Uh, Jock three more there." So we'd nine vodkas
in the space of about thirty seconds. I forget the rest of the day.'

Chapter 5

The Men of Sweeney

Music in Ireland evolved rapidly during the 1960s. The Clancy
Brothers appeared on *The Ed Sullivan Show* in 1961 and the
ballad boom was primed. With only a handful of recorded
singers and musicians over the previous twenty years, it might
have appeared that Ireland had forgotten about its inherent
musical urges as it struggled to establish an economic foothold in
the years since independence in 1921. But all those doubts were
washed away as a jubilant groundswell of song burst from its
underbelly. In Dublin, the cosy sanctum of O'Donoghue's pub on
Merrion Row was stuffed to the rafters with talent of all ages,
from the young apprentices Andy Irvine and Johnny Moynihan
revelling down the back, to elder statesmen of the tradition Joe
Ryan and John Kelly nestled up front.

The first notable group to emerge from this lair was the
vociferous gang of bearded gentlemen known, feared and loved

as The Dubliners. Ronnie Drew, Barney McKenna, Ciarán
Bourke and Luke Kelly performed initially as the Ronnie Drew
Ballad Group in 1961 before taking the name (from James Joyce's
collection of short stories) with which they would achieve
worldwide success. They were joined a couple of years later by
the fiddler John Sheahan. The Dubliners were something of an
anomaly amongst standard ballad outfits of the day, as they
had a well of musical depth that sprung from the instrumental
combinations of banjo and fiddle.

The Dubliners were a colourful bunch of renegades. Ronnie
Drew gnarled his way through Dublin street songs with a raspy
bite. Flame-haired Luke Kelly's impenetrable broad baritone
amplified the voice of the working-class citizen and, in turn,
amplified the true spirit of folk music.

The Dubliners became popular during Britain's folk revival
and even scored a top-five hit single in the UK with 'Seven
Drunken Nights', a song learned from the venerated singer Joe
Heaney and which was banned on Irish radio due to the lewd
nature of its lyrics. In 1968, just like The Clancy Brothers before
them, The Dubliners appeared on *The Ed Sullivan Show* to great
excitement.

Andy Irvine and Johnny Moynihan witnessed the exciting
ascent of The Dubliners from O'Donoghue's barflies to stars of
the international stage with mixed opinions. 'I loved them,'
declares Andy. 'Johnny had a falling out with Ronnie because
Johnny was totally idealistic and when The Dubliners became a
bit commercial, maybe around the time of 'Seven Drunken
Nights', there was a bit of a row and they didn't talk to each
other for a while. I always got on well with Ronnie and I liked the
group. I remember once being in London and meeting Luke in
Finsbury Park. I went down to the show with him and I thought
it was great. It was really kind of iconoclastic. If anybody said

anything from the audience they'd be put in their place immediately. I wished I'd had that talent.'

'I was a huge fan of the musicians in The Dubliners before they joined up together,' explains Johnny. 'As soon as they joined up, I turned the other way. I was a big fan of Ronnie Drew and of Barney McKenna and a big fan of Luke's. I didn't know John Sheahan. I met Ciarán Bourke at a couple of parties and I thought he was a likeable fella and I did appreciate his whistle playing. But when they got together, they were not better than the sum of their parts. I liked a cleaner sound, I didn't like accompanied Irish music and I tended to like unaccompanied singing too. Ronnie used to sing with the feel of a flamenco singer when he was on his own but, when they played together, the type of material tended to favour jolly balladeering. I thought it was crude compared to what those people could do individually. And then there was a mob assembling around them. That was all they were interested in, stuff you can tap your foot along to and shout, "Good man yourself." This might sound like sour grapes, but the adulation and following that they had seemed to revel in the cruder aspects of their music and they seemed to encourage that. I wasn't socially adroit enough to handle my disappointment with The Dubliners, so I ended up falling out with Ronnie Drew, which wasn't a good thing to do because I caused personal hurt where I shouldn't have. I did apologise to him before the year was out – on Christmas Eve, it seemed like a good time to do it.'

If Dublin, more specifically O'Donoghue's, was Andy Irvine's homebase in the early 1960s, the world at large was definitely his oyster. 'We followed the festival trail in the summers of 1964, 1965 and 1966. We would start at some fleadh in June and wind up at the Clare Fleadh at the beginning of August or late July and then on to Miltown Malbay, which wasn't a festival, it was a lot quieter. We'd sit in pubs like Friel's or Quealy's and watch Willie

Clancy and hope that he'd take out the pipes, and he usually did at some point during the day. I met Willie Clancy at lots of fleadhs from 1963 onwards and always tried to speak to him, not in a pushy way, but I hoped that he might go, "Howaya." In 1966 or 1967, I went up to him in Quealy's and said, "Hello Willie, how are you?" and he said, "Oh, you've been here before." That was a bit of an in-joke at the time. For all my attempts at ingratiating myself with him, that's as far as it got!'

Another eccentric musician and singer who befriended Andy around this time was Joe Dolan. 'Joe comes from Galway, but I imagine it was up in Dublin where I met him, probably in O'Donoghue's. We hit it off. He was a very extroverted, very loud, large character, especially in drink, which he usually was. He wasn't very predictable and not very controllable. Joe and another close architect mate of ours from Derry, Kevin Carroll, decided to go to Denmark in the winter of 1964. They asked me would I come along and I said no because I was exploring Ireland at the time.'

By autumn 1965, Dolan was itching to get going again and Andy, with wanderlust tingling in his toes, was ready to join him on the road. 'It was September 1965. There were five of us: Joe and his girlfriend, me and Muriel [Andy's future wife] and this lone character called Fred who Joe had met in London. So we were three different hitch-hiking units. Me and Muriel went to Munich and then we went to Vienna. Then we decided to hitch-hike down to Rome. We all met, fortuitously, on the road outside a small town on the Italian-German-Austrian border. They were sitting in a field and we said to the driver, "Stop! Stop!" It was amazing how you could just meet people in those days. We had a fantastic day in this meadow. It had a barn at the foot of it. Fred and Liz, Joe's girlfriend who spoke a bit of German, went into town with Fred's watch and a few other things that we decided to sell, and they came back with huge bottles of cheap wine and food and we had this never-to-be-forgotten sunny afternoon picnic. We continued hitch-hiking separately. The going was very difficult. It took about two or three days to get to Rome where we were supposed to meet at the post office. There was Fred. He said, "I'm done on one side." He'd been sitting there for half a day. We stayed the night at a rubbish tip on the outskirts of town and came back the next day. Joe and Liz never appeared and so we made the long journey home.

'The next thing was I got a letter in London saying they got a lift they couldn't refuse going down to Greece so they ditched us. Joe wouldn't think twice about doing that! He wrote from Copenhagen where the scene was absolutely wonderful and he'd been offered gigs and record deals and everything. Muriel and myself had just arrived back and were living in London at the time. I looked at her and said, "We've got to go!" We were ready to go the next morning when there was a phone call from Dolan, loud Dolan on the phone, and he sounded very close. I said, "Joe, where are you?" "I'm in Galway!" Once again plans had been made and shattered by the whim of Joe Dolan.'

Andy and Joe played as a duo in the Enda Hotel in Galway in June 1966. 'It was brilliant. We played five nights a week. All the usual suspects came to the gig every night. We had two little domestic cottages down the back in the kitchen garden. It was absolutely perfect. But Dolan was never great with putting up with perfection, so he had a row with the owner and we were thrown out. Johnny had been coming down and playing with us at weekends. He was a draughtsman and had a job in Roscommon at the time. He said, "Well, it's a real shame to break this up because it's going great."'

It remains unclear at which point the name Sweeney's Men was applied to the trio of Andy Irvine, Johnny Moynihan and

Joe Dolan, but it was definitely prompted by Flann O'Brien's
outstanding multi-narrative comic novel *At Swim-Two-Birds*, in
which he depicts the mad mythical tree-leaping pagan, King
Sweeney (Suibhne) of Antrim. 'There was one of those meetings
where the three of us sat for hours with crates of beer and
eventually Dolan, who was reading *At Swim-Two-Birds*, said,
"What about The Men of Sweeney?"' recalls Andy hazily. 'We
liked Sweeney because he was an early anti-religious person. So
it was Sweeney's Men. I remember Eamonn O'Doherty set about
painting Sweeney's Men on the front of the van from Johnny's
drawing [the van was featured on the cover of the first issue of
Folk magazine]. That summer of 1966 was absolute bliss. We
were still not professional musicians at that time but we travelled
Ireland and made money enough for a pint and for petrol and we
raided farmers' wives' vegetable gardens and things like that.
Eamonn was our manager at this time, and he'd change into his
managerial suit in the back of the van and go in and try and get
us a gig,' continues Andy. 'He was a bit of a musical dilettante in
his own way. He was an architect and a designer and an artist and
he played the flute, which he was quite adept at when he practised
it, but then something else would distract him. He never regarded
himself as a proper musician.'

Sweeney's Men were up and running and gradually a unique
sound was born around a bouzouki–mandolin interplay that
would later be cited as one of the key attributes of Planxty's
music. As legend reads, Johnny Moynihan introduced the Greek
bouzouki to Irish music. Much to his chagrin, this story has been
perverted and contorted in various articles and books through
the years. Johnny bought his first bouzouki from a friend called
Tony Ffrench who had brought the instrument back from
Greece. 'He decided he either couldn't play it or didn't want to,'
explains Johnny.

There will probably never be definitive proof of who first played or brought the bouzouki to Ireland, but Moynihan's application of the instrument to Irish music has led to it becoming a staple of the culture today. 'I heard there was a guy who played a bouzouki before that,' reveals Moynihan. 'But he wasn't on the scene and I didn't know who he was. And nobody ever told me where he played or anything about him.'

Initially, the Greek bouzouki wasn't well received by Moynihan's band-mates, but it soon became an integral facet of the band's sound. 'That was kind of invented by Johnny and me one night in his parents' kitchen, which I remember well,' says Andy. 'He was playing 'Rattlin' Roarin' Willy' and he was trying to get the phrasing of the tune and we suddenly decided to put a harmony to it and I think that was the beginning of the bouzouki–mandolin interplay.'

Having later swapped his bouzouki for a pre-war Gibson mandolin – 'an offer I couldn't refuse' – Moynihan's second bouzouki was a different shape altogether. It was a flat back rather than the traditional round back. 'I was in London with an old friend, now deceased, Trevor Crozier. Trevor knew a guy called John Bailey who made instruments for the leading lights of the English folk scene. John had a bouzouki that he made himself and was fed up with it hanging on his wall. Trevor heard that I no longer had a bouzouki and so he said he'd introduce me to John, which he did. Bailey had been in a Greek restaurant in London and he saw these bouzouki players and he asked if he could measure the instrument. He'd never made a round-back instrument, so he used a flat back and the sound was lovely. It hadn't got the depth or the punch of a normal bouzouki, but it actually had more sustain and it sounded like a Martin guitar with a real long neck.'

Johnny Moynihan was late coming to Irish music. 'One day I

was passing a radio and Ciarán MacMathúna's *Job of
Journeywork* was on and I heard this roots music from County
Tipperary and I couldn't believe my ears, it was the sort of stuff
I'd been listening to from all over the world. I was seventeen
before I realised there was such a thing as good traditional Irish
music. When I was at college Eamonn O'Doherty had a tin

History of the Bouzouki

The bouzouki was first popularised by the famed composer and
player Vassilis Tsitsánis. When Tsitsánis died in 1983, the streets
of Athens were filled with mourners carrying bouzoukis.
However, the instrument can be further traced to the longneck
lute of ancient Persia and Byzantium. The word 'bouzouki' is
thought to have evolved from 'bouzouk saz', a bowl-shaped
Turkish string instrument with a long, thin neck. However, the
bouzouki is most associated with a style of improvised Greek
music called *rembetika*. According to Paul Kotapish of *Acoustic
Guitar Magazine*: 'The *rembetik* culture bloomed in the
underworld of prisons and hashish dens in the port cities of the
Aegean Sea and western Asia Minor in the early 1900s, reaching
its zenith in the years between the world wars. A typical early
ensemble might have included a singer, two or more bouzoukis
playing melody and simple chords, and a tiny version of the
bouzouki called the baglama providing a staccato rhythm
accompaniment. The songs, with lyrics about drugs, hookers,
money, love, and death, were based on a variety of ancient
modes and traditional dance rhythms, and they were
characterized by expressive improvised introductions called
taxims, impassioned singing, and bouzouki breaks between
verses. Among the most influential of early players – or
rembetes – were Márkos Vamvakáris and Ioannis Papaioannou.'

whistle. I remember seeing one in the loft at home, so I went back and got it. Then Ronnie Drew gave me a present of a mandolin.'

Both Johnny and Andy were enamoured with old-timey American music from the 1920s and 1930s and they tried to emulate the sound of five-string banjos and Appalachian dulcimers with their open-tuned mandolins and bouzoukis. They made connections between traditional American music and Irish and Scottish songs and tunes, employing harmonica and tin whistle to accompany the stringed instruments. Sweeney's Men was an oddball trio in an age of showbands. 'Our ethos was based on an idealistic attitude of doing what we wanted to do and avoiding strokes of any sort,' explains Andy. 'Any kind of folk music was fair game, so we did American stuff and Irish stuff, Scottish stuff and English stuff.'

Joe Dolan had played guitar on the showband scene and it was through his connections that Sweeney's Men acquired their first official manager, the affable Des Kelly, leader of the Capitol Showband. Kelly hailed from Turloughmore in Galway and had played in bands since secondary school. 'That was back in what we called the "paraffin-oil shed days" because there was no electric lighting in the ballrooms,' Kelly remembers fondly. 'I did Agricultural Science in college and you had to go to Dublin to the Albert College for the last three years. I packed up all the music in Galway and went to Dublin, but I soon ran out of money and started playing music again with a couple of guys. We played at hops and stuff and relieved other bands and any way we could get a few bob. So I put the Capitol Showband together and that took on a life of its own. We had a rhythm section of drums, bass, piano and rhythm guitar, and a front line of trumpet, trombone, tenor sax and double clarinet. I played bass. It was a good band. I think it was generally accepted that we were the best musical band in the country of the showband type.

'Joe Dolan had been our very first guitar player in the Capitol Showband. He was a great friend of mine from Galway – a loveable, strange man. Later on, the Capitol Showband played the Puck Fair in Killorglin, County Kerry. It was a very long night. All the pubs had extensions. Joe suddenly appeared in front of the stage and said, "Ah God, you should come over to the pub across the road, I'm playing with a group called Sweeney's Men." So our interval came and my brother Johnny and I went across. I was totally knocked out. Straight away I took to them. It was so fresh, the sound of bouzouki and guitar. Before that it was The Clancy Brothers, Margaret Barry, all that sort of stuff, but this was a breath of fresh air. It was extremely musical. Before that when a group sat down and played, it was every man for themselves. But this was totally organised and harmonious, with Joe playing the big chords and the intricate playing of Johnny and Andy. I became an instant fan.'

As soon as he became the band's manager, Des Kelly imposed a neat and tidy code of uniform on these beatnik scruffs. 'We ended up wearing white shirts, dark waistcoats and dark trousers. We looked like three waiters,' chuckles Johnny in reflection. 'I didn't like the idea of the clothes, but Des wanted it and Andy endorsed that. I went along with it.'

Des Kelly, of course, will never be allowed to forget the uniforms. 'I remember bringing a set of shirts back from the States for them. The philosophy from the showband background was at least the musicians should be distinguished from the punters. It was an advantage. But the boys preferred to be totally anonymous. They were free spirits and we were all bourgeois bollixes to them. You didn't talk about money until they were totally broke. But I could laugh at all this. I thought the world of them. I loved Andy. I loved his integrity in his life and his music. There wasn't a crooked bone in him. He would shout and roar at you, but he couldn't hurt a fly. He's the most loveable man.'

'We were in great form,' continues Johnny. 'Especially Joe. He was a very jolly man. Andy was very humorous and very much into the craic. And I wasn't always the miserable old chap you see in front of you now. We didn't have a set list. We had a repertoire in our heads. We had a system where we'd each take it in turns to sing a song. Because I had more effrontery – I was more at ease in front of an audience – I would always do the first number, Andy would always do the second one and Joe would do the third and we'd carry on like that and occasionally throw in an instrumental. Within that lack of framework, we also had a sort of natural awareness that a gig should have a fetching start and there's got to be some slower, more serious numbers, but there shouldn't be too many on the trot. There should be humour in it and we should finish with a good rousing number.'

Folk-singer Anne Briggs also travelled with Sweeney's Men for some of the time. 'She was a great singer and a wild woman,' remarks Andy. Briggs is one of the great enigmas of folk music. Sandy Denny, Maddy Prior, June Tabor, Linda Thompson and Norma Waterson have all reaped inspiration from this mysterious and strikingly beautiful Nottinghamshire-born singer, as have many male singers such as Christy Moore, Dick Gaughan and Bert Jansch. 'The first folk club I ever went into in Britain was The Scot's Hoose in London and Annie Briggs was playing and she blew me away,' proclaims Christy. Even rock 'n' roll performers such as Led Zeppelin's Jimmy Page have cherished her music. Johnny Moynihan was her boyfriend for a number of years. They shared a dexterity on the bouzouki, a predilection for roving the countryside and performing music in informal environments. She also shared his difficulty with recording and reluctance to forgo artistic integrity for the trappings of commercialism.

'The one unfortunate thing about Sweeney's Men was the name, because we were supposed to be "men",' ponders Johnny. 'We had three fantastic singers who were practically travelling around with us: Annie Briggs, the late Caitlín Maude, who was a poet and actress and a figurehead of Gaelic culture, and, later, Gay Woods. Caitlín Maude knocked about with Sweeney's Men when we were starting out. In fact, I've a poster for a gig in Carlow with Sweeney's Men in big letters which reads "also featuring Anne Briggs and Caitlín Maude" in quite small print. They sang, not together, separately. Two fucking giantesses! Two huge singers and they were in little print under a poxy little ballad group. Bizarre. If we hadn't been called Sweeney's Men, we could have had a mighty group altogether. I suppose if we'd had a bit more of a taste for the bizarre we'd have had them on anyway.'

At the end of the summer of 1966, the band moved back to Dublin, to a house in Nottingham Street, North Strand. 'It was horrible,' shudders Andy. 'It was a cold winter and a miserable house. I slept in the kitchen. There were only two bedrooms. We didn't get much work in the winter of 1966. We were down on our luck altogether. In the early part of 1967, Des Kelly was throwing things in our direction. The Capitol Showband decided to put out a single a month and Des sang the first one, 'The Streets of Baltimore', and Dolan and myself played guitars on that. Anybody could have done it, but Des kindly gave it to us and we got twenty-five quid each, which was a huge sum of money. We eventually did a runner from Nottingham Street owing a week's rent and found another place on Ellis Quay, which became a sort of open house and was even more rough and ready and full of people all the time. I mean, we'd play The Neptune Rowing Club and half the audience would come back there afterwards.'

'There was no electricity or running water or nothing up there on Ellis Quay,' Des Kelly agrees. 'And there might be twenty or

thirty bodies in all states of disarray. But the music was absolutely
brilliant. The lifestyle appealed to me as well, maybe because it
contrasted with the rigidity of what we were doing on the showband scene. All of sudden, you had these three free spirits producing this great music. They were bohemian in their outlook.'

Sweeney's Men recorded their first single, 'Old Maid in the
Garrett', a sort of traditional comedy song, for Pye Records at
Eamonn Andrews Studio in Dublin. It was backed with the old
English mummer song 'The Derby Ram'. They also recorded Joe
Dolan's version of 'Sullivan's John', a song from the well-known
traveller Pecker Dunne, a colourful man renowned for
performing outside GAA football and hurling matches on a
fiddle he made himself. Much to the disappointment of the band,
this track didn't appear on the pressed single. Nonetheless, the
single was a Top Ten hit in the Irish charts.

'The week 'Old Maid in the Garret' was in the Top Ten, Joe
Dolan decided to go to Israel for the Six Day War. He arrived on
the seventh day,' recalls Des. 'I remember ringing him in
O'Donoghue's to tell him the big news about the single in the
charts. And Joe says, "Hold on, Des, there's something that's
after happening that's bigger than you or me or Sweeney's Men.
I've got to go to Israel." I actually bought a couple of paintings
off him to finance the trip. That's the sort of relationship I had
with Sweeney's Men!'

'After Joe left, I remember meeting Johnny in O'Donoghue's
and wondering what we were going to do,' recalls Andy. 'We did
ask Paul Brady, who was a friend, to join the band. He wasn't
really an O'Donoghue's regular and had only just moved into the
traditional scene. He was a rhythm-and-blues guy well known in
UCD. Paul actually played a gig with Sweeney's Men in Limerick.
I remember him playing that gig really well because we were
excited about his accompaniment to 'The Derby Ram', which

was different to Dolan's. I'm pretty sure it was Johnny who asked him, but Paul had just joined The Johnstons and he was regretful but there was nothing further to be done.

'Terry Woods had been pushing hard to get into Sweeney's Men. Johnny had doubts about Terry but we didn't know any other decent guitar players, and, of course, they also had to be people who would slot into our lifestyle. He was good on both twelve-string and six-string guitar. His entire animus was towards American music, which he did very well.'

Terry Woods was a Dublin-born multi-instrumentalist who, aside from guitar, played concertina, banjo and various other instruments, and sang in an old-timey-style American drawl. 'When Terry was in a good mood he was great fun,' says Andy. 'But he was a moody character and when he was in a bad mood he'd let everybody know. Johnny made no concessions to his bad moods, or rarely. So the two of them would be at loggerheads some of the time.'

The second Sweeney's Men single was an augmented version of an old Dublin song, 'The Waxie's Dargle'. It was an even bigger success and made number two in the charts. 'There was a show on RTÉ, a sort of hit parade type of thing,' remembers Andy. 'They'd start at number ten. You held your breath waiting to hear your name. It was exciting enough, I must say. After that, the record company brought out an EP, what they called a "maxi-single", which was a 45 rpm with all four tracks from the two singles.'

Despite chart success, there was little or no money to be made from records for Sweeney's Men. Live music paid the bills, but they really had to earn their fees. 'If all the people who say, "Oh Sweeney's Men, great gig, I remember seeing them in such and such" had actually been at the gig, we would've been huge, but we weren't,' reflects Andy. 'It was the time of the ballad boom.

There were an awful lot of bands around, most of whom were copies of the American coffee-bar scene bands like The Kingston Trio.'

In late 1967, Roddy Hickson took over as manager of Sweeney's Men, along with John Mahon and Gerry MacDonagh and started to get gigs for the band. Andy remembers that Gerry 'sold refrigeration spare parts and was the only guy I liked'. 'Can you imagine their delight,' says Andy, 'when, within a week of their takeover of management, 'The Waxie's Dargle' hit the charts! Roddy was a real whizzkid who drank coffee in The New Amsterdam on Duke Street, off Grafton Street, which was the real "in" place for people like him. He knew what was going on, on the street and all this kind of stuff, but he was a pain in the arse. He was opinionated and all his opinions were in complete contrast to how we felt. But they got gigs and we started playing these dreadful dancehall gigs where we'd play for about twenty minutes in between the showband sets and we'd get paid fifty quid. But the audience wouldn't listen.

'Two thousand people in a concrete block can make an awful lot of noise when they're not listening,' continues Andy. 'And you've only got two microphones, which is all the showbands had, and they wouldn't change the settings for you. It was desperate. I hated it. It was the most paranoid time in my life. There was no back door to get out. You'd get off the stage and go into the band-room to the side of the stage and sit there and think, "Fuck." And eventually you'd have to pluck up your courage to pack up your instruments and walk out through the people. I used to look straight ahead. There's the door. I'm going to be at it in a minute. Into the car and away!'

Andy really was thinking of getting away. He had gotten the bug from his previous hitch-hiking expedition around Europe. 'I'd given my notice just before Roddy and Gerry came on board.

They tried to stop me leaving, but they didn't in any way deflect me in my desire to travel.'

Before Andy left Sweeney's Men, they made their self-titled debut album in early 1968 for the Transatlantic record label with Bill Leader, an Englishman who kept tabs on what was happening in music in Ireland, as producer. 'Bill had been over in Dublin a good few times,' recalls Andy. 'He had wanted to record Johnny and used myself and Muriel's flat in 88 Lower Baggot Street and it didn't happen because Johnny, as ever, faced with the microphone, didn't manage to produce his best work. We also played on an album that Bill recorded, which I don't think ever saw the light of day, by The Grehan Sisters. He was a quiet, restrained kind of person. You wouldn't quite know what was going on there. So we respected him. We were inclined to think that his silences were due to his intellect. Whether that was true or not I've no idea, but one thing I do know was that he was a very good cook. The recording was done in Livingstone Studios in Barnet. I think we slept on his floor.'

Bill Leader remembers the first time he came across Andy Irvine in London. 'He always seemed to be coming from some exotic place well to the east like Bulgaria or somewhere like that, heading west to somewhere like Dublin, with yet another exotic instrument under his arm. He seemed to be someone who was exploring music and music-making and putting things together as he went along. In a way, I thought the music of Sweeney's Men was representative of Dublin. It was that strange mixture of the traditional and the intellectual and the poetic. If some distinguished Dublin writers of earlier years had actually got bouzoukis around their necks they might have produced songs somewhat similar to what Sweeney's Men were doing.'

The album's material makes for an intriguing miscellany of styles and hybrids. It begins with some sprightly bouzouki–

mandolin stitch-work and Moynihan's infectious free-flowing vocal on the Robbie Burns slip jig, 'Rattlin' Roarin' Willy'. Johnny also tackles what was previously Joe Dolan's baby, the Pecker Dunne ballad 'Sullivan's John', Andy takes lead on the woozy sea-shanty 'Sally Brown', which he later sang live with Planxty. He also sings lead on one of the album's outstanding tracks, 'Willy O Winsbury', the words of which were learned from Child's *English and Scottish Popular Ballads*, and were actually confused with an entirely different air. The resulting song is full of the quintessential Irvine poignancy and pathos. 'The Exile's Jig' is a lonesome whistle and mandolin tune learned from a recording of Seán Ó Riada's pioneering traditional ensemble, Ceoltóirí Chualann. Terry Woods brought the well-known American murder ballad 'Tom Dooley', a version not dissimilar to that of Doc Watson, and the old spooked-out southern ballad 'The House Carpenter', the latter's authenticity bolstered by Woods's eerily identical southern intones.

Despite Johnny Moynihan's claims that he 'can't listen to it', the debut *Sweeney's Men* album is a secret, treasured artefact of the Irish folk canon. Removed from the unappreciative context of the dreaded dancehalls and the frequently artless table-thumping of the ballad boom, *Sweeney's Men* is a luxury of imaginative musical ideas and cultural concoctions. Like any great record that surfaced before its time, *Sweeney's Men* was a vagrant sound roaming a world of preordained markets of acceptability. In hindsight, it is the missing link – the great innocent shot in the dark that helped dislodge the formulae of Irish folk music and later heralded in a new generation of fearless folk ensembles.

Andy Irvine left Sweeney's Men in style with a blow-out gig at Liberty Hall in Dublin, where he played the first half of the set in the old Sweeney suits with Moynihan and Woods. For the second half, he stepped down to make way for his replacement, guitarist Henry McCullough. 'The audience was aware of the fact that I was leaving. It was a big gig. For the second half, the band changed their gear and came out with Henry. Johnny wore a sheepskin waistcoat and Persian knee-length soft leather boots. Terry wore his jean jacket and jeans. They were a different band. Johnny had a big Shure microphone inside his bouzouki and Henry played the electric guitar. He was very good. I'd been party to rehearsals in Johnny's flat in Pembroke Lane. I was pleased to see the band going on and I was kind of into the music. They'd gotten into bands like Traffic by this time and had moved in a slightly different direction, and I would have had difficulty with that if I'd stayed in the band anyway.'

'I certainly wished him well,' says Johnny. 'I knew he wanted to go and it was a good idea. I had a fairly easy-going attitude, I suppose. I was smoking a fair bit of dope at the time.' Sweeney's Men would strive onwards, soaking up new psychedelic influences along the way, and making one more album in 1969.

Andy Irvine, meanwhile, was heading for adventures across the continent to the Balkans. 'Most people were thinking of going further afield and going to Nepal and places The Beatles had been to and where the Maharishi had stood on Mount Whatever and where drugs were cheap, and I'd no great interest in any of those things. I kind of remembered that, as a stamp collector, I had liked Bulgarian stamps because they had a weird script. And, of course, I had left-wing leanings. Also, nobody went there. So I decided to go. It was 1968 and, looking back on it, that became a period where a lot of people decided to broaden their horizons.'

That August in Kilrush when the rain was lashing down,
And our hotel was that hay-barn on the outskirts of
  town.
We were all sick and feverish and Dolan had the flu,

But Johnny produced some whiskey and the sun came
   smiling through.
Those nights in Sixmilebridge when the songs and
   music flowed
And when it came to closing, the lights were turned
   down low.
And the sergeant from Kilkishen, he would buy us all
   one more
And we never left that pub before the clock was striking
   four.
My heart tonight is far away across the rolling sea
In the sweet Milltown Malbay it's there I'd love to be.
So long ago and far away, but nothing can compare.
My heart's tonight in Ireland in the sweet County Clare
In the days of Sweeney, in the sweet County Clare.

'My Heart's Tonight in Ireland' – Andy Irvine

Chapter 6

Prosperous

As the end of the 1960s approached, the paths of Liam O'Flynn, Christy Moore, Dónal Lunny and Andy Irvine slowly began to converge. Like his father and grandfather before him, Liam O'Flynn spent several years working as a schoolteacher, but he was also slowly discovering the late-night world of folk clubs. Dónal Lunny, when not busy making jewellery, was making a name for himself as one of the most accomplished young musicians in the country. Over in England, Christy Moore was pondering the follow-up to his debut album. While Andy Irvine was discovering the joys of Eastern Europe.

It quickly became apparent that Andy's instincts were correct. It was the beginning of a life-long love affair. '1968 was the Bulgarian Year of Tourism and there weren't any tourists except Muriel and me. It was very good for us because the police had obviously been told, "Tourism is very important to us and we must nurture it. So don't say boo to foreigners." I remember Muriel and I walked for miles and miles down little narrow paths and on each side there'd be sunflowers as far as the eye could see, or maize, massive plantations of crops. It was very beautiful. They were lovely people too, very open people.'

From Istanbul to Bulgaria and on to Romania, Andy and Muriel hitch-hiked around the Balkans, living out of rucksacks. 'We were in a truck when we first heard Bulgarian folk music. I was bowled over by it. The driver was trying to talk to us and we didn't have enough Bulgarian and the engine was very loud anyway, so he turned on the radio. And this music came out and I thought, "Wow, that must be Bulgarian folk music!" I was hooked. It was like Woody Guthrie. From the first bar I was, "Yesssssssssss!" Bulgarian music was played on the radio a lot back then. The overthrow of Stalinism was a historical necessity, but it was a shame all the bathwater was thrown out as well because culture was much respected in those days. I couldn't understand it at the time. I couldn't understand the music any better than most people can now when I play it. The beat and the rhythm are totally alien to Western ears, so I had to get the hang of that first. And, of course, a little learning is a dangerous thing. I bought a kaval [a variation of flute played in Balkan folk music] and a gajda [or *gaida*, Bulgarian bagpipe]. I could get a few notes out of the kaval and very little out of the gajda, and never did after that. I failed systematically with my attempts to master Bulgarian instruments!'

When the winter cold hit, Andy and Muriel retreated to Ljubljana and then back to Denmark to earn some money at some of the folk clubs Andy had previously played in 1965. They returned to Ireland briefly for Joe Dolan's wedding, and stayed long enough to get married themselves, before heading back to Romania, where they listened to and learned about Romanian gypsy musicians. 'In Romania, the gypsies were the people who held onto the folk music. The peasants were largely losing the musical folk tradition at this time, I think. The gypsies were the professional people. If you were having a wedding or something, you would invite a local gypsy band to play at it, and their music would be taken from traditional music, but played in a gypsy fashion. In any country in Eastern Europe, they would take the basic tradition but they wouldn't have the same conservative respect for it that the peasant would.'

Andy sees parallels with the Eastern European folk tradition and the folk scene in Ireland, and tells the story of how Willie Clancy met Johnny Doran in the streets of Miltown Malbay at a fair one day. 'Doran was playing the pipes, standing up, I think (I don't know how he did that), and Willie Clancy was captivated by this. Later, he found Doran's caravan and said he would like to learn the pipes. Doran taught him how to play 'Rakish Paddy'. He practised all year and, the following year around the same time, Johnny Doran's caravan was sighted again and he went up to him and said, "I learned to play that tune." Johnny said, "Yes, very good, but this is the way I play it now." And it had changed completely. I heard this story on RTÉ, I think it was from Peter Browne, and to illustrate the story he played Willie Clancy playing 'Rakish Paddy' and then played Johnny Doran's version, and you could immediately see the difference between the settled peasant attitude to the music and the much wilder, freer, less respectful attitude of the travelling person. That's probably the same with gypsy music everywhere. At least that's the way I saw it.'

Returning home, Andy carried with him the magic of this mysterious new music. From here on in, it would continue to inform the music he played and enkindle the other musical cultures he was interested in. He penned a tune called

'Blacksmithereens' based on his impressions of Balkan music, and he segued it with the old English folk song, 'The Blacksmith'. 'I came back from Eastern Europe in late 1969. I did a gig in London and I played 'The Blacksmith' and the piece after it, and Peter Bellamy [English folk singer/folklorist] came up to me afterwards and said in his plummy, outright way, "I think your Blacksmith is a load of old Balkans!"'

While Andy was away on his travels, Sweeney's Men had seen a number of personnel changes. Henry McCullough's tenure with the band was short-lived. Moynihan had initially encountered McCullough when his band, Eire Apparent, was supporting the Jimi Hendrix Experience at Queen's University in Belfast in November 1967. McCullough was a Portstewart-born musician who became interested in the Sweeney's Men interpretation of traditional music, despite his own background in blues and rock. He played at the Cambridge Folk Festival with them in the summer of 1968. But not long after, he was invited to join Joe Cocker's Grease Band and became the only Irish musician to perform at Woodstock. He later went on to to play with Paul McCartney in Wings.

Popular Irish musician Al O'Donnell made a brief appearance with Sweeney's Men after that, but the rambling lifestyle didn't suit him. Moynihan and Woods continued on as a duo and recorded a second album with Bill Leader in 1969, also for Transatlantic, called *The Tracks of Sweeney*. The sound of this record veers somewhat towards American psychedelic bands and features a real somnolent treasure in Moynihan's 'Standing on the Shore' and a number of hillbilly humdingers from Terry Woods. It was to be Sweeney's parting shot.

Years later, in an interview with the *New Musical Express*, Terry Woods was quoted as saying, 'We confused everyone at Cambridge in 1968, they had no idea what was going on.'

He goes on to describe McCullough's appearance at Cambridge. 'He stood there with his bright red guitar, which amazed everyone. Henry, that red guitar and his long flowing hair! That was the end of Sweeney's Men. Henry just couldn't take it after that. We tried to keep the band going but that was foolish – I suppose I should have joined a rock 'n' roll band there and then.'

Andy, meanwhile, was at a loose end. 'When I got back to Dublin, I didn't really know what to do. The rest of my life suddenly loomed ahead of me. I said to Johnny in O'Donoghue's, "Any chance of getting back into Sweeney's Men?" But he was very reluctant to think about Sweeney's Men. By that time, he'd had Terry Woods up to the eyeballs. They weren't getting on. 'I played one gig with Johnny and Terry at Nottingham University in October or November 1969 and it was really difficult. Very little was said – I felt I had to introduce songs because no one was talking. The tuning up was incessant. They hadn't practised and it was very rough altogether. I think that was the beginning of the end.'

For a brief moment after the demise of Sweeney's Men, there was the very real possibility of an Irish-English folk supergroup, one that we can now only fantasise about. Ashley 'Tyger' Hutchings, bassist and founding member of the acclaimed English folk-rock band Fairport Convention, had quit that group not long after the release of their 1970 masterpiece album, *Liege and Lief*. 'Tyger's a nice guy. His plan was to form a new band with Sweeney's Men – the three of us – and Terry's wife, Gay Woods,' explains Andy. 'I was quite taken with the idea because I had nothing on. But Johnny decided that for "Moynihan" reasons he couldn't do it. I felt musically connected to Johnny and so I also declined. I didn't think it would be a good idea without him. But we had a band meeting and I don't remember much music being played, but I do remember singing 'Autumn

Gold', which was my new number, and it being hailed by Tyger as a minor masterpiece! The group eventually became Steeleye Span with Terry and Gay, and instead of Johnny and me it was Tim Hart and Maddy Prior. It pulled itself apart in a short time. Gay and Terry left and Martın Carthy joined.'

'I made it as far as the office of Nat Joseph of Transatlantic Records,' says Johnny. 'My idea of starting a band was to maybe play some music at a party, see if we can get a gig in the local pub, maybe make the price of a van and go off and have a great time. The idea for this group was obviously something different. So I said sorry for my earlier agreement, which wasn't very firm anyway.'

With Sweeney's Men laid to rest and no sign of a folk supergroup in the works, suddenly Andy's freewheeling life was hit with a dose of reality. 'I was already twenty-eight by this time and the whole thing about earning a living suddenly came more into focus. It's really weird how up until about twenty-five you're not worried about the future at all. By 1970, I was trying to think what I could do next. It was probably Al O'Donnell who introduced me to the Friday and Saturday night gigs in Slattery's on Capel Street. I sometimes played five or six times a week for all the clubs. It was a good time. There were clubs every night of the week there, upstairs and downstairs. On a Monday there was the Blackbird Folk Club downstairs, there were two clubs on a Tuesday, Wednesday was the Tradition Club upstairs, Thursday was something else. One week I played seven times, I literally played them all. I can see myself setting out winter, summer and spring with the big Peter guitar that I played, wrapped in a brocade bedspread that somebody had given me, and the mandolin, getting on a bus into town from Donnybrook and walking up Henry Street to Slattery's. It wasn't great money, but it kept me going. It was a godsend, really.

'Al and myself were interchangeable and we'd play in the middle. He'd been playing there before me and he was more popular than I was. There'd be someone to start with, which we never heard because we'd be downstairs having a pint. They'd be some ballad-type trio. And then Ollie Cassley, who ran the gig, would get up on the stage and say something like, "And now ladies and gentlemen, for my real highlight of the night, Irish traditional music!" Paddy O'Brien, a great accordion player, and Joey on the bodhrán would play reels, and Ollie would be shouting out "Hit 'er a diddy" and all these remarks and the audience would be way into it because they'd be well on by that time. It was very well supported, jam-packed and noisy. It was a difficult gig to play.'

It was around this time that Andy Irvine and Dónal Lunny forged a serious musical bond. 'I'd have known of Andy and Sweeney's Men for many years and I really wanted to get to know him,' admits Dónal. 'And an amazing thing happened. I was staying in a bedsit in Grove Park when I was in college and Andy came to the door, carrying all these instruments, and he asked me was there a room to let in the house. I was thinking, "Yeah! You can stay with us." But I didn't say that because there wasn't any room. That was the first time I met him. He actually had his two arms full of instruments. I don't think Andy remembers that.'

'We knew each other a little bit because Sweeney's Men and Emmet Spiceland were on the same circuit roughly,' explains Andy. 'I remember one gig when Sweeney's Men and Emmet Spiceland played together. There was a guy who had lived in Denmark who knew people who worked in the Folk Music Academy in Iceland. He put on a gig, which he paid for himself, and I'm not sure why. I think he didn't like the way the folk music scene was going and he put on this gig to try and get it back to a less pop, more credible state. He booked Sweeney's Men and someone else, who I can't remember. He then got cold feet I think and booked Emmet Spiceland. He got up before they went on and said something like, "Ladies and gentlemen, the next band is very popular and I'm *hoping* they will perhaps play music that I'm sure they know but which is perhaps not their normal repertoire." So then Emmet Spiceland got up and they probably brought the house down. I didn't like them. It was a bit soft soap, a bit sweet, but the girls loved them.'

According to Andy, Sean MacReamoinn was the instigator of his first real encounter with Dónal Lunny. 'I met him in a pub and he said, "We're having this big Irish–Soviet Union friendship conference and we're having a party after it. Would you come and play? Dónal Lunny is going to come and play as well." Ten minutes before we went on, we arranged two pieces, one of which was 'Reynard the Fox' and probably Dónal's one song at the time, 'When First unto this Country', which is great. Everybody was sitting around drinking and shouting Russian phrases. We went on stage and he was the best musician I had played with up to that point, and the quickest. Johnny Moynihan was the first musician that I played with that I really respected, but it took a long time for Johnny to get it together, as it did for me on his stuff. I saw the speed at which Dónal picked up on the way I was doing something and that was the first insight I had into what a great musician he was.'

'No doubt about it, Andy and myself are kindred spirits in our love of strange time signatures and syncopation and punctuation in our approach to music,' agrees Dónal. 'He had recordings of Bulgarian music. He had Le Mystère des Voix Bulgares from the late 1960s. I mean, they didn't really surface over here until the late 1980s. Hearing it back then was magical for me. It blew me away. Andy and myself were experimenting with drugs at this time. He was also into Soft Machine, who'd loop tapes manually. It could be a piece of tape twenty-seven feet long on the floor uncoiling out of the tape recorder and sort of picked up at the other end and going back in again. Steve Reich used that technique too. It was fantastic. It was before synthesisers kicked in really, very spacey music. Meeting Andy really fed my hunger for that kind of music.'

Andy Irvine and Dónal Lunny performed all over town as a duo, opening for popular rock outfit Horslips and the English blues-rock singer Duster Bennett at shows in the Exam Hall in Trinity College. This partnership also furthered the presence of the bouzouki in Irish music. Just as Johnny Moynihan had introduced the instrument to Andy Irvine, he in turn passed it on to Dónal Lunny.

'Andy had loads of instruments in his room in Marlborough Road,' recalls Dónal. 'He lived with Eamonn O'Doherty, but it was a kind of an open house. It was brilliant, a lovely place to be always. Very cool, very relaxed. He started bringing back all these strange instruments like the kaval, the gadulka, instruments I'd never seen. One day, I started playing the bouzouki and I really liked the sound of it. Because there were four pairs of strings, the chords were kind of easy. And even though it was upside down for me, I could still get chords out of it and I just really loved it. And Andy said, "Ah take it home with you, the strings are very slack for me." So he just gave it to me. Brilliant! That was the round-bodied Greek bouzouki and the bouzouki became the thing I used most. I think it has a great application to Irish music. It allows Irish music to be itself. I realised that pretty quickly because the openness of the chords didn't actually cloud the music too much. You know, the conventional shapes of chords on the guitar are so familiar and clichéd. There's nothing unusual about them. They're so ordinary. But the sound of the bouzouki and the configurations of the notes were different, it was a new thing. Andy at that time played more mandolin than bouzouki, so it was a good combination between the pair of us anyway.'

Folk singers performing in clubs with guitars, mandolins and bouzoukis is one thing, but live performance is not so straightforward for a student of an instrument as recondite as the uilleann pipes. Nonetheless, Liam O'Flynn was learning how to engage an audience with his instrumental prowess. He performed with other traditional musicians such as Matt Molloy and Seán Keane. The Old Sheiling Hotel in Raheny, Dublin was a popular spot. 'It was the height of the ballad boom when I played the Old Sheiling. The man who owned the place was Bill Fuller, but Dolly McMahon, Ciarán MacMathúna's wife, was in charge of the music booking and Dolly always insisted on having some pure traditional music there as well. So Matt Molloy and I played there two, three, four nights a week as a duo. That was part of the learning curve, playing to a live audience in that sort of environment.'

Beyond pure traditional music, Liam was becoming increasingly aware of a new generation of folk singers and bands. 'I remember the first time I heard The Clancy Brothers, I was blown away. I couldn't get over the energy. I'd heard all these songs sung in another style, but this was a completely new approach. It didn't seem like a corruption in any way. It was really catching the songs by the scruff of the neck.'

He first met Dónal Lunny at the music sessions in Prosperous. 'I guess he was really the first person I had direct musical contact with using guitar to accompany traditional music. He very, very friendly and it was obvious he was in it for the sheer enjoyment of it, the sheer buzz of playing music. I also heard Emmet Spiceland. They created an individual sound. It was immediately recognisable and had beautiful harmonies.

'I knew who Andy Irvine was from being in and out of folk clubs,' continues Liam. 'Sweeney's Men were very exciting. There was more of an instrumental dimension in there. You always got the sense from a band like Sweeney's Men that that was their way of life. They were a travelling, on-the-road style band. You got hints of another sort of tradition. There were shades of Woody Guthrie, who I didn't know much about at the time, and there were echoes of English folk music in there as well. It seemed like a hugely romantic and adventurous way of life.'

Andy thinks that he probably met Liam for the first time in 1970 at the Tradition Club upstairs in Slattery's, where the Wednesday night sessions featured the best musicians around. 'I was aware of the fact that even though he came from a different, a really different, musical background, that there was a mutual respect between us. You'd meet him maybe at the bar in Slattery's or somewhere and he'd detach himself from whoever he was talking to and come over and say hello.'

Still reeling from the experience of *Paddy on the Road*, Christy Moore had an idea. Inspired by the new sounds echoing across the Irish Sea, he decided he was going to attempt to put together his dream band. '*Paddy on the Road* was an odd album. I was very unhappy with the way it was made even though I was happy to have made an album. I grew to realise that it really didn't reflect anything. The Irish music I heard in London was a revelation to me. It opened up my ears. There was a whole attitude to the music and what it meant in the ghettos. I was over in England having heard Sweeney's Men, having heard Liam playing and being aware of different things that Dónal was doing, and I felt if I ever got the opportunity to make a second album, then I would do it with musicians I love rather than people with whom I was told to play.'

Christy's master plan was taking shape. He approached Bill

Leader, who had started up his Leader and Trailer record labels, to bring his mobile recording unit to Ireland in the summer of 1971. The musicians he invited were Andy Irvine, Dónal Lunny and Liam O'Flynn. Kevin Conneff, with whom Christy had frequently played in Britain, played bodhrán, and English musicians Clive Collins and Dave Bland contributed on fiddle and concertina, respectively.

'I wasn't very familiar with his work, but I was aware of Christy's reputation,' explains Bill Leader. 'I think he had made a bigger mark in the north of England than he had in London. Particularly around West Yorkshire, he was legendary. He and Mike Harding and Hamish Imlach and people like that had big reputations. I was London-based and I was very metro-centric at that time, to my shame. So I met him in London and it all seemed like a great idea, so we proceeded.'

'I can't say exactly what it was that was in my mind,' admits Christy. 'I can't say I was after a specific sound. But I certainly wanted to play with people whom I felt would understand what it was I was doing. It had to have pipes and it probably had to have a piper as well. Liam was the first piper I ever got in close to and I've always found a deep and moving soulfulness about his playing. Even as a young man, I heard that and without knowing much about the instrument or its history, it still touched me deeply. Sweeney's Men were a revelation to me; Andy's singing and hearing the first Sweeney's Men album ... it was head-turning. It was also the accents they sang in. There was something very real for me about it. They weren't just chronicling the music. They were living it. Dónal Lunny was the first guitar player I ever spoke to. He taught me the chords. I recognised from an early time that Dónal has a distinctive and sympathetic way of accompanying Irish music that very few, if any, have equalled.'

Liam O'Flynn was impressed with Christy's vision. 'I was aware of Christy Moore's existence from back in the day, but I don't think we were ever sort of introduced to each other. I guess the first time we really met each other was when he proposed the idea of this album. He got in touch and he had it really well sorted in his head what he wanted. He picked his guests very carefully. He brought a wonderful energy and excitement to the whole thing. I was amazed because traditional musicians, we play our tunes and we don't think much about them, and then someone comes along outside of your world who can talk about this very seriously and can identify a particular tune. It was a real eye-opener for me.'

'I didn't know Christy that well,' explains Andy. 'I thought he was kind of fast and loose, where I was more introverted. And that's probably still the case. I had respect for him, but I wouldn't say our friendship started until a little bit later. We rehearsed for the album at my flat in Marlborough Road and we got on extremely well. I still have that rehearsal on tape. I remember it well. I was married to Muriel at the time. We'd been in the habit of making Turkish coffee since the Balkans and she came in halfway through the rehearsal with a tray of little cups of thick sweet coffee and a glass of water for everybody, and they were all kind of, "Wow, what's this?"'

The final touch was the recording location. Christy decided upon the old cellar in Downings house in Prosperous, a place that was historically pertinent and possessed with great musical ghosts and memories of after-hours parties throughout the 1960s. Christy's sister and brother-in-law, Anne and Davoc Rynne, were very excited to have such a gathering of fine musicians back in Downings. 'At that stage, we had three small children and it was a very exciting and busy time,' recalls Davoc. 'The house was full and it was all a bit chaotic. I remember standing outside the basement kitchen door listening to the

sound and being awestruck. I also remember being rather concerned about the strange cigarettes some of the musicians were
smoking! But I soon got over that!'

Bill Leader was a good choice of producer. He had cognitive
respect for Irish music and plenty of experience recording it,
from Séamus Ennis to Sweeney's Men. 'He recorded a lot of Irish
music in London as well,' notes Christy. 'He recorded a lot of
traditional players who were in exile. I think he liked what was
good. He had an ear. He was very quiet and very focused, totally
unobtrusive. What he brought to the project were his ears and his
determination to let it happen. And when it happened, he
certainly didn't interfere. There's more to him than meets the
eye.'

'Bill Leader was a very personable man,' adds Liam. 'He
made the business of recording for an inexperienced recording
musician like myself a very enjoyable thing. There was something of the Ciarán MacMathúna about him.'

'He was a quiet, phlegmatic man and very pleasant company,'
agrees Dónal. 'It was a very neutral situation. He wasn't judgemental about the music we recorded. He just let us at it and we
just put it together. For me, it was an epiphany. I'd done the
Emmet Spiceland thing and I was interested in what was going
on. Bill had a Revox tape recorder and two mics, which on the
face of it were wildly incompatible. One was a mic that you'd
normally put into a bass drum, a d-12, a big box of a microphone, and the other one was a condenser mic of some kind. Bill
didn't have monitor speakers. He monitored on headphones all
the time, which was a more compact way to record. I remember
putting on the headphones and listening to a take and hearing it
three dimensionally. I could hear noises behind me and over in
the corner. It made me aware of balancing a mix. The way Bill
balanced it was by moving us around. He put Liam down the

back because his pipes were louder than any of the guitars or bouzoukis or other instruments. He just distributed us. Then it was just a recording of a situation, of an environment, really. It was in the cellar with a flagstone floor and stone walls and the reflections were strong. He actually got a great result. The music was raw and there are flaws in the recording, but generally speaking, he did a great job.'

Leader says he was very modestly equipped to do recordings, but that it worked for the sort of thing he was doing at the time for people like Bert Jansch and John Renbourn. 'They were recorded in rooms in ordinary homes, they weren't done in studios. A couple of microphones and a Revox tape recorder was all I could afford. The players on Christy's album were great players and it's not too difficult to catch that if they are delivering the music. It was great music and they were working together very well. Secondly, the fact that we were down in this haunted cellar gave us a very distinctive acoustic that we could work with.'

The finished record was titled *Prosperous*. It remains a milestone album, Christy Moore's second and the first to feature the combined talents of Moore, Irvine, Lunny and O'Flynn. The cover features the front door of Rynne's stately Downings house. The musicians are lounging on the steps surrounded by a jumble of Davoc Rynne's antiques. 'Davoc was particularly concerned when his "antiques" were hauled out of the showroom for the photo shoot!' jokes Anne. Also noticeable on the front sleeve is the uncomfortable manner in which Andy is seated, with his right leg stretched out straight, the result of a recent motorcycle accident.

The album includes two future Planxty classics, 'Raggle Taggle Gypsy' (listed as 'Raggle Taggle Gipsies') segued into 'Tabhair Dom Do Lámh', a tune written by the blind harper Ruaidhri 'Dall' Ó Catháin, (c.1570–1650) and 'The Cliffs of

Dooneen', a song learned from Andrew Rynne. Already, there was a noticeable improvement in Christy's voice. A deeper, more soulful sound was replacing the sinewy vocals of *Paddy on the Road*. The overall sound of the album is live and breezy. You can literally feel the room and the cold stone floors. Other songs include Bob Dylan's 'Tribute to Woody' and one by Woody Guthrie himself, 'The Ludlow Massacre'. Also included is 'Rambling Robin', learned from Manchester folkie Mike Harding, and 'James Connolly', which Christy first heard Johnny Moynihan sing. But it's the 'Raggle Taggle Gypsy' joined to 'Tabhair Dom Do Lámh' that is the real standout piece and possibly the first ever attempt to play a folk song straight into a traditional tune by an ensemble of Irish musicians.

'That was Christy's idea during the rehearsals,' explains Andy. 'Christy always had that ability to sense these things. He'd say things like, "Wouldn't it be great if we could get from here into this?" And then Dónal came up with the connection. He's good at that. He was recognised by the rest of us as being the person to do that.'

'It was magic to hear *Prosperous*,' declares Dónal. 'On at least one track I was playing slide bouzouki, which was ludicrous, but it was a symptom of the sense of experiment and discovery that was going on at the time. It was like, try any bloody thing. It was a wonderful learning time.'

The album was released in England on Bill's label, Trailer. Christy explains that it was a year or eighteen months later when Tara released it in Ireland. 'This guy called Jack Fitzgerald approached me and said he wanted to get the Prosperous album. He owned the Golden Discs record shops. I put him in touch with Bill Leader and he bought the album from Bill for two thousand quid in 1972. Bill Leader sent me a thousand pounds, half the money. Then Jack Fitzgerald came and gave me another thousand quid. So I had two fuckin' thousand pounds! I didn't see anything like it for another fifteen or twenty years. Prosperous was the first album on Tara and they went on to release all kinds of stuff, including Jolyon Jackson, Stockton's Wing, Planxty, Andy Irvine, Liam O'Flynn, a very good catalogue.'

Prosperous was a revelation. A musical chemistry had been spotted. 'I think maybe during the recording we began to think we could have a band here,' reckons Christy. 'Between the four of us there was some sort of gravitational thing and a mutual regard for each other,' adds Liam. 'That experience on the Prosperous album was a completely new musical direction for me. That was the start of my professional career, becoming a full-time musician. It's a kind of a testament to that time. I knew it was going to make a huge impact. I really did. It was a different sound.'

Chapter 7

The Mugs Gig

The free-flowing, hair-raising chemistry of Andy Irvine, Liam O'Flynn, Dónal Lunny and Christy Moore generated during the *Prosperous* album sessions implanted in them the notion of forming a band together. In theory, it seems like a straightforward plan, yet for these four particular musicians and the spheres of culture and lifestyle they inhabited, it wasn't clear-cut at all. Christy would have to deviate from his snowballing solo career in England, and Dónal and Andy would have to forgo their immensely enjoyable activities as a magnetic double act. Liam O'Flynn, though, would have to take the biggest risk of all. He was a traditional musician and rooted in an entirely different culture to that of the vanguard folk performer. He knew this was a move that would be frowned upon by some traditional purists, yet, unprecedented or not, it was a chance he was driven to take.

1971 was a watershed year in Liam O'Flynn's musical life: it was the year he first played with the combination of Christy, Dónal and Andy; it was the year he gave up teaching; and it was also the year he left home for the first time to embark on a journey of cultural exploration. 'Bill Fuller, who owned the Old Sheiling Hotel, had a place in New York, the Old Sheiling in Queens,' explains Liam. 'He was all the time bringing out groups and musicians to play there. He had Willie Clancy and Máirtín Byrne and many traditional musicians. I played out there for about a month. After that, I decided to stay on, I wasn't ready to go home. I played there every night. There was no pressure involved. If the arse fell out of it, I could just come home. That was an extraordinary experience because it was my first time away from home and here I was making music for a living and meeting all sorts of interesting and wonderful people from different parts of the States.'

At that time, there was a 'piping scene' within the Irish-American community, but, in the larger folk scene, they didn't integrate as far as Liam remembers. 'I really enjoyed being among the folkies. I went to the Philadelphia Folk Festival and met up with Paul Brady and Mick Moloney and The Johnstons, who were living in America at the time. I met a fella named Pat Sky. I remember there was a session of music, as there always would be in those situations. Pat Sky and myself and Brady were playing – Sky had never heard of uilleann pipes before and that was the start of his love affair with the instrument. He was a very active singer-songwriter at the time and he invited me to join him on tour as his opening act. That was an amazing experience. We played in some of the bigger folk clubs and coffee houses, wonderful places. And this was at a time when folk music in America was very much alive and a big cult thing.'

The first place Liam remembers them playing was Caffé Lena in Saratoga Springs in upstate New York. 'A wonderful place.

The atmosphere was very natural in the folk clubs. It wasn't like being forced into formal concert halls where a traditional musician wouldn't feel at home. I had an absolutely fantastic audience, a lot of whom were hearing uilleann pipes for the very first time. They were so welcoming to this young piper from Ireland who was green behind the ears. I was a revelation to them and they were a revelation to me. It was perfect. I also remember on that tour playing one of the great music colleges and the line-up was John Lee Hooker, Pat Sky and Liam O'Flynn!

'In the meantime, I had some communications from the lads. I received a letter, I think from Andy, to tell me there was a wonderful reaction to *Prosperous* and that excitement was in the air and would I be interested in getting together as a band. I had now sampled life on the road in the American folk scene, so the notion of coming back to form the group made all sorts of sense.'

Dónal Lunny's artistic pursuits at the start of the 1970s were pulling him in a number of different directions. 'Both in pottery and metalwork I had been making very small things, tiny little vases and stuff like that, so I quite naturally gravitated towards making jewellery. I did that for a couple of years after I left college. For two years, I was sharing a workshop with Vincent Browne, the sculptor. We had a great time together and managed to make a living out of it while still being peripherally involved with music. Emmet Spiceland had finished at this stage. I temporarily joined We Four, which was a sort of a folk group with a stand-up bass and was kind of verging on soft pop. Suzanne Murphy was singing with the band then. I remember being upset by this beautiful soprano voice. The vibrato did something to some of the songs. It didn't sit right. So I used to ask her, "Please, try and sing it without vibrato." It's funny when I think about it because Suzanne has been the prima donna with the Welsh National Opera for the last yonks.'

Dónal had also nurtured his partnership with Andy, gradually developing and mastering the mandolin–bouzouki tapestry. Not long after recording *Prosperous*, Dónal and Andy began their own club night at Slattery's. 'Dónal was offered the Monday night and he asked me if I'd weigh in with him,' explains Andy. 'We took over from Johnny Breen from Sixmilebridge who had a club downstairs called The Butterfly Club. We called it The Mugs Gig, with Ronnie Drew as our first guest on Monday, 5 July 1971. Paddy Slattery eventually had upstairs and downstairs working on most of the nights, except Sunday nights upstairs, which was reserved for the Happy Families Club for years and years. We never did find out who they were.'

The Mugs Gig was a happy family all of its own, a miscellany of music styles and personalities from traditional soloists to ballad singers and folk groups and odd hybrids of rock, jazz, folk or whatever was turning people on, so long as it was good. 'The Mugs Gig was considered to be a folk club, as they are known, but that term covered a much wider range of music than it does now,' explains Dónal. 'I would say in the previous four or five years, it went from traditional singing and ballads and opened out very rapidly, so by the time The Mugs Gig was happening it was really just about music. It's all a very happy blur. Generally speaking, Andy and myself did our bit. They were Andy's songs and I might have sung one or two as well, back in the days when I had the neck to do a song. And we would probably top and tail the gig with the guests in between.'

'There was no PA system, but I had the good fortune to be really good friends with the ballad singer Danny Doyle, who was a great guy and really supported me through hard times,' recalls Andy. 'Danny had his own PA and he usually didn't have a gig on Monday nights. He'd actually come down and set it up in the afternoon and then pick it up the following morning. Danny was a very, very generous person with his time and money. I could never really understand why he embraced me in his circle of friends because they listened to a different type of music. And they were all full of sparkling wit, always, and I wasn't. There was a weekly meeting in some pub with people like Danny and Jim McCann and Johnny McEvoy and all these people at the high end of the soft-pop end of folk music. I felt very out of place. I usually got very drunk.'

Mellow Candle and Supply, Demand & Curve were two groups who became regular guests at The Mugs Gig. Both acts fell between the cracks of genre. 'Supply, Demand & Curve were very interesting,' says Dónal. 'Brian Masterson played bass. Paddy Finney was the singer and his voice was quite close to the conventional tenor's voice and he played Spanish guitar too. The other member was Jolyon Jackson, who played cello and flute.'

'We didn't want any old crap,' confirms Andy. 'Sometimes it was difficult if Mellow Candle couldn't do it or the McLynns from Sligo couldn't do it. Generally, though, we maintained a higher standard of music. Mellow Candle were great. The lead singer, Clodagh Simonds, was a good friend of Dónal's, a very nice person. She went on to work with Mike Oldfield. Later on, she imparted the knowledge that he was quite inspired by Planxty's music.'

Clodagh Simonds and Alison O'Donnell formed Mellow Candle way back in 1963 when they were enthusiastic Killiney convent schoolgirls balancing a love of pop music with everyday studies. Simonds was fifteen years old when Mellow Candle released their first single. By 1972, and now a five-piece folk-rock band, they released the album *Swaddling Songs* on the Decca label. Where other groups of the time fused rock and folk with abominably clumsy results, *Swaddling Songs* is a great display of delicacy, building songs around piano and employing subtle electric guitar, a rock rhythm section and ethereal female vocal harmonies to create a uniquely mystical and superbly crafted and textured collection of psychedelic folk songs. Despite rave reviews, Mellow Candle never really took off in the 1970s. However, in later years, *Swaddling Swans* resurfaced as one of the most coveted Irish folk albums ever, with mint vinyl copies now changing hands for up to four figure sums. Mellow Candle perfectly fitted Dónal and Andy's criteria for The Mugs Gig.

'The place was always packed, and the atmosphere was amazing,' recalls Clodagh Simonds. 'I think one of the reasons it all felt so exciting was that you couldn't but be aware that they really were breaking new ground, even before Planxty formed. Something very powerful was germinating. The intricacy and the rhythmic complexity of their arrangements was something really fresh and unheard of – they were literally blowing the dust and cobwebs off some of that material and giving it this sparkling, dancing new life. It was exhilarating to witness – no other word. At that time Dónal was living in a flat on Merrion Square and we'd all end up there, playing, laughing, drinking, singing, smoking until daybreak. Dónal was more or less inseparable from his Afghan waistcoat in those days – so much so that I actually wrote a little piece called 'The Furry Lunny'!'

Back in England, Christy was building a reputation. The fresh new sound of *Prosperous* was going down a treat and his live shows were in big demand. 'Christy was big at this time,' Andy points out. 'There was one occasion when he was double-booked and he asked if I would like to fill in for him at a gig in Ludlow somewhere down in Shropshire. The fee was fifteen pounds, which was at least three pounds more than I'd ever gotten before, so I hitch-hiked down, which was the way we travelled in those days because public transport would eat up the fee. I got as far as Shrewsbury or somewhere and I couldn't get to the gig so I rang the organiser to say, "Look, I'm about twenty miles away and I can't get any further," so he came out and got me. There was a much bigger audience there than I used to get at this time, especially in a place like Ludlow. And the organiser came out to the stage and said, "Ladies and gentlemen, I'm very sorry to tell you that unfortunately Christy Moore can't be with us tonight. BUT! He has sent along … I can't remember his name, but here he is!" The introduction wasn't quite the boost I needed, but it was a good gig and I was thankful to Christy for that one.'

Despite his burgeoning profile, Christy was pining for home and eager to pick up where he had left off with the *Prosperous* recording. 'Basically we were having such a good time it just dawned on us one day we should try and put this together on a more permanent basis. Everybody was up for it,' recalls Christy. 'I was almost jealous at first,' confesses Andy. 'I said to Christy, "What about Dónal?" because I thought Dónal might have said, "Well, you know I'm playing with Andy" and Christy said, "Dónal's into it." Then I said, "Yes, but what about Liam?" He said, "Ah, Liam's into it." "Ah, okay," says I, noting I was the last to be asked!'

'It was a huge thing for us all, really,' adds Christy. 'Andy and Dónal were making nice music then. So was Liam, and I was doing my own thing as well. I'd been over in England for five or six years and, looking back in the diary, I'm reminded of how well I was doing over there. My music was really expanding and I was getting loads of gigs, so it was a big step down for me in one way, but it didn't matter at all because it was a huge step up from the point of view of music and fulfilment.'

Without doubt, it was the participation of Liam Óg O'Flynn that distinguished this line-up of musicians as something approaching radical. 'Liam was from Kill and certainly when we met first he would've been from a different kind of a set than we were from,' explains Christy. 'He would've been a bit more conservative. Both his parents were teachers. I knew both his mother and father, lovely people. Obviously, I lost my father when I was very young and my mother was rearing a young family, so our house was quite undisciplined. I'm sure I got away with things that Liam could never have got away with. We were all a bit mad and Liam was a bit more restrained. He caught up with us in the madness stakes later on, mind you.'

Liam O'Flynn's adventures in America had already sealed his determination to become a full-time musician. He could see a new era dawning. He could see different cultures connecting and new opportunities emerging for a musician such as himself. 'I'd come through the competition thing in my teens and early twenties and I'd won various competitions at the highest level at the time. I wanted to do that and I did it. So I suppose looking on from that I'd no worked-out ideas of how I wanted to become a professional musician. As an uilleann piper, the possibility of making your livelihood from music was pretty non-existent. There wasn't an audience there for it as there was for classical music or pop music. This band was an opportunity to make it possible, to make it a full-time way of life.'

Liam remembers listening to songs being accompanied on guitar by Dónal and, eventually, Andy and being gradually introduced to this greater world of folk music. 'I loved it on several different levels. I loved it in a musical way. I loved the sound of the guitar accompanying the voice. I loved the people who were involved. There was a certain bohemian element to it all – a great sense of freedom of expression. No one was saying you have to do it this way or that way. This was a new musical experience for me. Getting towards Christmas 1971, I felt it was time to get back home again and get to the whole business of this new band. Also, it was my first time away and I'd been five months in the States, so it really was time to come home.'

With all four members now convened in Dublin, the month of January 1972 was a hectic period. Everyone had previous commitments and tours to fulfil in between organising rehearsals and devising plans for this new unnamed band. One of the first things the band did was to get in touch with the old Sweeney's Men manager, Des Kelly, and he jumped at the chance of taking on this new 'supergroup'. 'I'd rung up Des Kelly because nobody knew any managers,' explains Andy. 'Des had been very good in Sweeney's Men until he got sick and had to slack off. I told him who was in the band and asked him would he be interested and he said, "Oh, Andy, I'd be two hundred per cent interested!" '

'We met up with Des and we all clicked,' remarks Christy. 'Even though he was from a different world than we were, we were very compatible as men. I still get misty-eyed thinking about him. He used to manage a singer called Dermot Henry who was quite big at the time. There was George Kay & The Smokey Mountain Ramblers. There was Kathy & The Fugitives, I remember, because we got their van. For months afterwards, we'd find photographs of Kathy & The Fugitives, which were used for roaches. We got their PA as well. We felt a little bit guilty about that, but Des assured us they were breaking up anyway.

'Des loved the band. I remember him coming to rehearsals and tears welling up in his eyes, that kind of thing,' continues Christy. 'That's always a great trait in anyone who is going to be promoting you or organising a tour or anything. If your music makes them cry, then you're in with a chance.'

'Des was very easy-going, very friendly and he'd give you the impression that everything was possible,' adds Liam. 'He loved the band and we loved Des.'

Apart from managing bands, Des Kelly was also running his own independent label, Ruby Records, from an office on Belmont Avenue in Donnybrook, along with his *Ruby Records* radio show on RTÉ. 'There were two or three guys in the office managing different bands,' explains Des. 'The Smokey Mountain Ramblers were very successful in a strictly commercial way. They'd be putting fifteen or sixteen hundred people into ballrooms. There was about seven or eight bands working out of the office at one stage. Andy dropped in one day and asked me bluntly if I'd be into looking after them. If Andy was involved, that was enough for me. So I went down to Madigan's to meet Christy, Liam and Dónal. I took one look at them and thought, "This is Sweeney's Men all over again!" I wound up going to The Embankment in Tallaght with Christy that night,' continues Des. 'He was doing a spot at it. He went on stage and Jesus, Mary and Joseph, I was absolutely flabbergasted. I'd never even heard of him because he was in Britain and I wasn't following the folk scene. I was absolutely knocked out.'

With a van and a PA and representation now in place, Andy, Christy, Liam and Dónal were all set to go for it – except, they had no name. The working title of CLAD – the initials of each member's first name – didn't quite cut the mustard. 'CLAD was only ever used in *Melody Maker* on one occasion,' recalls Andy. 'The heading for the article was "CLAD To Throw Down The Gauntlet".'

Although no one quite remembers which member of the band first suggested it, they all agreed on Planxty. This mysterious word was known to the band through the music of one of the most illustrious figures in Irish traditional music, Turlough Carolan, the seventeenth-century composer, bard and harper. As a result of smallpox, Carolan lost his sight in his teens, but no illness could stunt his genius. He became a travelling harper and bard of lofty repute. Carolan maintains an immortal presence in

Irish music to this very day. In his own time, his playing was in huge demand and his visits to the Big Houses and castles and the esteemed families of Ireland were deemed a great honour and privilege. 'Planxty' was employed as a prefix to the title of many airs he wrote in honour of his patrons, e.g. 'Planxty Irwin', 'Planxty O'Rourke', 'Planxty Fanny Power'.

'We used to meet Des in Kennedy's pub in Westland Row,' recalls Andy. 'I remember that as being where we decided on the name because Christy had this grandiose scheme of recording a series of albums all with the word Planxty before them. So there'd be "Planxty Moore", "Planxty Irvine", "Planxty Lunny" and "Planxty O'Flynn" and there'd be "Planxty Carolan" as well, where we played all Carolan music.'

The word 'planxty' remains a mystery to this day. Although the term wasn't exclusive to Carolan's work, we can gather from his use of it that he is referring to a toast or a tribute to somebody. Yet no one has been able to definitively source its origin. The fact that there is no "x" in the Irish language augments the mystery. The theory of another great composer, from a later era, Seán Ó Riada, suggested that 'planxty' was a corruption of 'sláinte', meaning 'good health'.

'It was a very odd word,' continues Andy. 'We got called various things in our early days. I remember one time Des got us a room in the Irish-dancing teacher Desmond Donnelly's rehearsal studio and we went for lunch and when we got back there was a message on the door addressed to "Frank's Tea". There was another one in England where someone called us "Plan XTY". It was a hard word for some people to pronounce. I remember some people from the country couldn't manage the juxtaposition of the "n" and the "x" and so it would be "planixty". On the continent, it was even more difficult, God knows what way they pronounced it there.'

Planxty transpired to be the perfect name, as Carolan music would feature prominently throughout the band's repertoire. In fact, the B-side of their very first single was an exquisite interpretation of what is reckoned to be Carolan's debut composition, 'Sí Bheag Sí Mhór' (titled on this pressing as 'Sí-Beag Sí-Mór'). The A-side was a rambunctious rendition of 'Three Drunken Maidens', an old folk song that Andy had learned from the English singers Tim Hart and Maddy Prior from the group Steeleye Span. 'Sí Bheag Sí Mhór', though, was the tune that properly captured the blossoming Planxty sound. The single was recorded in Trend Studios on 18 January. Donal Lunney [sic] is credited as the producer and F. Meyer as the engineer.

'I can remember the guy who engineered it. I think his name was Freddie Meyer,' reflects Christy. 'The vibe from him was he'd seen it all before with all these ballad groups coming in. We were treated with a certain amount of disdain, as I recall it. I don't think we were insulted or anything. But we certainly weren't treated with the seriousness with which we took ourselves!'

'I remember a large man was the engineer,' adds Andy. 'We did 'Sí Bheag Sí Mhór' and he would say, "She begs for more, take two!"' The very next day, Planxty performed their first TV performance on RTÉ for *Capitol Folk*, which was a programme about folk music in different capital cities. They did 'Arthur McBride' and 'Raggle Taggle Gypsy'.

Des Kelly had his sights on bigger things, though. He managed to book them on Ireland's leading chat and entertainment programme, *The Late Late Show*, hosted by the public's favourite broadcaster, Gay Byrne. 'I remember Des ringing up and he was very upbeat,' says Andy. "I have good news, I've got *The Late Late Show*!" It was for the following Saturday and I said, "Oh Jesus, Dónal and myself have a gig in Galway" and he said, "Well you'll have to fucking cancel it!" And sure enough we did.'

'We were in full flow then,' adds Christy. 'We were having such fun. Obviously, it was my first time being on *The Late Late Show* and I remember arriving out there, being full of it and meeting Gay Byrne in the lobby. To this day I always feel perhaps I was a little bit forward. He called me "Sonny". "Are you all right, Sonny?" Thirty years on, I still remember that. We became very friendly in later years. I've a fondness for him.'

'At the time, to get *The Late Late Show* was a huge achieve-ment,' explains Des. 'There was a fella called Tony Boland who was instrumental in getting it for me. The boys weren't impressed in the slightest. Not at all. They were all bollixes and suits as far as they were concerned. Gay Byrne! Who did he think he was! That sort of thing,' Des recalls in fits of laughter. 'I remember John Woods from Pye came out in his dressing gown and pyjamas and when they were over, he was waiting outside the door to sign them. His face fell about a foot when he saw me! "Ah, you haven't them, have you?" They made a tremendous impact on *The Late Late Show*.'

Andy, Dónal, Liam and Christy had been scheduled to play The Mugs Gig together on Monday, 31 January. However, on 30 January 1972, British army paratroopers opened fire on civil rights demonstrators in Derry, killing thirteen civilians and wounding seventeen, one of whom died later, in what is historically known as Bloody Sunday. Everyone was unanimous in the decision to cancel the show. On 6 March, The Mugs Gig featured popular balladeer Paddy Reilly. Andy, Dónal, Christy and Liam played together for thirty minutes. 'The first ever gig we played was at The Mugs Gig and it was in front of all these people we knew well,' remembers Andy. 'Morgan The Packer would greet people at the door and pack them in. We thought we'd done really well, but we met Des the next day and he said we were terrible. It was our presentation he didn't like.

It took Des a little while to get used to the fact that we weren't a kind of in-your-face showband.'

Like a true showband veteran, and echoing the days of Sweeney's Men, Des even suggested that the band wear matching suits. 'I think initially he thought that, as a matter of course, we would make a better impression with the suits, but there was one mention and that was the end of that. He was laughed out of the room,' says Liam. The following week, Planxty played a full set at The Mugs Gig, and Des began to see the light. And for the next month or so, in the bustling nest that was Slattery's, Planxty honed their set for the outside world.

'I'd have been used to a slick start and a slick finish,' explains Des. 'The Capitol Showband had played places like The Palladium and had worked with professional choreographers in London and all this kind of stuff. And while I wasn't expecting that from Planxty, I at least expected them to start on time and fellas not to be walking off stage in the middle of a tune. This is what The Mugs Gig was like. But they were still magical, though. What appealed to me was the musicality of Andy and Dónal, the interplay. There's this pent-up energy in Dónal and the serious-ness and dedication and concentration of Andy. And then you had Liam sat there like a rock and he would suddenly burst in from nowhere. He used the pipes so well in the sense that he didn't overplay. And then I never saw anybody like Christy who could get hold of a song and sing it as if he was singing to you personally and nobody else. He still has that. Very few have that gift. Put the four of them on stage and I believe there's a presence there they don't have individually.'

With the success of *The Late Late Show* performance and the general buzz of excitement that encompassed the band, Des Kelly's telephone line was jammed with offers from all over the country. During the first week of March, the band went into

The Metropole Cinema on O'Connell Street, Dublin to rehearse with a full PA. 'That's where I suddenly realised I was a part of something really worthwhile,' states Andy. 'I really bonded as a group member, because I had some doubts originally. My duo with Dónal felt like the next stage of my musical interaction with somebody else after Sweeney's Men. I was really enjoying it. When Christy asked me initially, there had been that feeling of jealousy, but I soon got over that. My memories of those rehearsals are great. The bouzouki–mandolin interplay was one thing, but then we found great sounds with the pipes and harmonica. We discovered how these two instruments sounded great together, and had never been played together before, I'm sure. I remember quite early on wondering what form this rehearsal would take. At about twelve o'clock, Liam said, "Anybody want a pint?" So then it was, "Yay, it's not a strict rehearsal. It's not nine-to-five."'

'There was a lot of laughter,' adds Christy. 'I felt I was on top of the world. I'd been trodding around England on my own playing folk clubs and suddenly to be back in Ireland again with three of my favourite musicians, it was heavenly.'

Liam agrees that The Mugs Gigs were very exciting. He remembers the line of people going around the corner waiting to get in. 'People who heard Planxty for the first time became instinctively aware of the chemistry between the musicians. The audience becomes really turned on by that. When we started Planxty we said we'd give it three months and if nothing was happening, then fair enough. By three months, the thing had really taken off. It was like a runaway train. You couldn't get off.'

Chapter 8

Plan XTY

There's something serendipitous about the formation of Planxty. You simply couldn't preordain such a band. Their configuration of instruments alone was unprecedented. Guitar, bouzouki and mandolin sat alongside the tentacled sound of the uilleann pipes at the forefront. Tin whistle, bodhrán and harmonica were prominent features too, while hurdy-gurdy, harmonium, dulcimer, portative organ and various other curiosities had a peripheral presence. Together, all these instruments found a common place, which wasn't rooted in one specific category, but rather was revealed on the unique cultural playing ground that can only be described as 'Planxty music'. Within this whirlpool of sound was traditional music from Ireland, Eastern Europe, America and Britain. From the very moment Planxty began, they drew from the vast amplitude of time. They drew from songs and airs so ancient nobody could possibly date them, from harp music that evolved through the sixteenth and seventeenth centuries and onwards through time, through different contexts and treatments, from folk music of the 1960s, right up to contemporary songwriting.

With ages ranging from twenty-five to thirty, each member of Planxty was already an accomplished and travelled musician by the time they activated the band in 1972. Each of them had already sampled different worlds and nurtured a unique musical personality of their own. Together, they addressed the art of arrangement rather than the formula of genre. And their diversity wasn't just defined by the instrumentation and influences, but also by the variation of time signatures and the creation of counterpoint melodies. They balanced this innovation with a delicate empathy for the music and with old-fashioned musical virtues such as thoughtful singing and intricate playing. As an acoustic band, they generated their own electricity. To this day, their live shows have a roof-raising dynamic that can match the best rock or electric folk groups. Furthermore, the band boasts two great singers, a great soloist in Liam O'Flynn, and, gradually over time, their own in-house producer and musical director, Dónal Lunny. All in all, this was a band charged with a serious arsenal of ability, history and diversity. Planxty's impact in 1972 was nothing short of dramatic.

'I wouldn't look at Planxty as a "traditional" band,' says Christy Moore. 'The ethos was not to make traditional music. The ethos was this music is beautiful and vibrant and fun, so let's have a fucking good time and not sit around in corners with long faces on us being miserable. Ninety per cent of the material was traditional in its make-up, but our approach was not traditional. Our approach was to rock, to have a bit of craic with it.'

'We had complete conviction about what we were doing,' declares Dónal. 'It had a validity and it had its own integrity.

We had unspoken criteria, some of which were in place because of Liam, because he was a pure traditional musician who had the nerve to step into a situation and take the traditional music in there. It very rapidly established itself that the music demanded to be treated on its own terms. It influenced our arrangements. As an arranger, it put me through the hoops. I think it was unfamiliar to people to hear traditional music with a chassis under it and it still sounds like traditional music. It was a bit of a breakthrough.'

As is the case in any context, those who break new ground will naturally have their detractors and sceptics. The most radical aspect of Planxty was the presence of Liam O'Flynn, a musician of the Irish tradition, a tradition that for many people existed as a very defined approach to music. In his decision to join this band of long-haired folkies, he was stepping outside of the traditional world. And, despite the fact that Liam knew he was neither betraying the tradition nor jettisoning anything he had learned, the inevitable criticisms and doubts ensued.

'Christy and Dónal and myself understood where we were all coming from,' explains Andy. 'But there were doubts about Liam at the beginning because there were a lot of traditional musicians who really didn't respect his decision to be in this band with mandolins, bouzoukis and guitars. The music must have been quite a step for him, playing all these folk songs. It was very much a step against the advice, surely, of the people he ran with. He balanced the whole thing really well as it turned out, but at the time, a phone call to say Liam had left the band wouldn't have been that surprising.

'Old John Kelly was the person who one tended to think spoke for the traditional music fraternity,' continues Andy. 'He had that shop on Capel Street, the one Tony McMahon famously called a "Huckster shop", a dark little place with things hanging from the ceiling. Kelly was a great player. He was also an irascible sort of a man. He was very much of the last generation of traditional musicians. He'd come down to Slattery's on Wednesday for the Tradition Club and sit and talk through anything he didn't really like. He would have held a puritan attitude regarding Liam's involvement. Liam's situation was never an issue as far as I was concerned. Liam himself didn't say that much. He was the least effusive and the most reserved member of the band.'

Dónal recalls that there were certain people who felt that the music should be played in its pure form as it was played a hundred years ago. 'But this is a museum mentality. It has its own value, of course, because it means that the music is actually preserved and it's not forgotten. And that the good parts of how it was back then are maintained and preserved and not sort of lost in a welter of flavour-of-the-month. What we were doing was much too radical for a lot of people. But then, I think the thing that would give one great faith in oneself was the approval of someone like Séamus Ennis, who realised we weren't screwing up the music. We had respect for it, total respect for it. Séamus Ennis was Liam's mentor. He was a giant of a man, a giant of a musician. He was a folklorist. He just had so much of the culture, of the land.'

To this day, Liam O'Flynn, in his own tolerant and sagacious way, plays down the situation and the potential anxiety and discord it may have caused him. Liam prefers to remain philosophical about such matters. Yet Liam's dilemma is a great case study for the theory that to achieve great things one must take chances, follow instinct and push the accepted boundaries. Liam did all these things in his decision to pursue music with Planxty.

'Traditional musicians were unused to that sort of approach, as indeed I was myself,' admits Liam O'Flynn. 'But I always had a terrific musical curiosity. I was never pushed into doing anything I didn't want to do. One really important element within Planxty was that there was a terrific mutual regard between us, and there was a high regard for the music itself. I remember we had one rule in the band, which was if there was any one individual who really didn't want to do this, that or the other, that was respected and there was no further argument about it. To me that was a terrifically important thing. I knew that it was going to cause a few ripples here and there and I wasn't sure how I was going to deal with that. There were definitely furrowed brows and people getting very worried about this young man being hijacked by these guys.'

Most of the critics came around eventually. 'There'd still be a few of them there, but so what?' shrugs Christy. 'We weren't making music for anybody except ourselves and we were happy with it. At the end of the day, what won out was the music. As time passed, most of the traditionalists viewed what we were doing as having respect for the music. I don't think we ever compromised it.'

'But at the same time as Planxty was happening, I was also ploughing my own furrow as well,' Liam picks up. 'I was expanding my own repertoire and my own musical experience within the tradition. I was living with Séamus Ennis. So it wasn't as though I'd jumped from one ship to another. And within the band there was a powerful awareness of all that as well. I remember Séamus had a terrific interest in Planxty. He gave us basically anything we asked for in terms of songs or tunes. Christy got songs from Séamus, and Christy was extremely kind to him as well. As a traditional musician, he was kind of unusual in that he had a terrific interest in the song side of the tradition, both English and Irish. He understood the approach that Planxty had to the music. He knew we weren't just slashing away at chords, Planxty was much more subtle in that we had countermelodies running together and one melody interweaving with the other. That was such a unique part of the whole Planxty sound. I think that attracted Séamus hugely.'

Liam remained close to Ennis for many years, through his mentor's illness and right up to his death in 1982. 'He got very ill, self-inflicted. He got in touch with me and told me he was coming out of hospital and asked if I knew of any place he could use for accommodation. And as it happens, I was sharing a place with my brother Micheál in Mount Street and we had more space there than we needed. And there was another flat two girls were sharing who were really into the music as well. There was a room upstairs and, between us, we set the room up and Séamus moved in. Obviously, then I got to know him very well and had access to him in that sense. Then we moved from there to a flat in Pembroke Road and from there to a house in Templeogue, again with my brother. All in all, I was around him a lot for two to three years. They were the early Planxty days as well and I was doing a lot of travelling. He was – to say the least – a fairly demanding sort of person. If my brother was alive today, he'd have the funniest stories to tell about Séamus. Séamus wasn't the most domesticated man. I suppose he didn't lead a regular type of life. He was much happier being up at night and sleeping through the day. At the time my brother had a day job and was also studying for a degree in university at night, so there was a conflict of timetables.

'Gradually, Séamus's health began to fail and, eventually, it just wasn't practical for us to continue. The responsibility was large. He moved to a flat on the northside of town and, while he was there, he organised a plot of ground for himself out in The Naul on a farm that his grandfather had had. The owner at the time gave Séamus this plot. He got himself a mobile home and lived out the rest of his life very happily there. I guess a lot of people thought that he must've lived a terribly solitary, lonesome sort of life, and in certain respects he did, but he was genuinely happy there. He felt he'd sort of come back to his roots because his father and his grandfather where both buried in the graveyard in The Naul.'

Dónal's brother, Frank, had watched Christy and Dónal develop from keen teenagers in The Rakes of Kildare into one half of the most exhilarating new band in the country. 'It was very organic,' says Frank. 'They grew from everything they had known. They had no place else to go but to form Planxty. Planxty designated a change, a musical movement. Life was never going to be the same again. I think the people who listened to the music knew that. It was a break from what had gone before. It was exciting. They brought in a tempo.'

Having honed their live set in residency at The Mugs Gig, it was now time to bring Planxty music all over Ireland. They played two concerts, an afternoon show and evening show, at Newbridge College on Thursday, 16 March 1972. Amongst the audience of excitable students and Kildare family and friends was Scottish folk star Donovan. Suitably impressed with this new Irish supergroup, he invited Planxty to open for him on his six-date Irish tour the following week. This, as it transpired, was to be the Irish public's perfect introduction to the band and their music.

'This was probably the most important thing in my entire life up to this point,' insists Andy. 'Donovan was touring with an Irish band at Easter 1972. The first gig was in The Hangar in Galway, which was a dancehall. We went on first. The soundman was Donovan's brother-in-law and he wasn't very interested in us. He wasn't even there when we got up to play. I kept the head down. I was trying to get everything right and I wasn't paying much attention to the audience until, after about twenty minutes, I heard them go mad. I thought "It's a fight. It's a fight.

A dancehall fight has started up here." And I turned to the lads, alarmed. They were all smiling. Then it dawned on me … it obviously wasn't a fight!

'It took me a while to realise we were going down like you wouldn't believe. It was like the audience discovered that night something they were looking for. I've never seen anything like it. They went berserk for us. Des had to go and ask Donovan if it was okay to play an encore. After the gig, we went into the dressing room. We couldn't believe it. Des came in laughing uncontrollably. Des was a great, thoughtful person. From under his coat he took out a bottle of vodka. I can remember grabbing it and glugging it back before somebody said, "Andy, Andy, for God's sake don't drink it all!" I'd never had an adrenalin buzz like that before.'

Looking back on the gig brings a smile to Liam O'Flynn's face too as he remembers the sheer excitement. 'The crowd got more and more into the music as it went on. By the end of the set, they were going wild. There was this terrific passing of energy from the band to the audience and the audience back to us.'

'The Donovan gig was funny,' chuckles Christy. 'It was the first time we'd seen a stretch limo, except for maybe the odd funeral. Donovan was in this left-hand drive stretch limo, just himself. It was great fun. There was an awful lot of hash. We were very stoned. Really, we didn't give a shite. This was a whole new world for us. Perhaps Dónal had sensed a bit of it in Emmet Spiceland, but for the rest of us to be doing these kind of gigs, even as support, was mega, going out on these big stages. Something was happening in our lives that we hadn't experienced before.'

'The crowd went for us,' agrees Dónal. 'We definitely eclipsed Donovan, who is the most gracious man. He's a lovely man, very, very sweet. I've met him since a few times. In fact, I was out in Japan five or six years ago with Maighread Ní Dhomhnaill doing a sort of showcase gig because her album was being released out there. And who was sitting in the front row only Donovan! It was great. We chatted about back then. He was lovely at the time as well. He did his gigs and he took this as graciously as one could. For us, it was a total shock. We didn't expect it. It was like, "Wow, we love the music. And they love it too. Yes!" It was a great moment.'

For Christy, though, it was the gig in the City Hall in Cork where the band was suddenly recognised. 'For me, Cork was the night people were turned on to us. I have a recording of that. We did 'Raggle Taggle Gypsy' and the recording is awful, but you can hear it. At the end of the song, the crowd start applauding and it goes on and on and on and we're all giggling up on the stage. We can't believe that it's happening. So in my mind that's the night Planxty took off.'

'My recollection of that tour, which was about six gigs, was that, apart from the Dublin one, we blew him off the stage every night,' adds Andy. 'We hadn't expected that. I'd given no thought as to whether we would be popular, or make a living or whatever. I hadn't even thought about that. I was just thinking about music. This was an eye-opener.'

A first-hand witness of Planxty's show-stopping performance opening for Donovan in Cork in March 1972 was musician and film-maker Philip King. King would go on to document the band on film years later, and this gig was the pivotal moment, just as it was for hundreds of other open-minded young men and women around the country. 'Prior to that gig, there used to be a folk club in a place called the Country Club in Cork City just up the hill there in St Luke's,' explains King. 'I remember going to see Andy there. He had just come back from one of his American jaunts, I think. We got to talking afterwards, and I asked, "What are you up to?" and he said, "We're waiting for Christy to come home from England. We're thinking of forming this band."

And that was the first inkling that I had that this was on the way.
I've a clear memory of the conversation. I had known that Andy
had listened to an awful lot of American music from listening to
Sweeney's Men. There seemed to be that amalgamation going
on already. There was a sort of a bleeding from one type of
tradition to another, into something that was forming some new
sort of unit.

The people around music in Cork were very eclectic. Seán Ó
Riada had happened and he was teaching in the University in
Cork. He died in 1971 and *Ó Riada's Farewell* had come out
that year. I was in university in Cork. Ó Riada was teaching
classical music, but he really was about the business of
interrogating the tradition. We were listening to what was
coming out of the West Coast of America at that time; records
like *The Rock Machine Turns You On*, which was a
compilation on Columbia Records, and had people like Taj
Mahal, The Electric Flag, Dylan, The United States of America,
Leonard Cohen. *The Notorious Byrd Brothers* by The Byrds had
just come out. And, at the same time in Cork, there was a real
sense of American old-timey music. Mick Daly and people like
that had got their hands on all the Folkways stuff. The
beginnings of the Lee Valley String Band were playing. The
Incredible String Band was very popular in one particular area.
And there was Rory [Gallagher], of course. Rory was Rory. Rory
was ours. There was an amazing music picture going on.'

At the time of the Cork gig, Donovan had been through The
Electrical Banana/Mellow Yellow stage and was coming out the
other end. 'He'd gone to India with The Beatles and all that stuff,'
continues King. 'Donovan had credibility, so we went along to see
him. Opening the show was this band, Planxty. These four guys
arrived on stage. Christy was sort of mythic at that stage.
Everybody had heard of him, but nobody had seen him.

Andy, I knew. Liam O'Flynn was known in Cork. Those aficionados would have known Liam was a piper, a very serious piper, a piper out of the tradition. They would have been listening to traditional groups like Na Filí. So we'd have known Liam was an important figure. We'd have known about Dónal through Emmet Spiceland. I also remember seeing Dónal with a ruffled shirt on television playing with We Four. He was in We Four for about five minutes. So was this a supergroup we didn't know about? Here seemed to be four individuals coming together to do something. And we didn't know what they were going to sound like.'

King describes the amazing sensation of being in the room. 'I heard something that I recognised to be true, that was *of* this place and claimable absolutely as ours. And whereas the blues was *of* us, and Radio Caroline was *of* us in a different, alternative way, the same as any youth culture striking out to hear what it wants to hear, that is not *of* its parents' generation, here was a music that was locked into a chain of tradition that we recognised as being ours, but most fundamentally was cool. It had none of the baggage you might think was associated with tradition. I think we were open to hearing that because Ó Riada had opened our heads. I also think that listening to it in Cork was sort of interesting. Cork is a city, but it's a country town, Macroom and Cúil Aodha are near to it, West Kerry is not too far away from it. Seán O'Riordáin, the poet, was living in Cork. There was a flourishing arts atmosphere. The Everyman Theatre was there at the time. The poets, people like Gabriel Rosenstock, Michael Davitt and Liam O'Muirthile, were all in or around the university at that time. And here was something that was undeniably true. You had 'Raggle Taggle Gypsy' with 'Tabhair Dom Do Lámh, you had 'Sí Bheag Sí Mhór', things purely out of the tradition. Then you had the magic of the Andy and Dónal thing. As Andy has said, Dónal would be playing two instruments at the same time, if he only could. That was the effect that he had on Andy. Andy's virtuosity, his understanding of the American thing, and also what had happened to him in Eastern Europe. When you think about it, they had been all over the world, they picked from everywhere, from the blues, elements of rock and roll, elements of the 9/16 time signatures coming from Europe, elements of old-timey music, and elements of the big ballad. The big ballad owes an awful lot to the English experience as well. In that repertoire they had 'Sweet Thames Flows Softly', 'Little Musgrave', 'The Blacksmith'. This was not folk-rock, this was grounded somewhere in a very rich seam of tradition and I think that's what we were looking for.'

By the time Donovan came on stage, King says he was 'gone'. Although he stayed for the gig, he didn't hear any of it. 'We were across the road in The Phoenix. This was it. It was revelatory. It was a happening. But it was the timing. I think Jacques Attali called music "the herald of the future". There's a sort of a moral authority in great music. It explores faster than other things can, what is about to come into existence. I think Planxty had that. At the time in Ireland, when you think about all the unemployment and emigration, the "national question" was beginning to bubble. And we were given this great gift, which was the gift of being able to see ourselves. We were able to go through the looking glass,' concludes King.

Perhaps the most rewarding aspect of this instant affinity between Planxty and the audiences on the Donovan tour is the fact that many of these kids were either unaware or simply not interested in traditional Irish music. 'That's true,' confirms Dónal. 'That was one of the most gratifying aspects of the whole thing. A lot of them were rock 'n' rollers, just kids like today. They listened to contemporary music. And we showed up and we had currency of some sort. And that was a lovely thing about subsequent gigs; the span of people from small kids of eight or nine years old to eighty- or ninety-year-olds as well. They'd be there to see Liam, but they'd get into the stuff. It was very, very sweet, very cool. We recognised the music as being beautiful. But what rock 'n' roller is going to sit down and listen to an album of unaccompanied uilleann pipes? Very few, without some sort of a handle. People have to relate in some way. That became a kind of raison d'être for me from then on. It was something I engaged with very much. How do you get the present generation of contemporary music listeners to relate to a very esoteric piece of traditional music?'

Nothing stifles the enthusiasm of youth more than something that appears static, permanent, routine, rigid … For many people, that's how the Irish tradition may have appeared, something that belonged to another time, the identity of someone else's generation. Yet when it is explained that the tradition is actually something that is moving, evolving, travelling, something timelessly inspiring, and hugely reflective not just of someone else's life, but also your own, then it suddenly becomes highly relevant.

The great Seán Ó Riada had enlightened people with his ostentatious arrangements of traditional music in the late 1950s and 1960s. His work as musical director in Dublin's Abbey Theatre and as a composer of film scores – most famously *Mise Éire*, a film about The War of Independence – in 1959 saw him marry Irish tunes and *sean-nós* songs with an orchestral arrangement. He put together an ensemble of traditional musicians called Ceoltóirí Chualann in the early 1960s. They presented traditional songs with accompaniment and traditional dance tunes and slow airs (including a lot of unearthed Carolan music) arranged with instruments such as harpsichord, bodhrán, accordion, piano, fiddle, flute, pipes and whistles. The members of Ceoltóirí Chualann eventually overlapped and morphed into the world-renowned traditional group, The Chieftains. Ceoltóirí Chualann made their last public performance in 1969, later released as the landmark album, *Ó Riada sa Gaiety*. Seán Ó Riada died a young forty-one-year-old in October 1971, yet in his lifetime he had widened the berth of possibilities for traditional music, and that vision resonated in the music of Planxty.

Planxty, though, were individuals of a very different era. The stringent codes of lifestyle that had been dictated and practised in Ireland for so long had unravelled by the 1970s. Unlike Ceoltóirí Chualann's formal code of bow ties and dinner jackets, Planxty were essentially unkempt free spirits. 'We were ourselves,' declares Dónal. 'We didn't dress up. We were scruffy. And the very fact that we were scruffy somehow made us cool or whatever. I had just been through Emmet Spiceland and we had been pretty elaborate about image. It was Beatles influenced. We had expensive hairdos. We wore expensive clothes, all the trappings. I'm sure that turned so many people off what we were doing. So Planxty was a departure. That was part of why we required credibility. It was just about the music – and maybe drinking afterwards. Life as you know it for many people.'

With a listening audience now drawing upon both aficionados of traditional and folk music, and also the average music-obsessed Irish teenager, Planxty rapidly became one of the most popular bands in the country. Yet there was another notable band that was also appropriating Irish music in a new way, Horslips. Horslips was a rock 'n' roll band that addressed Irish music and Irish mythology with electric guitars and drums. Their music was a million miles from the subtle, timeless treatments of Planxty, but it was massively in vogue with the Irish youth. 'Music didn't quite have the same pigeonholes as it has now,' says Andy. 'Somebody who was going to see The Small Faces one day may go and see Planxty the next, and enjoy both experiences.

'Horslips were huge at the time,' he continues. 'In my mind, Horslips were definitely the competition. They were out there. They had more virile management than we had, or so I thought at the time. A couple of them were graphic artists. They had a lot of tools at their disposal. My memory is that you could read about Horslips much more than you could read about Planxty. So I built up this big thing, which I never told anyone about before. I hated the fact that they were the competition. I'm embarrassed saying it, but when their debut album came out, which was shaped like a concertina, I actually rushed out and bought it because I couldn't bear not to know what it was like. After one hearing, I thought, "Oh, thank God. Crap!" I didn't care after that.'

On 21 April 1972, Planxty headed across the water for their first tour of England, which had been booked a couple of months previously by Christy. They would visit cities such as Manchester, Bolton, Leeds, Hull, Barnsley, Blackpool, New-castle, Chester and London. 'At some point, Nicky Ryan flew over and became our soundman and he worked miracles with the equipment we had. I remember staying at a house with him in Sheffield and he was walking around the garden listening to the band on some early cassette player,' says Christy.

Although they played in tiny folk clubs, Dónal believes the gigs were all the better for it. 'It was really successful. We were flying. It was great to go into a place with two hundred people stuffed in and people just lapping it up. It was also fairly haphazard. There was one occasion where we stayed in the pub, which is hilarious because the bar didn't close at all. It was demented. "Abandon" is the word you would use.'

'One night we were staying in a guy's house in Doncaster,' recalls Christy. 'And shortly after we left, he was busted. The poor fellow, he had given us his hospitality and he wasn't into smoking dope at all himself. But he got busted because there were loads of roaches and "afters" all over the place. I think he actually got taken to court and fined. Of course we were gone, but they were onto us. They visited a few other places we'd been in, enquiring about us. Word got back to us that they were watching out for us. There was a quite a lot of paranoia and a lot of stuff got dumped. In those days, dope was a big deal.'

'It was the drug culture tour,' declares Andy. 'We arrived back at this guy's house to stay and he met us at the door and said, "The Special Branch are after you, get out of here," and we got back in the van and drove off. Everyone was in a panic. We threw everything over a hedge. And we went back a week later and there was the grass kind of all sprouting. We found it by sheer luck! At the end of it we drove the last fifteen miles to Holyhead with the windows open. We cleaned out the fucking van. When we got to the boat, we were met by the Special Branch, and they said "Are you the Christy O'Connor Showband?" "No!" "What's your name?" "Christopher Moore." So they had to let us go, but it was kind of scary.'

By the end of the tour, the band was reduced to paranoid wrecks on the run from the police, yet nothing could suppress their contagious sense of humour. 'There's a recording of a gig in Chester, which was the last gig on the tour,' recalls Andy. 'There weren't many people there. You can hear Christy saying, "Thank you very much, probably time to introduce the band, this is Liam O'Flynn over here on the uilleann pipes, this is Dónal Lunny, Andy Irvine and I'm Christy Moore." There was a big pause and Dónal says, "What are your names?"

Excerpts from Andy Irvine's letters from Planxty's first English tour April–May 1972

21 April 1972 – on boat to England for first tour

We are about to dock in Liverpool. It is 5.30h and we all slept in a welter of sleeping bags in a corner of the saloon. The crack is mighty here, we are all excited and got smashed last night and giggled ridiculously.

We have to meet Nicky, our sound balancer at 16h in Manchester. 2 Roadies! It's really crazy!

We had a gank night in Rathangan the night before we left Ireland. Freezing cold marquee with about 100 people at it.

Jimmy [Drag] is a fucking great roadie. He's considerate, thoughtful and hard working and is definitely an asset, tho' I still don't know who – if anybody – is paying him. Is it a bit stupid doing £35 gigs and having 2 roadies?

Next time I see you, I'll be the proud owner of a Hurdy-Gurdy!

We got a five-page fan letter from a schoolgirl in Cahir the other day. Poor girl!

If I don't get a letter from you soon, I'm going to join the Foreign Legion....

24 April 1972 – The Van

Here I am after a fair night's sleep in the van in Manchester. The others stayed in a cheap hotel but I decided to save the 30/–. I think the others think I'm mad. But I'd rather have 30/– than a bed in a hotel…!

We had a long day on Saturday and were all disorientated and depressed which culminated in our being very nervous at the first gig. The audience was expecting the old full o'crack Christy Moore and he wasn't at all that way, so they were a bit nonplussed, I think. However, we played really well and won, by and large. The place was packed at 45p a ticket – 300 people and we got a measly £35! Still, we do the same club at the end of the tour and get the door.

One thing about the gig, we had Nicky our sound engineer and got a really beautiful sound. Between Jimmy and Nicky we don't have to raise a finger! They do all the setting up and all the fetching and carrying.

We went to a Disco afterwards, I can't remember why, and then slept on some guy's floor.

The zip of my sleeping bag is busted and I have a cold, which is a drag.

Last night's gig in Bolton was really good. An audience of about 60 but a really good crowd and we went down a bomb and were much less stiff.

We have a day off today – 'Holidays' as Donal says and then in Doncaster tomorrow night.

25 April 1972 – Dave Brady's, Yorkshire Moors

We drove out here yesterday and had a blast and then went into town and had a huge feed in a curry place. Had a couple of drinks and then back here where we got totally smashed. I retired to bag at 2:30h. The others were up till all hours and there's been little respite from dope and energy so far. The roadies especially just don't seem to sleep at all.

The weather here has been freezing and I have a heavy cold and am not far from losing my voice.

We are preparing to leave now for Doncaster. We have borrowed Dave's [Brady] PA, which means tonight we will have 400 watts and 6 speakers. If we don't get a good sound tonight, we never will! Dave is bringing his tape machine and we should have a good tape to show for ourselves.

I just hope I'll be able to sing …

Later:

Well, by Jasus, we didn't get a good sound in Doncaster. It was a cock-up and we didn't do too well. We got £60 however and many people liked it but it was definitely Jon Ledingham's [aka Jonathan Kelly] night and not ours. Poor Nicky was very depressed about the sound – which was a slight disaster – and we went to a friend's house and drank home-made wine and got pissed-ish.

I woke up at 7.20h lying frozen on the floor.

We had a farewell drink and blew.

Last night in Leeds was really good. The sound was excellent and so were we. We went down well but still not fully a smash. I think the missing factor is Christy's lack of crack on stage. He has not produced it on any of the gigs so far. The music was great, though, and Christy managed to sell 7 of his LPs.

Now we're off to Hull.

Last night was a financial flop, which was a bit depressing. There were about 300 people there and we made £46! We found it all hard to believe but the advertising expenses were £60, which is really ridiculous.

28 April 1972 – Hull

The concert last night was a smash! At last, we took an audience by storm. Wow! It completely restored our morale. The Watersons were on with us and went down a bomb. We thought we'd be in trouble but we really rocked the audience. Also made £63.
The lads scored just before the gig and I ate some before going on. (I didn't mean to, would you believe? I thought it was a throat tablet!)

Had a great laugh back at Lal and Norma's house.
The lads went elsewhere and I stayed and slept.
They're all gone playing snooker now.

I think Donal is losing his mind because of the shit.
Maybe he's just tired.

We got a harmonium last night. Don't know what it's
like yet. It cost £12, so can't be bad! Nicky disclosed
the other night, to our amazement, that he and I are
related. He's a cousin of Muriel's.

1 May 1972 – Mexborough

We are all totally smashed! We are about to play
cards, which should be something to see!

Liam's gone off and the rest of us are utterly zonked.

Every time I look up, somebody is rolling <u>another</u>
joint. We're not playing tonight ...

Next day:

Nicky and me are sitting in the sun and Christy is
making breakfast. Guess where Donal is...?

Christy is arranging for us to do an 8 hour recording
session in London, for a demo.

After the success of Hull we were back to the
ordinariness of folk clubs and the one in Barnsley

was far too boring. We did a concert here in Mexborough the day before yesterday, which wasn't advertised and about 30 people arrived to hear us. Still it was great crack and a lot of friends who had only heard us at the sound-wise disastrous Doncaster gig got a chance to hear us well.

3 May 1972 – Manchester

Here I am again having just woken up in the van. We had a night of drama last night. We had been in Blackpool and decided to drive home to Dave's in Bradford. When we got there, Dave rushed out and told us that the guy we had been staying with in Mexborough had been busted and the police had been up to Dave's and were looking for the van.

We hightailed it out of there and hid 2 ozs of grass in a field before deciding in a welter of paranoid melodrama to return to the Antrim hotel in Manchester, about 40 miles away.
We have one more gig in that area and that's tonight … But, we also have to return Dave's equipment. We'll probably all be in gaol next time I write!

Yesterday, we picked up Liam and lashed on to Blackpool, where we did a tiny club run by a huge man. Really enjoyed it and went a bomb.

Mary, Nicky's wife, came up to Blackpool and will be with us for the rest of the tour. She says that it said in 'Spotlight' that Planxty are being played every morning this week on 'Morning Airs'. That's great. I wonder what recordings they're using?

The lads are all in the hotel and it's raining and was all night and me snug in the van with the rain beating on the roof.

8 May 1972 – Manchester

This is just a short note because I'm hungover to the point of insanity.

Yesterday was Christy's birthday and we wound up in a drinking club, drinking about a thousand bottles of champagne.

We've one more gig, tonight in Chester and that's the end of live performances.

Newcastle, London and last night were really brilliant. In London, they wouldn't let us off the stage. Newcastle was fantastic. The Country Meets Folk programme was goodish except for the last number. 'Three Drunken Maidens' was brutal. We couldn't hear each other and were all playing in different times!

Des arrived on Saturday and tho' we were bolloxed after driving from Newcastle overnight, Liam and me stayed up half the night with him. And last night too.

We're all pretty jaded but happy to be a success!
Our Irish tour is every day in June.

We have two weeks till the end of May for rehearsing,
recording an LP, doing a couple of gigs perhaps and
having 4 or 5 days off.

John Peel was raving about us on the radio the other
night. I'm afraid we're going to be big!

Chapter 9

The Black Album

Planxty's eponymous debut album – universally identified as *The Black Album* in reference to its predominantly black sleeve – is a milestone recording in Irish music. It crystallises the 1972 set, the first year of Planxty, the incredible collection of idiosyncratic treatments and arrangements of songs and tunes plucked from a tantalising miscellany of sources. And even though *The Black Album* may not be the best-produced Planxty album, or as intricate and musically advanced as later records, it is undoubtedly the calling card for the new generation of Irish folk ensembles of the 1970s, and remains one of the timelessly enduring Irish music documents of the late twentieth century. But, like so many era-defining albums from years gone by, the circumstances surrounding its recording were less than illustrious.

1972 is remembered by all four members of Planxty as a cyclone of excitement and activity. Swept along by the momentum of the music and the contagious energy between artist and audi-ence, there was little consideration about how the band would sustain itself in the long term. Ireland at this time possessed little in the way of a music industry infrastructure. The showband era was rapidly fading into the distance and folk and traditional musi-cians had little or no acumen or interest in monetary matters. The Dubliners and The Chieftains, who had evolved from the core of Ó Riada's Ceoltóirí Chualann, had broken the ice overseas, but there was no clear course, especially for a band as unprecedented as Planxty.

On returning to Ireland after their debut jaunt to England in May 1972, Planxty regrouped at The Mugs Gig. By now, an album was beginning to take shape within their formidable live set. What was needed was a company to record the songs. Enter Phil Coulter, an old associate of manager Des Kelly. Coulter was a Derry-born songwriter of note – later to become a renowned producer, pianist and recording artist – who had penned the Capital Showband's 1963 hit 'Foolin' Time'.

Des Kelly knew Coulter through his collaborations with the Capital Showband and he invited him to come and see Planxty in action. Coulter attended The Mugs Gig in Slattery's of Capel Street on Monday, 22 May. According to Andy Irvine's letters, Coulter was so enthralled with Planxty that he described them as 'the greatest sound ever to come out of Ireland'. The following day, he met with Des Kelly and the band, minus Andy, who was jaundice-ridden and 'yellow as a primrose'. Coulter discussed plans to record the band for the Martin–Coulter production company. With no other offers on the table, it seemed inevitable that Planxty would take him up on the offer, yet there was a feeling of déjà vu for Dónal Lunny, the only member of the band to have already spent studio time with Coulter during the Emmet Spiceland album recording.

While the band deliberated over the decision to take this offer, they carried on business as usual, bringing the Planxty music all over Ireland, occasionally popping over to England and Scotland to play gigs or record a BBC session. The late, great John Peel was one of their early champions and they recorded a coveted Peel Session on 24 July, choosing 'Planxty Irwin', 'Merrily Kissed the Quaker', 'The West Coast of Clare' and 'Raggle Taggle Gypsy' – all titles in preparation for the forthcoming album. Planxty would go on to record two more Peel Sessions over the next two years.

One song that didn't make it onto the album was a loving ode to the spectacular landscape of Clare called 'The Cliffs of Dooneen', sung by Christy, though it was later released as a seven-inch single by Polydor in late 1972. Originally included on the *Prosperous* album, this song was a popular live number for the band and was known to lure audiences into kindred hushed singalongs. Both the words and the melancholic disposition of the pipes and whistle had a particular resonance for Irish people who had left their homeland to live abroad. There was a nostalgic aspect to these sorts of ballads sung by Christy and Andy, but with the musical depth of Planxty it became something more resonant again.

> *It's a nice place to be on a fine summer's day,*
> *Watching all the wild flowers that ne'er do decay.*
> *Oh, the hare and the pheasant are plain to be seen,*
> *Making homes for their young round the Cliffs of*
>   *Dooneen.*

> *Take a view o'er the Shannon, fine sights you'll see there:*
> *You'll see the high rocky hills on the west coast of Clare,*
> *Oh, the towns of Kilkee and Kilrush can be seen,*
> *From the high rocky slopes round the Cliffs of Dooneen.*

'The single is a very different recording to the *Prosperous* one because that album was recorded on one or two mics and so the pipes are very dominant,' says Christy. 'As I recall, the actual single had a better mix to it. That was recorded in the Eamonn Andrews Studios. Years later, I was recording an album there and my wife, Val, came in with our son, Andy, who was then in the pram, and I found the master tape of 'The Cliffs of Dooneen' and I stuck it in the pram. I think 'The Cliffs of Dooneen' got to number five in the charts and 'Three Drunken Maidens' to number seven. But as to what they sold, it's anyone's guess. It was at a time when the charts were probably totally rigged!'

On 4 September 1972, the band travelled to London for the recording of their debut album with Phil Coulter as producer. The contract, however, wasn't signed until the eleventh hour. The deal on the table was £30,000 to record six albums for Martin–Coulter Enterprises, which would then be licensed to the Polydor label in England. 'We were over in Bayswater in this kind of bed and breakfast, and the gun was at our heads,' explains Christy. 'We had to make the decision by three o'clock on Friday or there was no deal. The only one who was against it was Dónal. He didn't want to sign it. I didn't give a shit. All I wanted to do was make albums. Dónal dug his fuckin' heels. If I'm correct, I can remember us all kind of feeling "wish to fuck Dónal would sign this and let's get on with it". I think he was uncomfortable perhaps with Coulter. And also we weren't encouraged to be involved in production. I remember Des almost pleading with us and, eventually, we decided to go ahead and Dónal came along with us but he signed it under duress. The reason I can remember it so well was because I bought Val a lovely pair of earrings and they were stolen. I can still see the fuckin' earrings, they were lovely.'

Inexperienced in the intricacies of recording contracts, the band failed to realise that all production costs and various miscellaneous expenses would be deducted from the £30,000 advance. Furthermore, the band also seemed to be under the impression that it was Polydor they were signing to, rather than Martin–Coulter. 'That was probably our fault,' admits Andy. 'It may have been that no one told us. Or it may just have been that we weren't listening, but we signed to Phil Coulter and Bill Martin's production company. We were signed up for six albums in three years or something. I don't know how they expected us to do that. In the event, we made three and nullified the contract by mutual consent. Looking at it objectively, I suppose you could say that they took a chance. They didn't know we were going to be as popular as we were.'

'We were offered what sounded like a lot of money, a large advance,' continues Dónal. 'But it wasn't really. It was thirty grand. The budget for the first and second album was four grand, and it went up to five for the third and fourth and would've gone to six grand for the fifth and the sixth, just so it kept up with inflation. It was paltry enough. But the lump sum itself sounded somewhat impressive and we felt at least we could do our albums. We weren't wringing our hands in despair. We were happy being able to perform. A young band will do anything, will sign anything, and we did. I did. It puts a question mark over the validity of certain contracts. You can't mention morality and contracts in the same breath. You can't mention *business* and morality in the same breath. The conjunction of the words "business" and "ethics" is an oxymoron.'

Phil Coulter was an old friend of Des Kelly's from the Capital Showband days. Kelly explains that he was 'literally the only English contact I had'. Kelly avoided getting involved in negotiations for the band's recording contracts, feeling that it was really their territory. 'I remember Phil told us they were getting thirty thousand as an advance, but what nobody realised was that the group had to pay for everything, and that was expenses for anyone coming from England to see them and that sort of thing. I think they felt angry, and rightly so. I think they felt a bit used.'

For their debut album, Planxty chose titles carefully from the well of potential material available to them. Apart from the singles 'Three Drunken Maidens' and 'The Cliffs of Dooneen', other songs that didn't make the album included Dónal's 'When First unto this Country' and a beautiful vocal and harmonium version of the traditional Southern Appalachian song 'Down in the Valley', featuring all members of the band, including Liam on vocal harmonies.

'The material on the first album is drawn from what each of us brought to the table,' explains Liam. 'And a *lot* of material was brought to the table. It was sifted and sorted and selected.' Liam put forth his tunes, and Andy and Christy contributed four songs each. Dónal upheld the role of musical director. 'Yes, he had that role,' agrees Andy. 'He always had this ability to be able to hear the band while he was playing with it. I always found that impossible. When I was singing I tended to block out everything else. He'd be playing these great lines, but he'd be listening to everybody else as well. That's been a huge factor in the Planxty music and everything else he's ever done.'

'I was not one for going to books to collect material,' clarifies Dónal. 'In a way it suited me to be just involved in the treatment that we gave to the stuff because Christy was collecting his songs, Andy his and Liam his tunes. I was in the arrangement department and any time there was any slack I would come up with some kind of an idea that people would take on. That was a democratic process as well. Some of these pieces in their assembly went through several metamorphoses and that was sometimes a painful process. We would spend days building these complicated arrangements and then would have to face up to the fact that it wasn't really working. It would go down the toilet. And then it would start again and it was really agonising sometimes. And I would have to say that we got there. It always turned out better. Just managing to let go and start again was a positive thing.'

The album's opening shot was the epic 'Raggle Taggle Gypsy/Tabhair Dom Do Lámh' song-tune segue, the live centre-piece, a double-barrelled showstopper that captured so much of what Planxty was all about in four and a half minutes. 'Raggle Taggle Gypsy' was a song learned from one of Christy Moore's most profoundly significant influences, singing traveller John Reilly. Although previously recorded on Christy's *Prosperous* album, this was an altogether more striking take. 'I suppose we felt it would be nice to get a proper recording, as much as we liked the *Prosperous* one,' says Christy. 'I imagine Dónal and Andy would have been anxious to re-record it with a more balanced version of the strings and for everything to be in its proper place.'

Christy had heard other versions of the song in his travels and became aware of the fact that it was one of the 'basic' songs. At one time, there was a seven-week series of programmes on the BBC all about different versions of 'Raggle Taggle Gypsy' from all over the world. 'What makes this version so special for me,' explains Christy, 'are the pictures John painted in my mind when he sang this ancient ballad. It seemed like he lived it every time he sang it. This applies to all the songs he sang. When I first heard him, I had no idea of the historical value or the cultural ethnicity that was imbued when an illiterate Irish gypsy was found to have such a treasure chest of wonderful and ancient songs. For me, it was simply the joy of meeting a beautiful, innocent man who took such delight in young fellows like myself wanting to hear him sing. As a singer, I knew what a pleasure it is to encounter people who want to listen, who understand the core and sap of the songs and who are transported back to the place where these verses were first sung. John was a direct link back to those precious moments.'

The immortal legend that is John Reilly lives on through the music of Christy Moore and countless other singers. Christy first happened upon him in Grehan's pub in Boyle during the fleadh cheoils of the 1960s. The Grehan Sisters were much-admired singers, and they and their mother offered refuge to Reilly in his later years. Frank Lunny was also a frequent visitor at Grehan's and another witness to this mystical singing traveller and his great reservoir of songs. 'The Grehans were such generous, beautiful people,' recalls Frank. 'They fed him. They gave him his beer. On one occasion, myself and Pat Dowling went to Boyle and we took John out for a trip in the car and went up around The Coolies. He was a lovely, gentle old man and the thing I remember most about him as we drove around was he'd look out the window of the car and say, "Ah jaysus, there used to be a lovely premises in there" or "There was a terrible fight there one night" as he looked into a field with maybe one stone left in it.'

Christy went on to sing and record many songs heard from the mouth of John Reilly, but 'Raggle Taggle Gypsy' is certainly one of the greatest and most successful interpretations. Just like the *Prosperous* recording, but now with greater impact, Planxty bridged the song into the Ruaidhri 'Dall' Ó Catháin composition 'Tabhair Dom Do Lámh' ('Give Me Your Hand'). 'That was an obvious winner,' reckons Andy. 'It gathered momentum and more structure between Christy's recording and Planxty's recording. It's an easy enough joint, really, but the audience always roared from day one when we went into the tune.'

'Tabhair Dom Do Lámh' has been tackled and interpreted in many different manners through the years, but none so dramatic as that of Planxty's visionary arrangement. Audiences immediately picked up on the transition and it became customary to roar their appreciation at the very moment the music shifts from song to tune. 'It was very unusual at the time,' explains Dónal. 'It was a first, really, to have a song and then a tune. It was something that excited people. The whole thing was sort of widened out and it had a real sweeping feeling.'

The 'Raggle Taggle Gypsy/Tabhair Dom Do Lámh' set was one of many song-tune amalgams that would become a trademark of Planxty music. 'That idea of tacking a tune onto a song, I don't think I've heard that used before Planxty,' states Liam O'Flynn. "Tabhair Dom Do Lámh' is a tune I would've known long in advance of Planxty. I guess I would have heard it probably through Seán Ó Riada's music, he dug up so much of that early harp music. It's such a powerful happening. Definitely a lot of people see it as a defining Planxty moment.'

Andy Irvine takes the lead on the album's second track, 'Arthur McBride', an anti-recruitment song from Donegal that was collected by P.W. Joyce in his native Limerick in the early nineteenth century and documented in his collection. It's the tale of Arthur and his cousin being accosted by a British army sergeant, his corporal, and a 'wee drummer' petitioning them to sign up to the army and reap the benefits of a steady wage and a so-called good life. Arthur and his cousin, however, were having none of it and before the king's men could take their swords to them, our peace-loving duo cracked their heads with their 'whacking shillelaghs'. Despite this one act of violence, this witty song depicts a refreshing, almost Joycean portrayal of the Irish as true pacifists at heart.

This version of the song is executed with real gusto by the band, particularly with the rousing singalong of the closing verse of:

Rory Dall

Intrigue and conjecture surrounds the story of Ruaidhri Ó Catháin (Rory Dall), who was also a blind harper and who lived *c.*1570–1650. From the Ó Catháin clan, prominent in Derry and Antrim, Dall, like many other harpers and fiddlers, was stricken with blindness and encouraged to pursue musicianship. He did so loyally under the patronage of Hugh O'Neill, who titled the harper Oireachtaidhe Ó Catháin (Chief Ó Catháin). He himself was a proud and spirited man. The story of 'Tabhair Dom Do Lámh' is a great example of this.

According to Francis O'Neill's *Irish Minstrels and Musicians*, during one of Rory Dall's many trips to Scotland, he visited Eglinton Castle, the home of Lady Eglinton in Ayrshire. However, Dall was deeply offended by her 'peremptory manner' and he hastily left the castle before a note of music was played. When Lady Eglinton was informed of the great esteem with which her guest was held, she soon set about making a speedy reconciliation. In turn, Dall wrote 'Tabhair Dom Do Lámh' as a peace offering. The fame of the composition and the encounter that inspired it spread across Scotland even to the ears of King James VI, who invited Dall to perform in his court. Dall obliged and his inspiring performance prompted the king to lay his royal hand on the harper's shoulder. When asked by one of the courtiers if he realised the honour thus bestowed on him, Dall remarked, 'A greater man than King James has laid his hand on my shoulder.' 'Who was that man?' asked the king. 'O'Neill, Sire,' he replied, proudly standing to his feet.

As for the wee drummer, we rifled his pouch,
And we made a football of his rowdy dow dow.*
And into the ocean, to rock and to row,
And bade it a tedious returning.

As for the aul rapier that hung by his side,
We flung it as far as we could in the tide.
'To the Devil, I pitch you,' says Arthur McBride,
To temper your steel in the morning.
[*Rowdy dow dow refers to a drum]

Andy came across this tune while touring the northwest of England in 1971. 'I learned that song essentially for Planxty,' he says. 'I rarely played it at my own gigs. I couldn't play it solo, it was a band number. I stopped that process in 1972 when I went to a session in Tullamore and I couldn't play anything on my own at all. I realised then that it was all very well playing in a band, but you had to be able to play the stuff alone too!'

'Arthur McBride' is a song typical of Andy's socialist mindset and also a good example of his propensity for finding tunes in dusty old book collections. 'He did that quite a lot,' remarks Dónal. 'He went to the National Library and rooted around for days and he'd come back out with beautiful songs. There came a time when it seemed that everything had been mined, everything had been dug out, but Andy was still finding new things.'

The Black Album features two compositions written by the most famous of all Irish harp composers and the man seemingly responsible for the word Planxty, Turlough Carolan (1670–1738). The first is a short melancholic composition called 'Planxty Irwin', and the second is a re-recording of 'Sí Bheag Sí Mhór', which Planxty had previously recorded as a B-side. 'Sí Bheag Sí Mhór', allegedly inspired by two warring fairy hills in County Leitrim, is a spellbinding piece of music. Like much of Carolan's work, it embodies the decorative elegance of European music being written in the seventeenth century by the likes of Vivaldi, Corelli and Geminiani. Baroque music was becoming popular amongst the aristocracy of Ireland and Carolan would often hear it played in the Big Houses. It is even said that Carolan encountered the violinist and composer Francesco Geminiani on several occasions in Ireland and that 'Carolan's Concerto' was the result of a challenge laid down by his distinguished Italian peer.

Like his predecessor Ruaidhri 'Dall' Ó Catháin, accounts of Carolan's life are shrouded in myth. It is often impossible to determine fact from fiction. Unlike Ó Catháin, Carolan was an itinerant harper, bard and poet, sent off with a horse, harp and guide after becoming blind from smallpox around the age of eighteen. Nonetheless, he lived a successful life and, despite the oppressive climate of the Penal Laws in Ireland, he played and composed planxties for both Irish and non-Irish patrons and received national acclaim and great hospitality for his work. It is for his composition rather than his playing that he is most renowned. Over 200 pieces are recognised today as being his, with some seventy sets of lyrics.

Planxty's version of 'Sí Bheag Sí Mhór', led by Liam's pipes and accompanied by the delicate string interplay, also retains the baroque feel, giving Planxty music an almost classical dimension. It remains one of their signature tunes. 'That was the first one I heard Liam play when he came back from America and I thought, "Oh, yessssss!"' declares Andy.

They can, of course, thank Seán Ó Riada for reviving Carolan music centuries after it had faded from public consciousness. 'Ó Riada was the person, really,' declares Liam. 'He was taken with the music of the harpers. He delved into the collections and introduced all that music to a much wider audience, musicians as well as listeners. And the notion of doing that type of tune within the Planxty set-up seemed ideal. You had instruments that could accompany the tune very nicely. Andy and Dónal had those lovely ways of using countermelodies. According to Donal O'Sullivan, the man who wrote the definitive book on Carolan (*Carolan: The Life, Times and Music of an Irish Harper*), this was the first tune he composed. Fairies are a huge part of Irish folklore and the notion of the "little people" and the spirit world was hugely important. It still occupies a very important place in the Irish mind. It's a timeless tune. It proves that a good tune can be passed from generation to generation and stand the test of time.'

One of the few non-traditional songs on *The Black Album* is Ewan McColl's 'Sweet Thames Flow Softly', sung gently and soulfully by Christy and given a typically rich Planxty treatment. McColl originally composed the song for a London-based radio-play adaptation of *Romeo and Juliet*. 'I was booked to play at Ewan McColl's club in King's Cross, London in 1969,' Christy recollects. 'This was the premier venue in Britain at the time. At least, so it appeared to the apprentice twenty-four-year-old balladeer from Bognia. There I was shittin' myself and Ewan recognised my nervousness and bought me a large Glenmorangie single malt whisky, which did help. Later, I sat on stage beside McColl and Seeger and he sang this song, 'Sweet Thames Flow Softly'. I thought it the most wonderful love song I'd ever heard. Peggy later sold me the album and I was happy to sing this masterpiece. When we rehearsed it, Andy tried harmonica with the chanter and we had another magic Planxty moment. The song brings to the band an element that I love where the material springs from very diverse and unconnected sources.'

Two more great Planxty influences from the Clare tradition, Junior Crehan and Willie Clancy, receive tribute in the form of a beautiful duo of reels titled 'Junior Crehan's Favourite' and 'Corney is Coming'. 'I got the first tune from Junior,' explains Liam.

'I asked him if he had a name for it but he said no, so I decided to call it 'Junior Crehan's Favourite'. He said, "That'll do!" 'Corney is Coming' is a tune I heard Willie Clancy playing. He didn't have a name for it, but we asked Breandán Breathnach and he knew the name. I think both Willie and Junior were very pleased with this new band and new type of presentation of traditional music and that they figured in it very strongly. Also, I think the audiences and listeners were aware that we valued these people – the Junior Crehans and Willie Clancys – very, very highly indeed. They were our heroes. Both those men are still musical heroes of mine.'

Ask Christy Moore what his favourite song on Planxty's *Black Album* is and he'll answer Andy Irvine's 'The West Coast of Clare'. Never has a song so succinctly captured the pathos of the singer. When Planxty play 'The West Coast of Clare', the audience, who may have been yelping and hollering moments earlier, became ensconced in deep reflection. Andy's words portray a duality of sadness that is both personal and universal. Liam's accompanying tin whistle echoes out a sense of distance over a heart-melting melody. Again, it is a song born of nostalgia, yet so vivid and transcendent that one can't help but succumb to it.

Sorrow and sadness,
Bitterness, grief.
Memories I have of you
Won't leave me in peace.

My mind was running back
To the West Coast of Clare,
Thinking of you
And the times we had there.

I walk to Spanish Point,
I knew I'd find you there.

I stood on the white strand
And you were everywhere.

Vivid memories fade,
But the mood still remains.
I wish I could go back
And be with you again.

'If I was to pick one track it would probably be that,' confirms Christy. 'I really love that. And I would say it isn't really about the west coast of Clare as such. It's about everything. It's about your life. It's about heartbreak. It's about intense love. It just so happens to be placed there.' Dónal concurs, 'I think Andy's sensibilities at that time would've been to avoid sentimentality and mawkishness. It's sort of open.'

'It's become a classic,' declares Liam. 'I've heard other people do it and it's fine, but Andy's singing of it is just *it*. And so often that is the case. It's a moment of mighty reflection.'

Andy wrote 'The West Coast of Clare' in the late summer of 1968. 'I started it around the time of one of the last gigs Sweeney's Men did. We were playing in Quilty, which is the next town to Miltown Malbay, and I just felt sad at the thought that this was going to be the end of a period of my life. I was going away to Eastern Europe in a couple of weeks. I think I wrote the "Sorrow and sadness" verse there. I always remember that gig because we went to the pub in Quilty and there was a woman there made up to the nines, an older woman. She kept asking me for a light and every time I gave her a light she said, "Thanks for the hot connection."'

When writing the song, Andy says he was thinking back over the previous five years and times spent in Miltown Malbay. 'It was actually written with a Danish girl called Birte in mind, but the whole essence of the period kind of deluged Birte a little bit.

It very quickly became a memory of great times in Clare in 1963, 1964 and 1965. I finished it when I got to Ljubljana in August or September 1968. I came back for Joe Dolan's wedding at Christmas 1969. I remember singing that song, and some others I'd written, to Joe Dolan in O'Donoghue's and Joe saying; "Jeez, Andy, that's a fuckin' great song." So I was encouraged. That was the first song I ever wrote. When you start writing songs, it's a void, you don't really know if they are good, bad or indifferent because they're kind of personal. Then I sang another one and he said that was a great song too. Joe didn't give praise that lightly. I was much encouraged by that.'

'The West Coast of Clare' is directly followed on the album by a song of radically contrasting mood, 'The Jolly Beggar'. This jovial, lusty number, sung by Andy, details the divilish exploits of King James V of Scotland, who, according to legend, roamed the countryside dressed as a beggar in search of romantic liaisons with farmers' daughters. As Andy often points out when introducing this song at Planxty concerts, it was a good time for Scottish beggars, who were much in demand given their potential to actually be royalty in disguise. 'The Jolly Beggar' is segued into a reel, which is untitled on the album sleeve. 'We didn't have a title for that tune for a long time,' says Liam. 'In royalties it's always called 'Jolly Beggar Reel'. I think it was old John Kelly who eventually told us it was called 'The Wise Maid'.'

Christy's next contribution was 'Only Our Rivers', a song written by Mickey MacConnell from Bellanaleck near Enniskillen in County Fermanagh. This is a sad song that mirrors themes of tyranny and hardship against images of nature and freedom. 'I heard Mickey MacConnell's brother Cathal sing this song in Leeds in 1969. I'm between two minds about it,' says Christy. 'I feel that it's part of a trio of songs in my repertoire, the two subsequent songs being 'Irish Ways and Irish Laws' and

'North and South of the River'. I've had this feeling without ever analysing it, but I expect the songs describe how I feel about the territory known as Ulster, the Six Counties, the Occupied Territory, Part of Great Britain, The North, up above, or where "The Troubles" exist. Because of the songs I sing or have sung about this part of Ireland, I have been given many different labels. I came to Ulster for the first time in 1964 and did my first gig there in 1967. The songs I've sung reflect what I've felt, what I've experienced and what I've seen and encountered.'

'Only Our Rivers' was written specifically about experiences in Northern Ireland, yet lyrically and thematically it easily relates to so many different cultures and circumstances, rendering it a truly universal song. 'Yeah, I could hear Floyd Westerman, the Native-American folk artist, singing it just as easy as Planxty or the aboriginal singer Archie Roach singing it in Australia,' adds Christy.

'This recording represents a very considerable milestone in my musical life,' declares the original author, Mickey MacConnell. 'I left school at fourteen, having decided that the academic life was not for me. After a few dead-end jobs, I got a job as a cub reporter in my local paper, *The Fermanagh Herald*. It was there that I quickly discovered all about the misuse and abuse of power by the Northern regime at first hand. It was something of an eye-opener to see it in action and witness the despair and hardship it caused. I was playing a lot of traditional music at the time with my brother, Cathal, and I was also experimenting with guitar playing and song-writing. I wrote the song in 1965 when I was eighteen years old – this was long before the first stones were thrown in Derry or elsewhere. It was a personal reaction to what was going on around me and was written with no real expectations as to its future.'

MacConnell was a young reporter working with the *Irish Press* when Christy telephoned to ask if Planxty could record

'Only Our Rivers' on *The Black Album*. 'Needless to say,'
continues MacConnell, 'I was absolutely delighted. It was my
first breakthrough and an extremely significant one. I honestly
believe that it was the right song at the right time and recorded
by the right man. It grew "like Topsy" as the politics of the North
changed and, in time, became regarded almost as an anthem for
the dispossessed. I'm extremely grateful to Christy and the lads
for that. Planxty were undoubtedly the most important band of
perhaps any generation and established the benchmark by which
everything that followed was judged.'

Where Christy applies a very sensitive, clement style of
singing on the songs 'Only Our Rivers' and 'Sweet Thames Flow
Softly', on the old rebel-rousing 'Follow Me Up to Carlow', his
voice is sharp and stinging. 'Follow Me Up to Carlow' depicts the
battle of 1580 at Glen Malure, County Wicklow, where Fiach
McHugh O'Byrne overthrew the forces of the crown led by Lord
Grey de Wilton. 'This was old Frank Lunny's favourite. It goes
back to the repertoire of The Rakes of Kildare. It's a powerful
and much hackneyed ballad that was written in days of utter
tyranny. Its ferocity is indicative of the tyranny that prevailed,'
Christy explains.

> From Tassagart to Clonmore there flows a stream of
>   Saxon gore
> Well great is Rory Óg Ó More at sending the loons to
>   Hades
> White is sick, Grey is fled, now for black Fitzwilliam's
>   head
> We'll send it over dripping red to Queen Liza and her
>   ladies

Christy, Liam, Andy and Dónal had agreed from the outset that
they would not use Planxty music as a vehicle for politics. 'There

was a certain reserve in the band collectively in getting involved in politics,' confirms Dónal. 'There were other bands out at the time that were overtly involved in politics. That went from serious songs about the situation in the North to "rebel songs" where people would sing anything from 'A Nation Once Again' on. It was being serviced by other bands and it was something that we didn't feel the need to do or didn't feel it was appropriate. Indeed, much later on, after the second manifestation of the band, Christy amassed quite a lot of songs which had political messages and that indirectly led to Moving Hearts.'

However, both 'Only Our Rivers' and 'Follow Me Up to Carlow' could be clearly identified as political songs. 'This is true,' agrees Christy, 'the former being a modern nationalist ballad, and the latter being most certainly a particularly bloody rebel song from the early eighteenth century. Also 'Arthur McBride' is a political song in the sense that it's an anti-war song, typically of Andy's world view. It's the first time that I've realised that now. God, that's a bit odd. But they are two good songs. I would have to say at the time of assembling my repertoire in those days, and to a certain extent right up to the present day, if a song appealed to me it would have to be the structure of the song, the music, the vibe of the song, before the politics. 'Follow Me Up to Carlow' would be a song from my very early repertoire before I had a view of things, whereas 'Only Our Rivers' appealed to me because of what it said, and the time it was coming at. But very few songs would I have learned or written purely because of their politics.'

Liam's other contribution to The Black Album was another tune learned from Willie Clancy, 'Merrily Kissed the Quaker', a single jig, or 'slide' as they are known in Kerry, where they are performed to accompany a unique style of set-dancing. This short but buoyant piece of music became a real Planxty signature tune and it gleefully employs the marriage of chanter, drones, regulator, strings and the tribal rumble of the bodhrán. 'That music comes from East Kerry, Sliabh Luachra,' explains Liam. 'I've always had huge admiration for people like Padraic O'Keefe, Johnny O'Leary and Denis Murphy. It's a rich, rich music. This was a very popular "in" tune at the time. It was nice to have that sort of variety in the instrumental music, as well as the jigs and reels and hornpipes, to have some Kerry slides.'

Just as *The Black Album* opens with a breathtaking seamless segue, it concludes in equally fine style with 'The Blacksmith', an old southern English folk song that Andy had adapted to an East European signature. The song bleeds into an extended wild and trippy outro – later dubbed 'Blacksmithereens' – driven by a pummelling bodhrán and bouzouki rhythm and some hair-raising uilleann pipe phrasing that is as electrifying as any great psychedelic guitar riff. Andy had performed this song regularly in his partnership with Dónal. 'Andy and myself had a shape on that before Planxty,' explains Dónal. 'So then it was a matter of adding Liam and Christy to the arrangement. 'The Blacksmith' is a very obvious reflection of the influences Andy gathered in Eastern Europe. That piece of music was right up my street as well.'

'It's a great example of introducing elements of the Eastern European tradition, which were quite unknown to me,' admits Liam. 'That presented me with an interesting challenge because of the time signatures, but it worked.'

Despite Dónal's scepticism, the recording process of *The Black Album* at Command Studios in London appeared to be painless. 'We stayed at the Irish Club in Eaton Square. There were nights of merriment and days that started late,' declares Christy. 'Phil Coulter was the producer, but he had nothing to do,' adds Andy. 'He just sat there and said diplomatic things. I remember after the recording we went out for a drink and he was talking about the 5/8 time signature of 'The Blacksmith' and he seemed to be generally impressed by the music we played.'

'I would say we were swept along,' ponders Dónal. 'By the time we got to the studio, we'd been playing it for almost a year. So we recorded it in three days without any intervention or changes. We just got it right. It was all very quick. We just rattled it off. It was a matter of just getting a nice take of what we did. If there was a tuning problem or something like that, well fine, there might be a quality-control element to what Phil was doing. Fair enough. Phil would have had considerable experience at that time in studios, but not of that kind of music.'

Liam thinks that Phil Coulter was somewhat in awe of the band. 'He was bright enough to realise that you don't mess with something that's working,' he continues. 'He could have tried to arrange all manner of dressed-up arrangements, but I think he knew the band wouldn't have any of it. He took a back seat in the studio. He realised, I'm sure, that it was the best way to deal with the situation.'

'I remember we got a copy of it I think on reel to reel format and we listened to it in my flat in Donnybrook and we were blown away,' adds Andy. 'We were heavy into it. We thought it was great!'

Polydor released the album in early 1973 in its now iconic dark-lit album sleeve with a photograph taken by Tom McIlroy of the band silhouetted under a spotlight, as they played live at the National Stadium. The album was launched with a concert in the Carlton Cinema in O'Connell Street in Dublin on 7 February and was promoted by Jim Aiken.

Marcus Connaughton was a young Dubliner who joined Polydor Ireland in 1973 as a trainee label manager. 'Polydor was located right in the heart of the city on Middle Abbey Street just across from Independent Newspapers, so the whole street was vibrant at the time. My wife Helen is always staggered that I can still remember the catalogue number of *The Black Album*, which is 2383 186. Because it was doing such incredible quantities, these numbers stuck with you. The sales figures were dramatic at the time. You're probably looking at about 200,000 vinyl albums initially. *The Black Album* was the start of a huge interest in Irish folk music. It was kind of a bridge from Seán Ó Riada and Ceoltóirí Chualann into the modern idiom. It was very, very exciting to see those guys on stage. If you went to a concert in the National Stadium you probably knew most of the people at the gig. We were starved of live music in Ireland. You might get to see Fairport Convention or Steeleye Span, but all of a sudden we had our own heroes that we could go and pay homage to.'

Excerpts from letters from a jaundice-inflicted Andy Irvine in Dublin, May 1972

16 May 1972 – Dublin

We have just had a rather non-practice and I have been playing the hurdy-gurdy which is beginning to sound more musical.

Last night, The Mugs Gig was jammed to the door-o and we made £8.50 each. (It's little because we have decided to cut Des in, as he is paying Nicky's wages – we also had to pay various people who had subsidised the debacles of the three previous weeks.)

Dónal and me got pissed as rats-o and I stayed the night in his place.

I'm not well again today. I'm sweating and weak and my back is sore. It feels ominously like Glandular Fever but maybe it's just the flu virus.

We have rehearsal at 14h and then tonight I'm going to The Tradition Club because Cathal MacConnell and Tommy Peoples are on.

22 May 1972 – Sick with Jaundice in Dublin

The lads came over to practise but I was too ill to take part. Had a really horrible evening and night. I thrashed around in a high fever all night and this morning, my temperature is normal but I still feel terrible. I meant to go to the doctor last night and today but don't seem to have the strength. Haven't eaten anything since you went back to Galway. I feel too sick to eat.

23 May 1972

We did our two gigs last night and I didn't come out of it as well as I expected. After the concert, I felt a bit weak and, after The Mugs Gig, I was fucked with a pain in my liver. When I got home and looked at myself in the mirror, I got a big fright. I looked exactly like a clown! I had very red rimmed eyes and my yellow face. The crowd and heat in The Mugs Gig last night was immense and intense. And the reaction, as usual, incredible. Christy was in his funniest mood.

Phil Coulter came up afterwards and was speechless with admiration. He said it was the greatest sound ever to come out of Ireland! He hadn't been so knocked out since the first time he heard Ó Riada, so things look very promising in that direction...

The night before in The Swamp they made £37 and elected to cut me in on a share on account of my woman and child! I used that expression one day in Manchester and they have never let me forget it!

24 May 1972 – Dublin

This morning I feel a bit better, somehow, I don't know why. I'm still as yellow as a primrose.
Last night in the Royal Hotel, Howth, was quite

exhausting and I hope the doctor will not notice, as I didn't tell him I was doing it – or Monday's gigs either. As far as he is concerned, he thinks tonight is the first night.

I quite enjoyed the singing last night, Luke Kelly and Barney McKenna were there and quite enraptured by 'Planxty'. The audience was not all that big and we made £25, which doesn't really seem worth fucking up one's liver for...

I hope The Chariot tonight will be better. To my annoyance, I find that we are in The Berni Inn on Thursday. It's not even a professional venue. Still, we may make some bread. We have this guy Gerry Doyle playing with us this week. Christy picked him up. He's good enough but he does just about every number from Neil Young's newest album and the rest is James Taylor. He does it all as a perfect copy. We still have no one booked for the tour with us.

I think I told you Phil Coulter was over the moon about the group on Monday night. The lads had a meeting with him yesterday and he's going to record us. That means we have to go to England for a week in July. Poor old Dónal is very wary, as Phil Coulter's production of the Emmett Spiceland LP was the straw that made Dónal leave the group. Still, he sounds sincere...

Christy was in great and obscene form again last night – he has this story about finding me with jaundice where he says, 'I went into his room and he has his walls painted yellow, a yellow carpet on the floor and a yellow bedspread … it took me half an hour to find him.'

Rumour hath it that The Woods Band with whom we are supposed to be playing in The Stadium has broken up again! Fuck's sake…

25 May 1972 – Dublin

I'm feeling just a little, tiny bit better today.

We did 'Morning Airs' yesterday and it was <u>quite</u> good. We don't seem to be able to do our best in studios yet. This is strange because I have always thought it the most rewarding.

Anyway, we went on to The Chariot and had a pretty boring gig. I hate The Chariot like poison.

We were quite good and went down well. The audience was full of celebrities. I snuck off quietly at the end and walked home.

Chapter 10

On the Road

In their first year of existence, Planxty were unstoppable. The combination of Moore, Irvine, Lunny and O'Flynn had spawned music of great significance. It didn't just bridge genre, it bridged generations. The music was *all* about people, all about the trials and tribulations of the human existence. Whether the characterisations were based on raggle taggle gypsies, military snubbing latchecos or deceitful blacksmiths, every story had resonance in both traditional and modern life; heartbreak, sex, violence, deceit, nostalgia, freedom … It was all there on *The Black Album*, and it was all there in those fascinating, unifying performances.

The showband era had generated a soundtrack for revelling couples to jitterbug and neck to, but Planxty had something that made people sit up and listen. They had something that struck a chord, something rich and deep that people could immerse

themselves in. And people all over the country did. They dived in.
They drowned themselves in Planxty. It was infectious and it was
cerebral and neither band nor audience could get enough – so
they toured Ireland tenaciously, barely stopping for a breath.
'The first eighteen months of Planxty were some of the most
exciting times of my life,' says Christy. 'It felt like there was this
generation being turned on to this music that we were playing,
people were discovering their roots and their heritage and their
Irishness, the same way I did when I heard The Clancy Brothers.
To be part of that and to be on stage providing that was a huge
turn on.'

At the end of November 1972, Planxty reached a landmark of
sorts in Ireland. They played the National Stadium, selling out all
2,500 seats a good week before the show. Their previous
appearance at the stadium had been a shared bill with The
Woods Band. The fact that a mere five months later they were
selling out the venue themselves highlighted their snowballing
impact on the country that year. The entertainment magazine
New Spotlight raved about the concert, commenting on several
highlights of the set, including Christy's 'I Wish I Was in
England' (from *Prosperous*), a raucous version of 'Three
Drunken Maidens', 'The Blacksmith', Dónal's *sean-nós* piece
'Bean Pháidín' and Liam's pipe solo, 'Rakish Paddy'. Andrew
Means from *Melody Maker* magazine was also present. In his
review, he portrays a harmonious ensemble of musicians in full
flight. 'The pipes alternate smoothly between a decorative
supporting role and the calm assertive instrumental lead in tunes
like the emotive 'Sí Bheag Sí Mhór' and 'An Phis Fhliuch'. It
would have been impossible to guess from Planxty's excellent
performance that they were all sweating with nerves.'

Planxty may have had the midas touch onstage but, behind
the scenes, there was a more haphazard process at work. A

perfect example was the opening night of a national tour of cinema venues at the Grand Cinema in Cabra in Dublin, which turned out to be a calamitous false start, witnessed and then documented hilariously by Peter O'MacBrady in an article for *The Music People* magazine.

> *The concert is supposed to start at 10.15 on a wet and windy Thursday night. Nobody knows how many tickets have been sold, whether or not the PA is strong enough to fill the large arena, or where Christy is. Andy last saw him earlier this morning when he left determined not to return 'til he had drunk a tenner at least. At the moment, the seats are full of elderly ladies – all busily scribbling out numbers on their bingo cards. Dónal Lunny almost collapsed when he arrived – he thought that the ladies were assembled to hear Planxty. Liam Óg O'Flynn wanders in and out but never says anything.*
>
> *Just as Christy arrives a major power problem arises. Christy decides to change into a clean shirt in honour of the occasion. Another problem, he does not have a clean shirt – so he wears the dirty one inside out. Everyone is upset now because it doesn't look like the group can go on. Andy is sitting in a corner looking very pensive – perhaps remembering similar situations from his days with Sweeney's Men.*
>
> *Dónal goes on stage and explains to the audience what has happened. The audience are disappointed but one of them shouts up that he'll 'see yis at the Stadium.' Christy gets annoyed at the cinema staff concerning their antiquated electrics system. Then he disappears for a while. Everyone is pissed off, so I explain that John Peel has said that he would like to have them on his show. Spirits are now high again. Christy reappears and makes*

wholesale apologies. News arrives that tomorrow night's gig in Waterford is booked out. Jubilation is the order of the moment and bottles are quickly opened and then emptied.

Sharing the highs and lows of the Planxty road show was a crew of roadies, drivers and technicians just as eccentric as the band members themselves. 'Early on we had two brothers, Seamus and Sean McCabe, who both drove the band – they were from Cavan and smoked fags endlessly,' remembers Andy. 'They were sent up rotten by Christy and Dónal. They didn't quite fit the image of the band. They were more like showband people who were dressed in suits and collected the money. Seamus was famous for that line that a lot of people are famous for where the promoter after the showband dance says, "Well we didn't have a great night tonight, maybe you could take a bit of a cut in your wages," and Seamus would say, "Ah sure no point in us all having a bad night."

'Sean was a rally driver. Sometimes late at night going back after the gig, maybe after a few pints, people would be asleep and you'd wake up as we took some corner at break-neck speed and Christy would be sitting next to you muttering, "He's rallying, he's rallying." Sean had been a policeman in Cavan, but got sacked because he didn't arrest anyone. He is a great guy.' Des Kelly remembers having high hopes that Sean would 'put manners' on the band, but this never happened.

'The first eighteen months was unbelievable,' confirms Andy. 'I've never been incarcerated in a van with such witty people. The jokes and the humour … It was magic. It was magic.' Another man who witnessed many priceless Planxty moments first-hand was renowned Irish folk singer Mick Hanly. He knew the boys from the Dublin folk scene, gigs in Slattery's and Trinity College, and was adopted as a support act when they first formed Planxty.

'There was a whole entourage that surrounded Planxty,' recalls Mick. 'There were a lot of people who were just there for the craic. And who wouldn't be? There was a lot of it to be had!'

Hanly laughed his way through many hours in the back of Planxty's infamous white transit van. 'I remember it with great affection. There were the four members, Nicky Ryan, the soundman, an assortment of different drivers, myself, and all the gear all piled into this transit van. Planxty were one of the first bands ever to have their own sound system. I remember they had these special Bunsen burner holders on the microphone stands. I don't know where they got them. The mic was squeezed into one of these Bunsen burner holders so they could have a microphone for the vocal and a microphone for the bouzouki or whatever instrument. I travelled all over the country with them. The band was a phenomenal draw. They played a lot of cinemas. They played the Carlton in Dublin and the Savoy in Cork and the Savoy in Limerick, which were huge theatres, and they pretty much filled them every time.

'The first time I ever sat in the van I was passed a joint and I didn't know what it was. I said, "It's okay, I have my own, thanks," which was a large box of Players. Of course, I was ridiculed roundly for it in later days. When there'd be no dope available, Christy would joke, "Jays, Mick has great Players there, break 'em out there, Mick." This was all new to me. I was a complete greenhorn. I didn't know anything about smoking dope or anything like that.

'I remember one particular trip in 1973,' continues Mick, 'we were all in the van on the way to some big venue somewhere. Myself and Mícheál O'Domhnaill were recording that day and we were picked up at the Eamonn Andrews Studios. That same day three of the IRA lads were lifted out of Mountjoy Prison in a helicopter. So the guards immediately put up all these roadblocks, which we all found very amusing, the idea of: "Well if they're in a helicopter, let's put up a roadblock." The driver Sean McCabe was an ex-guard and no one has more contempt for the guards than an ex-guard. We were stopped four or five times before we'd even half the journey done. Every twenty miles we'd meet another roadblock. Eventually Sean said, "I'm fuckin' fed up, I'm not stopping for the next one." So we came to this little village and there was a guard with a torch and I'm sure the last thing this guy wanted to be doing was to be on the road flagging down traffic to see if there were three IRA boys in the back, who were actually long gone. Sean says, "I'm not stopping, I don't care." So he slowed down as your man was flashing him down, and as he was drawing near to him he yelled in his gruff Northern accent, "Did you catch them yet?" Your man didn't know what to say. And Sean adds, "They're hardly flying this fuckin' low," and he booted off and left your man standing in the middle of the road. Well, Jesus, there was uproar in the van. Everyone thought this was the fuckin' funniest thing they ever heard.'

Des Kelly brought in another old college friend, the colourful and fondly regarded Johnny Divilly, who was a piano-playing butcher from Galway. 'Johnny Divilly was my best friend,' exclaims Des. 'We sat at the same desk in secondary school for three or four years. We went to Dublin together on the train to do our third year in college and we were in digs together. Johnny was a bit of a wayward man.'

John Divilly had his own butcher shop in the 1960s, but was forced to sell it after the bank strike of 1970. 'Des was flying high,' begins Divilly. 'He had finished the Capitol Showband and had taken on Planxty. He knew that I was in trouble. I was married with three kids. I didn't know what to do. So Des asked me to get involved. He said they're playing support to Donovan in The Hangar in Galway. See what you think of them and get back to me on it. So I went along to see Planxty. It was the funniest thing. I'm waiting outside The Hangar and there are big boulders outside to stop people from parking near the venue. So Christy arrives in a grey 1963 Jag. The first thing he did was to drive over one of the boulders. The boulder got caught between the mudguard and the wheel. I am standing thinking, "What in God's name is this?" He gets out and he thinks this is hilarious, off his head. Can't move the bloody car. My first job for Planxty was to get a mechanic out the next morning and extricate the Jag from the boulder.'

Divilly was more of a showband fan at the time and admits, although he thought the band were good, it wasn't really 'my kind of music'. He met up with Des in Dublin, where Des explained that he wouldn't be able to pay him yet. He asked him to start booking bands into venues and said that he'd give him 10 per cent of the profit if a gig went well. 'So I was working out of Des's office on Belmont Avenue,' continues Divilly. 'I did that for a while, but it didn't work out. I went back home. And then Des got back in touch and asked would I be Planxty's road manager. So I went to Dublin in my best suit, shirt and tie, clean-shaven. I think I'd only met Christy at this stage, so I didn't really know them at all. I remember going into the office. One of them had his legs up on the desk, wearing jeans and looking dishevelled. But this time I *had* to get a job and so I was taken on. But my impression of the lads was they were awful dirty looking.'

Johnny Divilly drove Planxty around Ireland and beyond in the white transit van. The van was eventually christened 'Hewlett' and the reg remains indelibly etched in his memory. '9500ZH! It had ferry seats. The first gig was at The Hunter's Moon, a pub about fifteen, twenty miles from Dublin. This whole world was new to me. I remember when we arrived I saw

Luke Kelly down the back reading a book. He was there to meet
the guys. The next one was in Cork. I wasn't quite sure how to
get out of Dublin. I didn't have a clue but I was smart enough to
wing it. So I got on the road, out on the Naas dual carriageway
in my suit and tie and the whole lot and I'm driving at a very
conservative forty. There was a sort of an air of anarchy in the
back of the van, is the only way I can describe it. Nicky is sitting
up beside me. He starts rolling a cigarette, or so I thought. I'm
thinking, Jaysus, he hasn't much money anyway. He takes a few
puffs out of it, savouring it. Then he passes it to someone else.
I'm looking at this thinking, "What on earth?" They take a few
puffs and pass it back to someone else in the van. I'm thinking,
"Oh God, they can't even afford to buy ten cigarettes. They have
to roll their own." Six weeks later, I've long hair, a big black
beard and I'm stoned!'

Johnny Divilly's role in the Planxty team was vital and
constantly shifting. After a spell as road manager, he became
responsible for booking concerts. 'I was going ahead booking
halls all over Ireland, meeting people, contacting local
newspapers, putting up posters. The best gigs were in Scarriff in
Clare in The Merriman, which was run by Aidan and Sheila
O'Beirne, lovely people. We loved going there because we knew
we'd be staying for the night. We knew we were in County Clare.
We knew the people wanted to hear Planxty. Afterwards, we had
great fun playing snooker and throwing darts all night. Christy
was mad for the snooker. There was an old piano there and I
started playing piano and we'd have a singsong. It was magic. If
we could have played in Scarriff every week, we would have.'

With particular fondness, Divilly remembers Planxty's
legendary visit to the Aran Islands in August 1973 when they
played two concerts on Inishmore and one on Inisheer. 'We were
playing all around Ireland and I thought to myself, Jaysus, it

would be great to play an aul island. So I went to the Aran Islands
to check it out. I fell in love with the place. I was out there about
two months on and off. I got to know everybody. So I booked the
halls. The first problem was: how do I get them out to the island?
A chap called Bertie Hernon had a lobster boat. I was warned
he'd charge an awful lot if I didn't fix a price with him. I couldn't
get a price from him. All he kept saying was, "I'll look after you,
I'll look after you." "How much?" "I'll look after you." It was in
the back of my mind the whole time. This is going to ruin us! We
went to Inisheer on the lobster boat. Christy was trying to feed
the seagulls with Bertie's old mackerel bait, but they weren't
taking a blind bit of notice. Christy didn't like this. So he ended
up trying to knock the seagulls out of the sky with the mackerel.
It was hilarious. So we got to Inisheer. We needed transport to get
the gear up to the venue. They had an ass and cart waiting for us.
So we piled all the gear up, with Nicky leading it and the rest of
us marching behind him. It was like the Flight into Egypt!

'The venue was a little school hall. There were three prices;
seven-to-twelve-year-olds, twelve to sixteen and sixteen to adults,
so we could accommodate everyone. I never saw so many twelve-
year-olds who actually looked like eighteen-year-olds! Everybody
was there. No motor cars or nothing. The concert was superb.
The music was heavenly. Afterwards, we came back on the boat
to Kilronan and there was great music. The whole experience
was fantastic. I've a great recollection of going for a walk the
next morning and Christy diving off the pier into the harbour.
He loved swimming. On the way home, I had all the money,
which wasn't a lot. I still had to pay Bertie Hernon, the guy with
the boat, and I thought he'd take most of it because he was
driving us everywhere over the three days. He actually only
charged us ten pounds. I couldn't believe it. He wouldn't take any
more. He was such a gent. He said, "You don't know what you've

done for the island." It was all over the papers about the music happening on the Aran Islands. So we got him a present. We got him a tape recorder because he was so taken with my one. We had a brass plaque on it: "From Planxty to Bertie, thank you so much."

Without doubt, the most important member of the crew – of any Planxty crew – was legendary sound engineer Nicky Ryan. 'Nicky Ryan joined us on the first English tour,' recalls Christy. 'He came up from London by train to meet the band. That same night he did the sound for us in The MSG Club. We had four mics, a 100-watt Marshall amp, a Binson echo unit and two Hurley Crazy Box speakers, plus a piper's stool liberated from a ballad lounge in west Kildare.

'Nicky had a reputation for being very interesting in the area of sound. The guy who drove the band on the first UK tour, a guy called Jimmy Drag, put us in touch with him. I think more so than anyone who was connected with the band in all its years, Nicky was the closest ever to being a fifth member, and that includes the other people who played in the band. That would be my opinion and I'm not sure if the other three would agree with that. Certainly, from the point of view of the spirit of the music, I feel Nicky understood it more than the others. He was very emotionally involved, and he really was a fantastic soundman. There was always a dichotomy between the attitude of the band towards Nicky and the attitude of management. There was no such thing as soundmen in the showband scene, so Nicky might have been seen as a bit of an upstart because he wanted really good gear and specific microphones and certain amps and various equipment, all of which was mad expensive. But he was invariably right. In a way, it's a pity he wasn't allowed to have more input into the albums.'

'Nicky had worked in the School for the Deaf in Dublin, he was absolutely enthusiastic about sound,' continues Dónal. 'He was also totally idealistic. He was hyper-attentive to how we sounded, to the fidelity of the instruments, what's coming out of the speakers. For Nicky, it was a vital necessity to try and achieve the natural sound of an instrument. He was totally uncompromising. When you're on stage with a band, you need the monitors because you've got the PA out in front of you and the sound is coming back at you from the hall and it's a bit muffled. Christy is over one side and I'm over on the other side, we might be twenty feet apart, but we need to hear each other. So monitors overcome this by giving you the sound straight and direct from the speaker at your feet. This way I can hear Christy directly rather than just his sound drifting across the stage to me. The problem was that the sound from the monitor speakers on the stage would find its way into the mics for the instruments, so it would have a double effect and it would colour the sound going out front. Nicky couldn't abide this. He really couldn't bear it. On some occasions, the stage set-up was such that the monitors affected the front sound very badly. On those occasions, Nicky would announce, "No monitors tonight." Our hearts would sink. Because of the lights from the back of the hall shining on the band and because of the lack of monitors, we wouldn't be able to see anything and we wouldn't be able to hear anything, so you're operating almost by instinct. It was very difficult.'

It was Nicky who discovered the PA that the band eventually settled on after about a year together. 'It had these electrostatic speakers, which were absolutely amazing,' says Dónal. 'You could see through them. They had this sort of mesh all around them. Seventy-five per cent of the sound went out front, twenty-five came back and, in certain circumstances, we didn't need monitors because we could hear the PA because these speakers would be informing us of what was going on. But also the fact that sound was coming back out of the speakers towards us onto the stage would cause feedback. Nicky counteracted that by building a screen for each speaker on each side of the stage. I think the power of the PA was only about 1,000 watts, 1k. These days people go out with about 25k and play a small club. This was a delicate PA, but the sound was brilliant, beautiful. The best sound I ever heard for acoustic instruments was through this PA that Nicky created. He was passionate for it. I'm sure he still is. I'm quite sure that the best sound that Planxty ever had was with Nicky because he cared so much. Nicky and I shared a room very often. We'd talk about anything and everything from 1 a.m. to 5 a.m. and then just collapse, fall asleep. We had great conversations and became very close. For me, Nicky was always great to be with.'

Compared to the vital, energising, communal experiences of the Irish concerts, Planxty's progress in Britain was often an uphill struggle. However, they made many new friends at the Fanfare for Europe concert at the Royal Albert Hall on 15 January 1973. Planxty were sandwiched between headliners Steeleye Span, who, by now, were one of the biggest electric folk acts in Britain, and eclectic London folk-singer-cum-comedian, Derek Brimstone. This was the last of a series of concerts at the prestigious venue to herald Britain's entrance into the EEC with Ireland and Denmark on 1 January. British Prime Minister Ted Heath was in attendance and seated in the royal box. According to reports, when his presence was announced from the stage, he was booed resoundingly by the audience. Unsurprisingly, the late Tory Prime Minister was unpopular with an audience of folk music fans. One might suggest this was largely due to his decision to imprison trade unionists, not to mention the events of Bloody Sunday, now approaching its one-year anniversary, and the introduction of internment, over which he presided, and the subsequent rise of violence in the North in 1972.

Nonetheless, the concert was a success for Planxty, who received vigorous demands for an encore at the end of their set. 'There was a guy called Joe Lustig who was a heavy duty manager who looked after Pentangle and Steeleye Span, and I think for a while Ralph McTell,' recalls Christy. 'He had a fairly serious stable in the early 1970s. I remember him at the side of the stage holding on to Liam. The crowd were cheering for an encore and he was determined we weren't going to play one. We didn't really know what to do but there was no way he was letting us go back out. He literally had his arms around Liam. I also remember Ted Heath, who was then the Prime Minister, going in to shake hands with Steeleye Span and he inadvertently walked into our dressing room as I was about to spark up a huge fuckin' rocket! And there's the British Prime Minister standing there looking at me! It was a golden moment.'

The Black Album was released a couple of weeks after the Royal Albert Hall show. In the 17 March 1973 issue of *Melody Maker*, Planxty were awarded 'Album of the Month'. The article stated: 'During the past year there has been little in the field of traditional music as promising as the emergence of Planxty.' Polydor Records stepped in and placed Planxty on a co-headline tour with another recent signing, rock band Iguana. 'That was a dreadful tour Polydor put them on,' laments Des Kelly. 'They put them into The Marquee Club, which was a rock venue, and they put them out on the road on one of these promotional things with vocal groups and strippers and, ah Jaysus, it was terrible.' The Marquee was a club famous for its rock 'n' roll happenings, yet Planxty made it theirs on the night. According to the *Record Mirror* of 24 February 1973, 'Planxty took the bit in their teeth and came home clear winners … a triumph for pure music …'

'It was the first time the sort of muscle of the record company was applied in a fairly indiscriminate way by funding this tour and taking up the shortfall, as it was called, meaning they were subsidising the gigs,' explains Dónal. 'Iguana was a great band in a way. The line-up was Hammond organ, a lead singer and maybe two brass players. The Hammond player covered every-thing. He had bass pedals. He was unbelievable. His name was Don Nutt and he had roundy glasses. So there we were, touring England and Scotland. We had a proper bus. Money was being pumped in by the record company. We were being promoted. It was a new experience. We were out in totally uncharted territory.'

'I think we rotated headlining every night,' remembers Christy. 'But it didn't last very long. It was a fuckin' disaster. The tour manager was abrasive and non-committal and would take absolutely no responsibility for anything that went wrong. His cry on that tour was, "It's not my responsibility!" That was the most muttered phrase. Throwing the Planxty and Iguana banners out of the window of the bus on the motorway was one of the more memorable moments. It was a hard tour, though, really. In actual fact, looking back on it now, it possibly could've sunk the band. After the initial success in Ireland, we were totally at sea in the UK. We were thinking, "Is this what it's all about?"'

In their bid to win over the audiences of Britain, Planxty encountered an array of agents and promoters. 'On one of the first Planxty, trips there was Harris and Appleton, who were two Manchester guys,' recalls Andy. 'They also addressed each other by their surnames. "We did our best, didn't we, Harris?" "Oh we did, Appleton." They were a double act. There was another guy, a big agent. Dónal was great at taking off his accent.'

'That was Barry Perkins,' remembers Dónal. 'He had no idea what he was dealing with. I think the last band he'd worked with before us was the Bay City Rollers. His suggestion of Planxty

T-shirts seemed completely outlandish to us at the time, and we fell about the place laughing at the notion. If we'd done what he wanted, we'd probably have made it on to *Top of the Pops*!'

Dónal remembers the tour with Iguana as a very strange time. 'We were going to places we'd never been. Myself and Nicky had an amazing experience in Stoke-on-Trent. This place had a very odd atmosphere about it. There were two beds in the room that Nicky and I were sharing. Nicky was at one end of the room and I was at the other. There was a fireplace and a mantelpiece, but in front of the fireplace there was a wardrobe. The disposition of the room was very uncomfortable. We were talking away and it had got to the point where there was a longer and longer gap between exchanges as we drifted off to sleep. After a while, I started to become conscious of this rather heavy, measured breathing. Gradually, I started coming back up to full alertness again. There was silence in the room except for this breathing. I realised it was coming from the bed I was in. It was coming from the pillow, as if there was somebody in the bed soundly asleep and breathing accordingly. I sat up. Without thinking, I pulled the pillow up. Nicky, at that stage, was beginning to rouse himself to see what was going on. I pulled up the corner of the mattress and I was looking under the bed. Where was this coming from? I said to Nicky, "Can you hear this?" He said, "Yes." It was really heavy breathing, in and out, in and out, in and out. Then it suddenly stopped. Every hair on my body was standing on edge. We summarised for a few moments, but we didn't have an explanation for it.

'I went to the loo, which was outside the room,' continues Dónal. 'When I came back, Nicky was sitting up in the bed shivering. He'd heard it again. It had started up and was from my bed again. So, basically, I slept with Nicky that night at the bottom of his bed. It was very odd. We went down to the breakfast room the next day, still shaken by the events of the night. The breakfast room was this sort of mock-Tudor style with all these peculiar ornaments around the place. There was a broom on the wall and little statues and urns and odd stuff that reinforced the strangeness. There was no real explanation for what had happened. It's something I'll never forget.'

The ill-fated Polydor package tour appeared to be cursed in one way or another and, eventually, the bands gave up and went home. Whatever way Planxty was being promoted wasn't working in Britain. They simply weren't finding the right audience and they weren't capturing the celebratory nights of music and culture and uproarious craic that were occurring regularly at home. It's reasonable to say that they were a band that fell between the cracks of genre. They weren't rock, they weren't quite traditional – and they were distinctly different to the electrified bands of the British folk revival. They were Planxty; four oddballs with an oddball band name. They were ahead of their time and no one had a clue how to promote them. So they just played tour after tour and lived day to day, because no one had any better ideas.

'In those early years in Planxty, the amount of travelling we did was outrageous,' Liam says in weary reflection. 'You couldn't but feel everything was out of control. There was no plan. The constant grind was hard. As a young person, there was this whole element of adventure, naturally enough, because you're visiting new places, countries, peoples and cultures. But with the sheer grind of it you sometimes felt like you'd like to get back to a nine-to-five job. It's so difficult for bands to try and control that. It's so easy to say you can break the year up and do that, that and that, but it doesn't work that way. You have to grab opportunities. And very often what seemed like a great opportunity turns out to be a waste of time. It's not an easy way of life.'

Planxty may have found the road gruelling at times, but there was one thing that bound them together. Without a dark, surreal sense of humour and a certain appreciation for the ridiculous, they may never have made it past a first album. 'It was the zaniest year of my life!' declares Christy. 'There was a lot of hilarity and a lot of humour that could be viewed as very dark. There were a lot of funny things going on. Dónal was always drawing funny stuff in the back of the van.' In between sleep, sound checks and the hour and a half they played on stage, most of the time was spent drinking and getting stoned. 'We would be drinking and smoking *and* trying to maintain a level of togetherness!' laughs Christy. 'Certainly we were in ways undisciplined. Although Andy was always disciplined, even in those days. I marvelled at Andy's discipline. Andy would spend what seemed then like an inordinate amount of time preparing for a gig. But, later on in life, I've come to understand what he was at and I started doing that myself.'

Johnny Divilly offers a good example of the frequently hilarious drunken antics of Planxty on tour. 'For tours abroad, we'd get the St Patrick ferry in Rosslare. We'd get the van parked and straight into the duty free. I'd buy a bottle of gin. It was twenty-two hours on the boat, so there wasn't much else to do. All the truckies would be there. I got to know all the truckies very well. After a while, the musical instruments would come out and we'd have a great singsong. On one occasion, a German television crew were on the boat over to England. They'd been in Ireland doing some documentary. All of a sudden, they realised Planxty were on board, they were big fans and had recognised them. So I said to the band that the boys here want to film you doing some music. So Dónal says, "Get the instruments, we'll do it!" We're all pissed at this stage. So we got the gear out of the van, speakers, the whole lot. The German guys are delighted,

setting up all their cameras, this is gonna be great, we're getting
Planxty on film. So Planxty start up – "It's been a hard day's
night…" The lads played all Beatles numbers, not one Planxty
track. The Germans were disgusted. But it was a great laugh. The
band used to come and collect me last because they all lived up
in Terenure and Christy would be in the back of the van maybe
having just dropped a tab,' chuckles Andy.

'It was pretty hefty stuff,' continues Christy. 'We definitely
used to push it to the limit from the point of view of our late-
night activities. And that went right through into the next round
of the band as well. We would party. Every night we would party.
There was a lot of acid around in those days. There was one
night in Planxty were I took this acid, I think with one of the
guys that worked with the band. I think I was the only one
tripping on the stage. I didn't take a full tab. It was an eighth of
a tab, but it was that microdot acid on blotting paper, very
powerful stuff. It was very, very strange.

'But I think we more or less always delivered. We had great
gigs and some gigs that weren't so great. I can recall a few
occasions when I was too drunk to play, but it didn't happen very
often and it might have happened with one or two other
members of the band as well, but not regularly. It would be
utterly, utterly exceptional. My behaviour was shambolic and, at
times, my drinking was completely out of control. There were
times when I went on stage drunk and let the band and myself
down very badly. I remember one night out in Fillmore East in
Bray, one Stephen's night when the band were so disgusted with
me they actually went off and left me behind after the gig. That
was a chilling moment.'

'Drink was one of the pitfalls of being a musician, and there
were a lot of casualties to drink at the time,' explains Dónal.
'When you played gigs you were kind of considered staff.

You'd be in the dressing room afterwards and the public would be seen out. They'd be mopping up and they'd ask, "Would you like a pint?" So you sit down and have a quiet pint after the gig, of course, but that could actually turn into another session, which would go on to four or five o'clock. In certain cases, it became a nightly occurrence, so it was a slippery slope. I think we were lucky not to have succumbed. I stop drinking from time to time, but I know that, when I am drinking, I'm drinking too much, well over the average. But I keep it away from the music. I won't drink before I'm playing.'

The scene for much of Planxty's merriment was The Irish Club in Eaton Square in south London. This was home base for Planxty in England, a place supposedly designed for elite Irish and Anglo-Irish figures of note. But, from all accounts, behind the façade of haughty sophistication was a complete and utter madhouse. 'The Irish Club was an incredible place,' explains Christy. 'It was like a relic of old colonialism. Lord Longford would be in there. Gerry Fitt, John Hume, Christine Keeler; exotic people used to stay there. It was where I first met Dónal McCann, God rest him. Ciarán Bourke and The Dubliners stayed there. They were wild times. We used to rehearse there as well. It was madness around the clock. You'd be coming down for breakfast in the morning and people would still be up drinking.'

'The main body of The Irish Club was on one side of the road, but they had a few rooms, including one of the only two double bedrooms, across the road and a tunnel underneath the road,' recalls Andy. 'On one side of that there was a little room were late-night drinking would happen. Unless I'm misremembering, I once passed Ian Paisley and John Hume in conversation. And I thought, "Wow, that's fucking amazing, they actually talk to each other!" The barman was called Michael. One of the receptionists was called Olive. She was quite a sassy woman. The other one was a romantic type. I'm sure she fell in love with someone, Dónal probably. You had to be a member of this club, but I don't think we ever joined. We were let stay there anyway. I think we even played a gig there once. The main clientele were crusty old farts really and I think they looked down on us. We were sometimes out of hand and not clad in the way that they would expect. I think they wondered who the fuck we were and how did we manage to get to stay there. It was like an old-fashioned club in that respect.'

Dónal thinks it was because of Des Kelly's connections in the club that they were allowed to stay there. In present-day terms, the building would be worth about £50 million. 'It was the most fantastic property. At the time we were there, it was not very well managed. It was very inefficient and probably losing money hand over fist. It was frequented by a most peculiar bunch of people, eccentrics as far as I could see, there was a kind of motley clientele. A lot of them were Irish people who had been in England for many years. Some of them would purport to be aristocratic and had a great sense of themselves and who they were and their family and all this sort of stuff. It's a very subjective thing, but I associate the word "Hibernian" with the feeling I got from The Irish Club. It was The Hibernian Club. It was slightly different. It wasn't quite Irish, and in other ways it was more than Irish. You had these people who were throwbacks. They reflected an Ireland that had existed twenty years before we were there. They were people from the Midlands and from all over Ireland who had spent their lives working in England and *being* in England.

'It was a very weird place and a brilliant place as well,' continues Dónal. 'On certain levels it was chaotic. The socialising in the bar was hilarious. There were a good few people who would

drink far too much for their own good and would be rattling
around the corridors of the hotel after hours. I remember one
time when we were staying there we met this guy in the bar. He
had befriended some of the staff, who, out of the goodness of
their hearts, had found an empty room for him to stay in. I think
he wasn't in regular work or something. He ended up in our
room. We were playing some music and sitting around with some
people from Brittany. And there he was and, at one stage, he got
to his feet and journeyed across the floor towards the bathroom.
We just carried on. Twenty minutes later, he still hadn't
reappeared. Someone went into the bathroom to see where he
was. He had fallen into the bath. He was on his back and his
arms and legs were still waving. He was like a beetle that had
fallen over on his back and couldn't get up. But he had been living
in the place for a couple of months, unofficially. That was the
nature of The Irish Club – a really demented place. The perfect
place for us!'

Chapter 11

The Well Below the Valley

Months rushed by as Planxty's maelstrom of touring continued throughout 1973. The transit van rattled from town to town, stopping off at colleges, cinemas, concert halls, hotels, folk festivals, with sometimes two gigs a day, sometimes never actually making it to the gig at all, but with plenty of fun and laughter and fighting and drinking and smoking and singing along the road.

The itinerary was packed solid in Ireland for the months of April and May, followed swiftly by another jaunt to England, and, before they knew it, it was time to record the second album. They were beginning to realise the impossible demands of their recording contract. Today, recording artists are given time to write and prepare new material before they go into a recording studio. Most major artists spend two or three years before they make a new record but, back in the 1970s, the luxury of time was not afforded to a band such as Planxty. The Martin–Coulter contract was beginning to feel like a stranglehold.

'A first album is a lot easier than a second,' reckons Andy Irvine. 'The first album we were getting together for twenty-five years, whereas for the second one we had six months. After the first album, I had a big problem with what we were going to do to top it. Where is the material going to come from? I used to get up at six o'clock in the morning in the freezing cold and listen to tapes and play along and work things out.'

The recording of Planxty's second album, *The Well Below the Valley*, began the week of 18 June 1973, again with producer Phil Coulter. The band arrived at Escape Studios in Kent, not quite sure how the songs would be arranged, what sets of tunes Liam had settled on or how this album was going to become a reality. 'The studio was a converted farm complex,' remembers Dónal. 'It had an original oast house – a circular building with a conical roof – used in the production of cider. Jeff Beck was around and appeared to have some connection with the place.'

Dónal was now armed with his famous 'teardrop' bouzouki. 'Sometime shortly before Planxty recorded *The Well Below the Valley*, I went with Andy to Peter Abnett's workshop in Kent. Andy was going to have Peter make him a hurdy-gurdy. While we were there, I started thinking about asking Peter to make me a bouzouki. I knew I could have a say in the design of the new bouzouki – it didn't have to be round-bellied like the authentic Greek one that Andy had given me. There was a little wooden-bodied five-string banjo hanging on the wall in Peter's workshop. It had an absolutely beautiful sound. The body was tear-shaped and more or less flatbacked, much smaller than a bouzouki body. When I discussed specifications for the new bouzouki with Peter, I asked him if he could give it the same body as the banjo, but make it proportionately larger. And he did.'

According to Dónal, Peter later made several hundred more bouzoukis to roughly the same design for musicians who'd seen him play. 'Because Planxty, and later on The Bothy Band, performed to so many thousands of people all over Europe, the bouzouki became popular in the world of acoustic music. Also, Alec Finn was playing a bouzouki in Dé Danann, who were touring extensively at that time, and would have added to the growth of its popularity. But probably because I was seen by more people – and possibly because of what I was making the bouzouki do rhythmically – I gradually became the person most closely associated with it in the music public's consciousness. This led to me being described from time to time in the media as the person who brought the bouzouki to Irish music. This is a claim I never made personally. I'd accept that I may be the person most responsible for the general presence of the bouzouki in Irish music today – but Johnny Moynihan brought the bouzouki to Ireland, and a historic moment it was too!'

At this stage, the band members started to feel the pressure of gigging and touring and not having time to prepare material. 'Little bits of trouble were starting to show,' admits Christy. 'A lot of the material was rehearsed in the studio as we recorded it. I can remember there being a kind of a bad vibe because Liam couldn't decide what tunes he wanted to play, which meant that we couldn't work out the arrangement. I can remember Liam in the studio, still agonising. But I suppose he was under pressure from outside the band. Certain peers might be looking at him in a certain way for being in the band. And that was always difficult for a young piper. "What do my peers think of this music?" I think Andy and Dónal were okay. But, in my own case, I was certainly drinking too much. That would've been taking its toll a bit. The recording of this was painful, but also I would have been very stoned a lot of the time. I was smoking a lot those days as well. I was starting to use hash kind of habitually, so my memory of it is not as vivid as it might be.'

'The second album was still being put together when we got to the studio,' agrees Dónal. 'We hadn't finished arranging everything and being in the studio affected how we finished it off too, it always does. Sometimes it's great, but sometimes it's quite strange. You can put music together in the studio and it sounds really nice, but when you bring it out to the stage, you might find there's a big hole between the verses. So then the arrangement actually gets finished in performance. It's a strange thing. It probably doesn't apply to all kinds of music, but it certainly applies to what we were doing and a lot of the things that I've done since. When you put it together in the studio, the values are different. So, really, it's always best to take music onto the stage because the weaknesses are immediately apparent and you can immediately compensate for them and fix them. That's the test, really.

'Phil tried to become involved,' continues Dónal, 'but we wouldn't allow him to *touch* a piano. There was no room in our music for a piano. He desperately wanted to play and was very hurt when we turned him down, but he kind of put himself in that position. It wasn't his place to play. And it affected our relationship at the time, because it was obvious to us that Phil didn't have a sense of our music. When you listen to the music we made then and you listen to the music Phil Coulter's been making ever since, it's easy to see why. It's not a quality thing, but the fact is that it's chalk and cheese. We were working on our instincts, so it was very hard for us to articulate what we were doing verbally. It was like we would *find* what was good and take that. So to have Phil sit down at a piano and festoon it, to do a conventional piano treatment, would have been disastrous for us. We were lucky to have been able to draw the line.'

There's no doubt about it, the odds were stacked against Planxty making this record. From the outset, the mounting pressure and the stifled atmosphere was not conducive to recording a great album. It could have fallen apart before it even started. It was a test. How would the musicians react to the circumstances? Well, the evidence is there for everyone to hear. *The Well Below the Valley* is a dark, tense, exhilarating album. It's the sound of Planxty in motion, free-wheeling on the momentum of the music itself. In a sense, it's the perfect second album, a raw and windswept document of a band captured in a state of confusion and spontaneity. They had made their finely honed, perfectly rehearsed debut album. This was another Planxty; on the hop, caught in the moment, thriving on the energy of the live performance.

Dónal Lunny sums it up perfectly. 'Even if it was a case of being up against it, I think it was a thing we took in our stride. That album turned out really well and that very element of by-the-seat-of-our-pants and getting the stuff together and bringing it in and finding out what to do with it sort of added to the whole thing in a way. It forced us to be creative and think on the spot. I thought some very good things came out of it.'

Although it appears to be a subconscious reaction more than anything else, *The Well Below the Valley* is an album that clearly veers towards the Irish tradition. The album's repertoire features a set of slip jigs, a set of reels, a set of hornpipes, a solo jig, a Carolan-style instrumental and a *sean-nós* piece, alongside six songs. Some of the same sources that were present on *The Black Album* reappear on *The Well Below the Valley* – John Reilly, Turlough Carolan and Willie Clancy. They are joined on this record by a further roll call of traditional music giants – Padraic O'Keefe, Denis Murphy, Séamus Ennis, Sean Mac Donncadh and Brigid and Paddy Tunney – all of whom lend this record a weighty depth of character and history. Planxty may have been caught at sea, but the spirits, some alive, some long deceased, were guiding them ashore. Christy opens the album, snappily singing and lilting a Connemara song called 'Cúnla' accompanied by a pacey duel of pipes and strings. He first heard Kevin Conneff sing 'Cúnla', but it was Liam O'Flynn's mentor Séamus Ennis, who had translated the song from its original Irish many years earlier.

'In 1968 or 1969, Séamus Ennis came to stay with me for four days in Halifax in Yorkshire where I was hanging at the time,' begins Christy. 'It was our first meeting. He was doing three folk-club gigs in the area and I undertook to be his roadie for the duration. He sang this song at the Grove Folk Club in Leeds and afterwards told me how he had come to translate it and perform it in the bilingual form. Some time later, I was doing a tour with Kevin Conneff (subsequently to play on *Prosperous* and later to join The Chieftains) and he too performed it in the Lancashire clubs where we played.

'My feelings about it today are that it would be better sung in its original form and that the translation somehow lessens its worth. I've no doubt but that the old version has poetry and subtle humour that does not come through in the translation. I have neither the Irish nor the scholar in me to make such broad statements, but with the exception of people like Michael Hartnett, Liam O'Muirthile and a couple of others, most of it gets lost in translation. I could not translate the Angelus, but I deeply appreciate the scholarly dedication required to deliver such wonderful songs to poor auld monolinguists like myself. Of course, when I was drinking, I was quite fluent, but sobriety has left me Erseless. I recall nothing of this being recorded, but I do recall it was never a song that I particularly liked to perform. I wouldn't really be happy with this recording of 'Cúnla'. The odd time I hear it now, I squirm a little bit. I hear in my singing the way I'm trying to have that humorous thing in my voice. I'm trying to sing funnily. Ugh.'

Andy takes up the lead on the second track, 'Pat Reilly'. The theme of this song mirrors that of 'Arthur McBride', where a devious recruiting officer petitions an unsuspecting youth to sign up with the king's army. Sadly, Pat Reilly was nowhere near as cute as Arthur, and he succumbs to temptation, only to later bitterly regret his decision. The accompaniment of bouzouki-mandolin and tin whistle furnishes this song with a gentle, melancholic finish. 'I like that recording very much,' remarks Andy. 'It was never a popular song. It never went down that well, and I had to carry a second mandolin in order to play it, but I think it's good.'

Liam's first set of tunes, a duo of slip jigs entitled 'The Kid on the Mountain' and 'An Phis Fhliuch' (translated as 'wet pussy'), were learned from two of his great inspirations, Séamus Ennis and Willie Clancy, respectively. We can trace them back a further generation to the fathers of both these men, James Ennis and Gilbert Clancy. 'According to Séamus, this is exactly how his father use to play 'The Kid on the Mountain',' Liam says. 'The other slip jig, 'An Phis Fhliuch', Willie got from his father, Gilbert, who was a well-known flute player.' Once again, old tunes were brought to life at the hands of Planxty. The beat of the bodhrán tumbles from the distance and a subtle rhythm provides an emotional lift.

Despite his indecision, Liam's selections worked out beautifully. He describes 'The Dogs Amongst the Bushes' and 'Jenny's Wedding' as two real solid tunes. Then the pipes take on an elegant pace for the ancient composition of 'Hewlett'. The exact origin of this piece is unclear, but is commonly accepted as a Carolan tune, and whether or not that is true, it certainly possesses all the ornate properties and baroque sensibilities of the work of the great blind harper. Similar to 'Sí Bheag Sí Mhór', it lends itself generously to the Planxty treatment. 'I would have first heard that from Ó Riada's music. It's just a lovely tune,' says Liam.

The hornpipe set, 'Fisherman's Lilt/Cronin's Hornpipe', is taken from the Kerry fiddling tradition of Denis Murphy and Padraic O'Keefe. 'Denis Murphy spent a lot of time in America,' Liam remembers. 'It was kind of reflected in his personality, in his clothes, the way he dressed. He was flamboyant. He was a great man for colourful ties.' Liam describes the solo jig, 'The Humours of Ballyloughlin', as 'another that came from Gilbert Clancy to Willie Clancy. Apparently, Gilbert knew the blind piper Garrett Barry from County Clare and he got a lot of his music, which he then passed on to Willie.'

'The hornpipes were really odd,' remarks Andy, 'because Liam misses a bar, and he's not sure whether he missed the bar or if it was some sort of tape fault.'

There are two songs on *The Well Below the Valley* that share the same title, yet are different in every other way. Andy Irvine's 'As I Roved Out' is savoured on this album as an absolute classic in the recorded Planxty works. In typical Irvine style, this is a sad and wanting love song, definitively sung with every word drenched in sorrow and set to a pastoral string arrangement and perfectly forlorn accompaniment from Liam's pipes.

> As I roved out, on a bright May morning,
> To view the meadows and flowers gay...
> Whom should I spy but my own true lover,
> As she sat under yon willow tree.
>
> I took off my hat and I did salute her,
> I did salute her, most courageously.

When she turned around, well, the tears fell from her,
Saying, 'False young man, you have deluded me.'

'A diamond ring I owned I gave you,
A diamond ring to wear on your right hand.'
'But the vows you made, love, you went and broke them,
And married the lassie that had the land.'

'If I married the lassie that had the land, my love,
It's that I'll rue 'til the day I die.
When misfortune falls, sure no man can shun it,
I was a-blindfolded, I'll ne'er deny.'

Now at nights when I go to my bed of slumber,
The thoughts of my true love run in my mind.
When I turn around to embrace my darling,
Instead of gold, sure 'tis brass I find.

And I wish the Queen would call home her army,
From the West Indies, Amerikay and Spain.
And every man to his wedded woman,
In hopes that you and I will meet again.

'As I Roved Out' was learned from the singing of the late Paddy Tunney, a hugely influential traditional singer who was born in Glasgow and raised in Belleek, County Fermanagh – the son of one of the great doyennes of Irish song, Bridget Tunney. According to Tunney, the song dates back to famine days, when the temptation of land would likely prompt a man to forsake his one true love.

All four members of Planxty agree that this one is a real classic. The other 'As I Roved Out' is sung by Christy and sports an altogether more buoyant mood. 'I learned it from Andy Rynne, but the source is John Reilly,' he says. The song is enhanced by a delightful tin whistle and strings accompaniment, over which he sings the story and lilts something to the effect of, 'With me toor ay ah faddle diddle da, diri faddle diddle derrio.' The song details a soldier-boy visiting a 'pretty fair maid' late at night where he and his horse are both fed and watered. The pretty fair maid and the soldier boy then retire to bed for a night of passion and, typically, the soldier boy bids farewell the next morning with no promises of when he might return.

> And she took me by the lily-white hand and she led me
>   to the table,
> She took me by the lily-white hand and she led me to the
>   table,
> Saying, 'There's plenty of wine for the soldier boy, so
>   drink it if you're able.'

> Then I got up and I made the bed and I made it nice and
>   easy,
> Oh then I got up and I made the bed and I made it nice
>   and easy.
> I got up and I laid her down saying, 'Lassie, are ye able?'

> And there we lay till the break of the day and divil the
>   one did hear us.
> Oh and there we lay till the break of the day and divil the
>   one did hear us.
> Then I arose and put on me clothes saying, 'Lassie, I
>   must leave you.'

> 'And when will you return again and when will we get
>   married?
> And when will you return again and when will we get
>   married?'
> 'When broken shells make Christmas bells, we might
>   well get married.'

Christy Moore

Liam Óg O'Flynn

Andy Irvine

Dónal Lunny

A young Christy Moore, 1967

Sweeney's Men scale the Hit Parade

Above: Planxty with Pat Dowling

Left: *Prosperous* album cover

Below: Early Planxty publicity shot

Planxty live at the National Stadium, Dublin

Advertisement for UK tour

Andy, Christy and Dónal in good humour

Programme for 9th Cambridge Folk Festival

German festival programme

The Planxty Songbook

Planxty (left to right): Andy, Christy, Johnny Moynihan and Liam, 1974

Above left: The Bothy Band on vinyl

Above right: *Andy Irvine/Paul Brady* album, 1976

Left: Planxty, 1978: Christy, Liam, Dónal, Andy and Matt Molly

Below: Moving Hearts (left to right) Dónal Lunny, Christy Moore, Brian Calnan, Declan Sinnott, Keith Donald, Eoghan O'Neill and Davy Spillane

Planxty take a bow at The Royal Spa, Lisdoonvarna, October 2003

Planxty live at Vicar Street, Dublin, 2004

Christy's other vocal on this album is one of his most intriguing and is the title track 'The Well Below the Valley'. 'I wrote this version of a song I heard sung by John Reilly, and which was popular among the Travelling community. They say it's from some version of the Old Testament. The scholars define and sift, compare and shuffle, redefine and blarr on, but I don't care. This song is about what I perceive it to be. I learned it via Tom Munnelly. Tom is a Dublin guy who has been living in Clare for about twenty-five years now. He works for UCD as a folklorist, a collector of music, songs and stories. Basically, he has spent his life collecting. He's a very interesting man, very wry, witty and sardonic. Without Tom, Reilly's work would not have survived. Tom was the man who recorded him. He's a very important man. He's given his life to it.'

'The Well Below the Valley' is a dark and brooding song based on the story of Jesus at the well that incorporates a multitude of murders and acts of incest, and hell and damnation within its macabre verses. Plucked strings, eerie tin whistle, foreboding bodhrán and the portentous chant of the backing vocal all conspire to augment this song of dastardly deeds and fearful taboos.

> *A gentleman was passing by*
> *And he asked for a drink, as he was dry*
> *At the well below the valley-o.*
> *Green grows the lily-o*
> *Right among the bushes-o.*
>
> *My cup is full up to the brim*
> *And if I were to stoop I might fall in*
> *At the well below the valley-o.*
> *Green grows the lily-o*
> *Right among the bushes-o.*

If your true love was passing by
You'd fill him a drink if he was dry
At the well below the valley-o.
Green grows the lily-o
Right among the bushes-o.

She swore by grass, she swore by corn
That her true love had never been born
At the well below the valley-o.
Green grows the lily-o
Right among the bushes-o.

He said young maid, you're swearing wrong
For six fine children you've had born
At the well below the valley-o.
Green grows the lily-o
Right among the bushes-o.

If you be a man of noble fame
You'll tell to me the father of them
At the well below the valley-o.
Green grows the lily-o
Right among the bushes-o.

There's two of them by your Uncle Dan
At the well below the valley-o.
Green grows the lily-o
Right among the bushes-o.

Another two by your brother John
At the well below the valley-o.
Green grows the lily-o
Right among the bushes-o.

Another two by your father dear
At the well below the valley-o.
Green grows the lily-o
Right among the bushes-o.

If you be a man of noble 'steem
You'll tell to me what did happen to them
At the well below the valley-o.
Green grows the lily-o
Right among the bushes-o.

There's two buried 'neath the stable door
At the well below the valley-o.
Green grows the lily-o
Right among the bushes-o.

Another two 'neath the kitchen door
At the well below the valley-o.
Green grows the lily-o
Right among the bushes-o.

Another two buried beneath the well
At the well below the valley-o.
Green grows the lily-o
Right among the bushes-o.

If you be a man of noble fame
You'll tell to me what will happen meself
At the well below the valley-o.
Green grows the lily-o
Right among the bushes-o.

You'll be seven years a ringing the bell
At the well below the valley-o.
Green grows the lily-o
Right among the bushes-o.

You'll be seven more a-portering in Hell
At the well below the valley-o.
Green grows the lily-o
Right among the bushes-o.

I'll be seven years ringing the bell
But the Lord above may save me soul
From portering in Hell
At the well below the valley-o.
Green grows the lily-o
Right among the bushes-o.

'There's one flaw in the song that I've only recognised this year,' continues Christy. 'It needs a first verse and I've written a first verse for it. It actually opens with: "A gentlemen was passing by, he asked for a drink, as he was dry." It doesn't actually set the scene, so I've written a first verse that says: "A servant girl took up her pail to draw some water from the well. Down below the valley-o." It kind of sets it up.'

Planxty's second album holds the distinction of containing the only recorded Dónal Lunny lead vocal on 'Bean Pháidín', a song in the traditional *sean-nós* form. 'I learned 'Bean Pháidín' from the singing of Seán Mac Donncadh, of whom I was completely in awe. When I met him I hadn't much to say because I felt guilty for having taken his song,' says Dónal. 'But looking back on it, I think he was pleased that I'd sung it.'

Dónal really gets under the skin of this song – his understanding and mastery of the language being an obvious asset – and there's a raspy resonance to his delivery. The primary sentiment of the song is jealousy towards Bean Pháidín, the Woman of Páidín, from a woman who clearly wishes she was Páidín's wife or lover. In fact, it's quite a violent song, as the jealous woman goes in search of Bean Pháidín to break her legs!

This recording also begs the question: Why didn't Dónal Lunny sing more lead vocals? 'In the earliest days, I used to give a stirring rendition of 'When First unto this Country', which I learned from Terry Corcoran, who was with me in NCAD. But I felt it didn't really fit into the Planxty repertoire, being an American old-timey song. As for not singing more songs with Planxty, I was happy enough to apply my energy to the arrangement of the songs Andy and Christy were doing, and to the challenge of Liam's choice of instrumentals. In fact, before too long, we had each found our respective roles, and mine was in the navigation room, which suited me fine.'

The Well Below the Valley closes with its only fully original composition, 'Time Will Cure Me', penned by Andy. Always the self-critic, he describes his performance as 'too fast and too high'. Not everyone would agree, of course. The tempo of the song demands a poetic fluidity to this typically lovelorn piece of lyrical romanticism. Couplets such as 'Rosy the lines you wrote with your hand/Reading between them, to misunderstand' are pure Andy Irvine gold. On the album sleeve-notes, he explains the girl was Israeli, that Sabra is the name of a particularly hardy cactus that grows in the Negev Desert and that time did, indeed, cure him.

> *Lonely the life that once I led,*
> *Strange, the paths on which we tread.*
> *Led me to you, unlikely but true.*
> *Sabra girl, clouding my view.*
> *Rainy the day, the first time we met.*
> *Deep was the talk as we lay on your bed,*
> *It didn't seem wrong to sing a sad song.*
> *Sabra girl, soon you'd be gone.*
> *Early the morning and sad the good bye,*
> *With a wave of your hand and a smile of your eye.*

So lately did meet, no sooner to part.
Sabra girl, homeward must start.

Rosy the lines you wrote with your hand,
Reading between them, to misunderstand.
I made the mistake you said not to make,
Yes, reading your letters, conviction did grow.
I thought it a chance and I knew I must go.
It's hard to believe I could be so naïve.
Sabra girl, flattered but to deceive.
And now you just told me that friendship is all,
I'm forced to repair the breach in my wall.
Illusions and dreams, as usual, it seems.
Sabra girl, they have been my downfall.

Lonely the life and dismal the view,
Closed is the road that leads to you.
Since better can't be as friends we'll agree,
Sabra girl, time will cure me.

The last sixty seconds of music on *The Well Below the Valley* is a sublime, harmonium-led swirling outro to 'Time Will Cure Me'.'

Planxty's second release of 1973 was complete and packaged in an ornate yet frisky Celtic art sleeve. Who actually designed the sleeve was the subject of some confusion. The design and illustration is credited to the well-known Irish artist and Thin Lizzy collaborator Jim Fitzpatrick, yet the body of the design was by two artist friends of Dónal's. 'The overall form of the graphic is in the shape of the number 2, and came from Rai Uhlemann and Francis Drake, both brilliant graphic designers who were in NCAD at the same time as me,' says Dónal. 'The design was given to Jim Fitzpatrick who, without changing the basic form, applied his prolific talent with Book-of-Kells-type motifs with customary profusion. His illustration of this original design parallels the musical arrangement of a melody already created.'

Oddly, for the German release of the album, Polydor opted for a completely different sleeve design, featuring a somewhat bizarre and garish-looking cake decorated with a confectionery dove and surrounded by confectionery roses. The motivation and the concept behind this design remains a complete mystery to the band and in no way appears to be connected to any of the music or themes contained within.

Beth Lester at the *NME* gave *The Well Below the Valley* a rave review, proudly stating: 'I love this album' and describing the title track in particular as 'overwhelmingly and deeply moving'. As always, there were those who didn't quite get it. The reviewer for *Disc* magazine appeared to be completely at a loss describing this foreign music. The writer credited as A.H. disas-trously, some might say offensively, wrote: '…it's real Irish folk music, not a folk/rock synthesis, complete with Irish bagpipes (they're plain green not tartan, did you know?).' Back home the semi-imagined Horslips feud was mildly rekindled. 'I think it was Eamonn Carr who was asked had he heard the new Planxty album and the reply was something like "Oh yes, The Well Below the Average!" Thirty-one years later I still remember that!' giggles Christy.

After the recording sessions in Kent, Planxty embarked on their first tour of Germany at the end of June. It was a breath of fresh air to travel somewhere other than Britain and it was an experience that Christy, in particular, relished. 'The Dubliners paved the way really. It was Karsten Jahnke, the guy who promoted The Dubliners in Germany, who brought Planxty over. He's a major player over there and has a thing about Irish music.

He liked Planxty and understood the music. Germany was a revelation to me. It was so exciting to go there because I'd never been anywhere except Ireland and Britain and I can still vividly remember arriving in Germany and the excitement of it all. The first gig we played was just fantastic. It was at the Musikhalle in Hamburg, which is one of the principal venues, and it was full. The Germans took to Planxty hugely, and very quickly. To this day I believe German audiences are amongst the best in the world.'

Back home they were back in the bus and back on the road, zigzagging across Ireland from the Aran Islands to Dún Laoghaire, from Ballybofey to Waterford. By this time, the band was making more frequent trips abroad to festivals in Brittany, to the Durham Folk Festival and, of course, the coveted Cambridge Folk Festival in England. Liam O'Flynn was ill and couldn't make the trip to Cambridge, so rather than turn down the opportunity, Christy, Dónal and Andy performed with René Werneer, the fiddle player from Alan Stivell's band, because he knew a lot of Planxty's material.

Polydor Ireland's young label manager, Marcus Connaughton, was at Cambridge to witness Planxty amongst an exotic line-up of acoustic virtuosos and electric-folk experimentalists. 'It was a brilliant experience,' says Connaughton. 'I was representing the company. I was in my early twenties and I was actually getting paid to go there and not have to stay in a tent, but stay in a hotel in Cambridge. I was used to camping at these festivals. My abiding memory was standing around a campfire late at night with Diz Disley, who had been playing with Stephane Grappelli, Alan Stivell, Dick Gaughan and all these legends, and you had to pinch yourself and ask if it was really happening. Davey Graham played that weekend and wowed everybody. Everyone had heard about him, but no one had seen him on stage. People were seeing artists that they'd heard a bit about but had never had the opportunity of catching live. It was very well choreographed and organised. There were no laminates. There weren't particular areas where you could and couldn't go.

'Nicky Ryan was doing the sound for Planxty,' continues Marcus. 'Nicky had a short temper. He handed me Christy's bodhrán and said, "Here, get that tuned." I was twenty-two, I didn't know what he was talking about. I barely knew what a bodhrán was for, let alone how to get it tuned. Martin Carthy had a caravan beside the stage, himself and Norma Waterson. So I went into his caravan and asked him. He said, "Oh I'll turn the gas on." I thought, "Jaysus, what's he doing here." So basically he warmed the skin over the gas and tuned it and gave it back to me and said, "That should be okay for Christy now." I just thought, "Wow." So I went back and Nicky said kind of gruffly at me, "Did you get that done?" I said, "Yeah, yeah it's tuned now." He had a look at it and mumbled, "Fine, grand," and handed it to Christy.'

In the space of less than two years the original four Planxty members had collectively experienced a sequence of extraordinary events and circumstances, fantastic musical moments, fiascos and triumphs, endless hilarity and treasured camaraderie – but they were faced with their first real catastrophe, one they would never really recover from, not during the 1970s anyway. Dónal Lunny announced he was leaving the band.

'I remember the time well,' reflects Christy. 'He came around to my place and told me. I knew that he was uneasy. I had recognised this uneasiness in him for quite a long time. He may even have hinted at it, but I don't think we thought he would leave. Then he announced he was going and it was a bit of a bombshell. He said, "I just called over to say that I've decided to leave the band and I'm forming a band with Shaun Davey." He left Planxty. I was pretty shocked. I couldn't imagine Planxty without Dónal Lunny. I still couldn't. He's the engine room of the band.

'He helped as best he could in the transition when Johnny Moynihan came in to replace him,' continues Christy. 'As to why he left, I couldn't pin it down to any single reason. I don't even know if Dónal knows. I remember eventually going to Liberty Hall to hear Bugle's [Dónal's new band] inaugural concert. I got the impression that it was a hard night for everyone concerned. I seem to remember Dónal playing a left-handed Fender Strat and he seemed ill at ease. It was very difficult for them. They were under the microscope.'

'I was very comfortable making music with Dónal,' says Liam. 'I'd done it before Planxty and I knew how interested he was in the business of accompanying traditional musicians and his skills in that area. But, at that stage, things were so disorganised and sort of in a bit of a heap as far as the band was concerned. I was getting pretty disillusioned with the fact that no sort of coherent plan existed, not that I was able to supply a plan.'

Andy felt 'gutted' by Dónal's departure. 'He'd always promised Shaun Davey and James Morris he'd be in a band with them,' he says. 'I think, at that point, Dónal was musically a little frustrated. Dónal is a great musician. He had parameters that he wanted to explore and Planxty was basically playing the same material. Our repertoire didn't change that rapidly. And I suspect that was probably more of a reason than anything else.'

The last concert Andy remembers Dónal playing with the band was at the Edinburgh Festival at the start of September of that year, again on a bill with Steeleye Span. He remembers it as a great gig, and, according to the *NME*, it was just that. Stuart Hoggard wrote: 'Planxty came on and hit the audience with 'Merrily Kissed the Quaker'; no fuss, no messing, clear and distinctly Irish. The Irish pipes immediately grabbed the Scots blood and wrenched it into some sort of nationalistic fervour ... A couple of jigs and Planxty's set was over ... "No way," yelled the rabble and cheered for more. And they got it, the first support band to whip up enough excitement in the crowd to be asked for an encore.'

'I don't think I was bored with what Planxty was doing, but things seemed to be moving very slowly,' reveals Dónal. 'Forty minutes of music a year didn't feel like good progress – although later I realised the difficulties of adding to the repertoire of a gigging band. My musical objectives at the time were much less focused than later on, but I knew that the Planxty mould had hardened, to the exclusion of many other influences and ideas. As it happened, given how hard we worked at constructing definitive arrangements, this was a positive thing because it protected our musical integrity – such as it was. However, I met Shaun Davey, who was writing what I considered to be great songs, original in approach and form. Shaun had recorded a very creditable first album with James Morris, who later formed Windmill Lane Video and Sound Studios.'

Shaun Davey had subsequently written enough new songs for another album, and Dónal remembers feeling pulled away from Planxty by the sheer profusion of new ideas. 'We started rehearsing in earnest, while I made a very modest living from session playing in studios, and producing various albums of traditional ballad groups. At the same time, we were trying to form a band. Our bassist was Kieran White and John Donnelly played drums with us for a while, replaced later by Robbie Brennan. Shaun called the band Bugle and we eventually did a handful of gigs. The music was hard to classify, as it didn't fit in any of the main genres such as rock, jazz, etc. But I loved the imagery and ideas in the songs.'

Dónal's departure had huge repercussions on the band. He was the arch arranger, the engine room powerhouse, not to mention the roguish back-of-the-van comic. It triggered so many questions about Planxty's future. Could the band continue without him? Could they really fulfil the outlandish demands of their recording contract? Could they persist in the endless trawl of life on the road? Was the most exciting band in Ireland ready to implode after a mere two years?

Maybe these musicians really were asking too much to sustain this strange vehicle of eccentric personalities and disparate musical sources.

Chapter 12

Cold Blow and the Rainy Night

Still reeling from the shock of Dónal's departure, Planxty regrouped in Andy Irvine's flat in Donnybrook to discuss a solution to the gaping hole in their band. This is where Johnny Moynihan re-enters the story. Moynihan had been absent from the folk scene since just after the days of Sweeney's Men. Now, his furlough was over and he became an official member of Planxty. 'I think I suggested Johnny,' reckons Christy. 'He was approached and he came in. It was exciting for me that Johnny was coming into the band. I held Johnny in high esteem from his days in Sweeney's Men.'

'It was a bit of a shock,' declares Johnny himself. 'Funnily enough, I'd been doing a solo gig in Moran's Hotel in Dublin and I'd been playing an Irish tune on the bouzouki in the course of that gig. I became aware that Planxty were at the back of the room, and I think I remember Andy saying something complimentary to me about the tune that I played on the bouzouki. He said you wouldn't realise there was a plectrum involved at all, but I didn't twig that the reason they were there was to suss me out. But seeing as how Christy and Andy were both fans of mine, they might have been trying to convince Liam. So it might have been karma that I played an Irish tune.

'They were lucky to find me doing a gig at all – that's for sure,' recalls Johnny. 'I'd been working as a draughtsman for a sort of back-street architect, someone who didn't have qualifications but prepared drawings for people who were building extensions to their houses. I had also been doing a bit of busking. I got a phone call from Des Kelly when I was actually out in Peggy Jordan's, funnily enough. Maybe it was the day after a party. Des kept stressing that it would involve a lot of work. I now realise that I should have taken him seriously! To me, the idea of music and work didn't really fit. Still, it was a bit of, you might say, a dream offer to play choice Irish music along with the likes of Liam. Obviously, I always enjoyed playing with Andy and I was an admirer of Christy from his solo gigs. Unfortunately, at the time I was about to join Planxty, I was also, for the first time in my life, experiencing a susceptibility to drink. Maybe I was sub-consciously under stress because there were lots of complicated arrangements, which wasn't my style.'

Dónal and Johnny hadn't really known each other that well in the past, but Dónal acknowledges that he had great admi-ration and respect for Johnny. 'He's a very colourful and romantic character. Johnny has always played wonderful music. He's been an artist in the truest sense. You can draw parallels between music and painting, or other art forms and there's a strong validity for accidental occurrences. But Johnny goes after very specific things in his accompaniments and his treatments and his singing. On top of that, I would say Johnny is less interested in projecting this to a great number of people. He's more interested in having it exactly the way he wants it, which is the ultimate, really.'

Johnny was propelled straight into the thick of Planxty's feverish touring schedule. However, it soon became apparent that he would not directly fill Dónal's role. Johnny and Dónal are both bouzouki players and both have a strong empathy for Irish music, but that's where the similarities end. Dónal's bouzouki was robust and rhythmic, whereas Johnny's playing was lyrical and never chord-driven. 'Johnny was about as different from Dónal, in the way he played the bouzouki, as one could imagine,' comments Andy.

Nonetheless, Johnny Moynihan – a great player, a fine singer, a mean tin whistle player and an occasional scraper of the fiddle – would be an asset to any band. The problem was that he wasn't an engine room player. 'It was asking too much of him to replace Dónal,' concedes Andy. 'And he wasn't prepared to take on Dónal's mantle, probably quite rightly. So the repertoire changed a lot and things that really required strong rhythmic bouzouki probably got dropped for lighter stuff.'

Johnny Moynihan is a notorious perfectionist and, as the other members of Planxty soon discovered, not a man to be rushed when it came to tuning instruments. 'The tuning with Dónal and me was drastic enough, but when Johnny came in it was just outrageous,' chuckles Andy. 'Johnny was very, very eccentric,' remarks Christy. 'He would spend more time tuning than you really had when an audience was waiting. There has to be a line. In a studio, it's a different thing, fine. But you can go too far and actually tune an instrument out of tune!'

'I think of Johnny as a law unto himself,' says Liam. 'He would get stuck on minutiae. For example, I remember we had a huge gig in London and he had devised some sort of holder for an instrument, possibly his harmonica, and it was attached to the mic stand, and he couldn't get this thing to work and this just took over completely. I remember being completely at a loss to understand how this became more important than doing the sound check. But his commitment was absolutely wonderful. You could never doubt his commitment and his desire to do things in absolutely the best possible way he could.'

Despite his pedantic disposition, Moynihan was a good man to have around and fitted right in with the wry Planxty comicality. 'He's a very witty man and he'd have us in stitches,' tells Andy. 'Despite any difficulties we may have had in the collective, I found it rewarding to be in a band with Johnny Moynihan,' adds Christy. 'Johnny was a completely different kind of player to Dónal. He was more gentle, sparse and specific. He was a good buddy on the road. I learned things from Johnny Moynihan that I still value to this day. He taught me the importance of games, sport, and I liked his attitudes towards food and eating on the road. It's always very important to have a bit of bread and cheese and a tomato and an onion and a knife when you're on the road. He's a great gamesman, competitive to the last and was a connoisseur of cheese long before it became common. We used to play handball and Subbuteo, pool, darts, squash played on a handball alley, great stuff. Serious Subbuteo playing coupled with wine drinking! And a unique game called handball-football that I think Johnny might have invented.'

The other problem that Planxty was, once again, faced with was how to record another album with very little time to prepare new material. Furthermore, the absence of Dónal's arranging talents made a new album a tall order for a band already run ragged from the road. 'Whatever about the previous album, this was definitely a panic situation!' declares Liam. 'There was so much touring and I'm the sort of person that a home base is really important to, to come back and renew yourself, a place where you can relax and unwind.'

It wasn't until the summer of 1974 that they finally settled down to rehearse material for their third album, *Cold Blow and the Rainy Night*. Rehearsals were undertaken at Johnny Moynihan's family summer home in Rush on the north coast of County Dublin. 'Rush is where I grew up,' explains Johnny. 'It featured on a Sweeney's Men song, 'Standing on the Shore'. It just came into my mind, a mental picture. It could have been any beach when deserted, which it was quite a lot of the time I was there. My mother's from Rush and every weekend and every holiday we'd been down there roaming around. It made much more of an impression on me than life in Dublin. It was a totally different, much freer life. The house was close enough to the sea so that, even in the calmest weather, you could hear the waves breaking on the shore. You could actually get the taste of the sea, the sea mist and the sand. It was very different to the constant stream of buses and ambulances and fire engines when I was at home in Dublin.'

Christy Moore's abiding memory of this time in Rush is of Johnny walking along the beach with a duffle coat and an old tape recorder hanging from his neck, 'like you'd have a pair of binoculars'. 'On the tape he had every possible riff for "P" Stands for Paddy, I Suppose', and he was trying to figure out which riff he was going to use. The three of us would be sitting in the fuckin' house looking at Johnny on the beach, waiting for him to come back in and tell us what he'd decided. On one hand you had that, on the other you had Liam trying to figure out what tunes he was going to play.'

'It got to the point where, in the panic that was mounting, I demanded that Dónal should be co-opted back into the band to play on the album,' explains Andy. 'I was living in Anglesea Road

at the time and Dónal came over and we practised "P' Stands for
Paddy' and more or less decided where the notes should be and
almost railroaded Johnny into it, which I don't think he was ever
too happy about. I think Johnny always felt he had been rushed
into it a bit, but it's a standout track and definitely the best thing
he did in his time in the band.'

Dónal was happy to answer the call of help from his old
band-mates and his presence on this new album helped Planxty
turn a difficult situation around. 'We'd all found our respective
functions in Planxty, and mine had been arrangement,' explains
Dónal. 'With Andy's songs, he usually had his own instrumental
accompaniment completely worked out, and I would devise
parts for Liam, Christy and myself to complete the arrangement.
Not that it was as cut and dried as that, but I did put the main
elements in place to start with. All of which would help to
explain why Andy asked me to come in on *Cold Blow*; there were
areas of arrangement not being covered. Of course, much of the
album was more or less in place before I got involved.'

The resulting album, *Cold Blow and the Rainy Night*, is a
flawed but infectious collection of marvellous experiments,
proving Planxty was a rare and peerless group in 1974. It was
recorded in Sarm Studios, Whitechapel in London, during a very
hot August, once again with producer Phil Coulter and his
engineer Barry Ainsworth. The mood was tense and, at times,
reached boiling point. Christy recalls Andy violently kicking Phil
Coulter's BMW on one occasion. 'Yeah, I remember kicking his
car,' confesses Andy. 'There was a conversation between myself,
Phil Coulter and one or two other members of the band. I just
suddenly got sickened by Phil Coulter's BMW and us making
three per cent royalties or something like that. Yeah, I gave it a
good hard kick.'

No such drunken vulgarity was reflected in the music,

thankfully. It begins with a whimsical idea that somehow blossoms into something lovely, blending the old Scots song 'Johnny Cope' with the hornpipe of the same name. The six-part hornpipe was collected by Séamus Ennis from the playing of Padraic O'Keefe, the Kerry fiddler. Liam O'Flynn reckons it's 'an almighty tune'.

Sir John Cope was an English general who was defeated by Bonnie Prince Charlie's Jacobite forces at the Battle of Prestonpans on 21 September 1745. Although credited as a traditional arrangement on the album sleeve, the song itself was actually written by Adam Skirving, a wealthy farmer of Haddingtonshire, in celebration of the Jacobites' victory against its numerically larger enemy. Despite his many honours of distinction, Johnny Cope is immortalised in this song as a figure of ridicule for his retreat from the field of battle. The pipes whir into action and Andy's lead vocal on the verses is interchanged with a band sing a long on the chorus to superb effect. The song is actually sung to the tune of the fifth and sixth parts of the hornpipe.

'This was our period of experiment,' declares Andy. 'It has the Appalachian dulcimer, which never saw the light of day after this album, and the hurdy-gurdy. On 'Johnny Cope', Dónal tuned his guitar down five semitones [a fourth] so his bottom string was B; this made it a into baritone guitar, though we didn't know that at the time. It had a fabulous bass sound. But, when the album came out, there was no bass on the guitar at all. I don't know whether they remixed it or what it was but I always wanted to get hold of the multi and remix that one.'

If the 'Johnny Cope' combination was a fine opener, the music was only to get better. A set of three polkas follows – 'Denis Murphy's Polka', 'The £42 Cheque' and 'John Ryan's Polka'. This set is an electrifying example of Planxty's building block-style arrangement, the way different sounds are gradually introduced, each adding their own dramatic effect to the unfolding texture of the music, and culminating in a fantastic final polka with the galloping bodhrán and Liam's regulators providing the final magic lift. It's a fiery send-off for the great 'flamboyant' Kerry fiddler Denis Murphy, who had passed away that year and who was a great influence on Liam in particular. The first polka is a widely performed tune, perhaps too common for some players to deem it credible, but married into this charged arrangement it seems right at home. The band didn't know the correct title of the final polka, so it was named after the Clare concertina player John Ryan, from whom it was first heard.

The middle polka, 'The £42 Cheque', was written by Johnny Moynihan himself. 'It's sort of an amalgam of different tunes,' he explains. 'I'd been on a bit of a skite with a girl I'd met. I had my van at the time. We'd been going around the place a bit. We didn't have very much money, the only money we had at the time was mine and that was coming to an end. But she had this cheque for £42, a sort of a pay cheque. We stopped outside a bank on the corner of O'Connell Street and Abbey Street. She went in to cash the cheque, so we could continue with the skite. I was sitting in the van and this hybrid of a polka occurred to me with a certain sort of a lift in it that I started playing on some instrument while I was waiting for her. The tune stayed in my head and I decided to call it 'The £42 Cheque'.

'When we played it in the studio, the first proper take was great,' continues Johnny. 'I was holding my breath as we came towards the end of it so nothing would go wrong. And nothing went wrong. It was perfect! And then the voice came over the intercom. "Sorry, chaps, we'll have to take that again, the machine wasn't working. I don't know why, it's never happened before." But I knew why. And that was the reason I came up with my aphorism: recording studios are places I'm dragged scream-ing into and led weeping out of.'

'I like the polkas,' says Andy, echoing the sentiments of the rest of the band. 'It shows off Johnny's playing, but, as ever, I don't think he was terribly happy with the way he'd done it. On the last polka, you can hear the difficulty Liam was having with the intense heat affecting the tuning of the pipes. But overall the polkas are very nice. It was very fluid, very *Johnny*.'

Also very *Johnny* is "P' Stands for Paddy, I Suppose', for many people the album's standout song. It was first heard from Joe Heaney, a giant of traditional singing and a frequent visitor to O'Donoghue's around the same time as Sweeney's Men. 'I think this is excellent,' declares Andy. 'We tried to do it live after that with Johnny singing the first verse over his own harmonium, but it just didn't work. But it's one of the best things we recorded and Johnny's singing is great.'

The actual words of the song were acquired from a recording of Colm Keane of Glinsk, County Galway, although various versions of the lyrics appear to be in circulation. It seems those many hours soul-searching on the beach in Rush agonising over what way to sing this song had finally paid off. After a slow drawl over the first chorus, the instrumental break of whistle and strings sets the pace. Johnny's cadence reclines over each word, drawing out this fluid poetry that rolls in perfect harmony with the song's very beautiful air. This song is also one of their finest recorded achievements.

P stands for Paddy, I suppose,
J for my love John,
And the W stands for false Willy-o.
But Johnny is the fairest man.

Johnny is the fairest man, my love,
Johnny is the fairest man,
And I don't care what anybody says,
But Johnny is the fairest man.

As I went out one May morning,
To take a pleasant walk,
I sat meself down upon on an old stone wall
To hear two lovers talk.

To hear what they might say, my dear,
To hear what they might say.
That I might know a little more about love
And before I go away.

P stands for Paddy, I suppose,
J for my love John,
And the W stands for false Willy-o,
For Johnny is the fairest man.

'Come and sit you down beside me,' he said,
'Together on the green.
For it's a long three quarters of a year or more,
Since together we have been.'

'Oh I'll not sit by you,' she says,
'Now nor at any other time.
For I hear you love another little girl
And your heart's no longer mine.'

Your heart's no longer mine, my dear,
Your heart's no longer mine.
It's a just three quarters of a year, no more
And your heart's no longer mine.

P stands for Paddy, I suppose,
J for my love John,
And the W stands for false Willy-o,
But Johnny is the fairest man.

And I'll go climb the tall, tall tree
And I'll rob the wild bird's nest,
And when I come down I'll give a little hug
To the girl that I love best.

The girl that I love best, my dear,
The girl that I love best.
And down I'll come and I'll go straight home,
To the girl that I love best.

P stands for Paddy, I suppose,
J for my love John,
And the W stands for false Willy-o.
But Johnny is the fairest man.

Johnny is the fairest man, my dear,
Johnny is the fairest man.
And I know a little more about love
Before I travel along.

Christy Moore openly admits that this was a period of personal struggle for him. Seized by the inexorable grip of alcohol, he was zapped of inspiration and straining to find songs. There were occasions during the recording of this album that Christy didn't even make it to the studio. 'I was drinking a lot. Anytime I didn't make it to the studio it wasn't to do with disinterest, it was more to do with my oblivion. I was really out of it.'

However, the three songs that he settled on for this album all stand to him loyally. 'The Little Drummer' was a song passed on by the late, great Dublin singer and collector, Frank Harte. 'He is perhaps the single most important collector of songs,' says Christy.

'I remember Christy and myself going up to Frank Harte for songs,' adds Andy. 'I'd known Frank since very early in my career. He was an architect living in Chapelizod and I first met him in about 1963. He was always slightly to one side. It would be Johnny Moynihan and myself and our clique, and Ronnie Drew and The Dubliners, all more or less of the same age, and Frank was probably seven or eight years older than I was. I liked him a lot.'

'I had run out of songs and the inclination to find them,' confesses Christy. 'The poor old band was a bit weary and stuck in the classic third-album rut. I think Andy pointed me at this wee song, a bit of a ditty but beggars cannot be choosers, and I was a songless minstrel riding the high stool and feeling sorry for myself.'

The title track is a version of a song learned from the well-known Manchester folkie Mike Harding. 'It's yet another of our wonderful all-night sex songs, which in no way represented our real-life experiences at the time!' Christy tells us. 'The song itself came to me in Blakeley, Manchester, after I made my debut at the Crumpsall Folk Club, where I was booked as the main turn in the autumn of 1967. My fee was £3 plus floor space and I went down big-time.'

Similar in theme to Christy's 'As I Roved Out', 'Cold Blow and the Rainy Night' tells of a downtrodden soldier caught outdoors on a bitter cold night beneath the window of a lady he is petitioning to let him in. 'Me hat is frozen to me head, me body is like a lump of lead/Me shoes are frozen to me feet, standing at your window.' The lady eventually succumbs and welcomes the soldier into her house and, indeed, into her bed. Typically, the lady falls in love and asks the soldier to marry her, but alas she gave up her virginity in vain, for soldiers never hang around for long in these old folk songs.

'It was a song we used to do right at the beginning, almost pre-Planxty,' explains Andy, 'and maybe that was a little bit of a reflection of the difficulty with repertoire we were having at that time. It was almost as if we had discarded it before we properly started and here it was coming up again. I liked the song, but it could have been done better. I think it suffered from the tensions that were going on a little bit in those days in the studio.'

Christy's other song on *Cold Blow* was perhaps his most enduring contribution to the album, 'The Lakes of Pont-chartrain'. Tracing the origin of very old folk songs is rarely an exact science and certain songs become the subject of ongoing scrutiny, postulation and conjecture, not to mention bouts of territorial umbrage. 'The Lakes of Pontchartrain' is one such case in point. Innumerable versions of this song have been recorded, reported or documented in some form or other through history under several different titles and combinations of lyrics and melody, and alluding to many different styles of music, be they Irish, British or American. The information contained in Sam Henry's *Songs of the People* reads: 'Source: Paddy M'Closkey (Carnamenagh, Corkey, County Antrim), learned from Frank M'Allister (Carnagall, Corkey) *c.*1905, learned when a woodsman in America.'

Lyrically, this version of the song is certainly American and suggests it was set in Louisiana, referencing a man falling in love with 'a Creole girl' and featuring the great line: 'If it weren't for the alligators, I'd sleep out in the woods.' It's a love song, but the love doesn't reach fruition as the Creole girl awaits the return of her intended, who is away at sea.

Although made plural in this version of the song title, there is in fact just one Lake Pontchartrain, a twenty-four-mile spread of water on the north boundary of the city of New Orleans. Many Irish emigrants found themselves working on the New Basin Canal from Lake Pontchartrain to the Mississippi River during the mid-1830s, where they were subjected to tough work and at the mercy of tropical diseases, such as yellow fever. It's therefore possible that the song could have been written by or about an Irishman, although that theory is purely speculative.

Christy himself learned it in the less exotic locale of Hull. 'I remember it well,' he relishes. 'It was a Sunday night in Hull and I was booked to play at The Folk Club run by the Waterson family in the Olde Blue Bell pub. It was a grand gig in a room that held eighty people – no PA used or needed. The Watersons were the biggest act on the folk circuit, but they still ran their club notwithstanding. Later, after the show, I was billeted in their house and Mike insisted on singing and teaching me this song. He was convinced that it was an Irish song despite its geographic location and historical significance. That night neither of us knew where Lake Ponchartrain was, but I was fairly certain it wasn't around Killarney. Anyway, I brought it home and slept on it for a few years before tentatively showing it to the lads and bejaysus but didn't it pass muster and the rest is history. This is one of the great songs to sing.'

Perhaps rather than labouring over unattainable dates and location of origin and various nugatory details, it is sometimes just better to listen and enjoy and sing along to great songs such as these. 'I think I played the dulcimer on that and Dónal played the portative organ,' adds Andy. 'We hired this sort of flute-organ at my behest. Shirley Collins, the singer, had a sister called Dolly, who was a classical musician and who accompanied her on one of her albums on a portative organ. It was a bellows-driven thing played with one hand and it had little wooden flutes as organ pipes.

It had a really lovely breathy sound. When we went into the studio on the first day, there it was sitting right in the middle of the floor. It had been rented for about fifty quid a day. You plugged it in and the bellows were driven by electricity. When we did 'The Lakes of Pontchartrain' it was miked up quite averagely and it doesn't really sound its best. It sounds like it could have been a synthesiser. However, later when we came to do 'The Green Fields of Canada', we miked it up very carefully and got a great sound.'

Liam chose a fantastic set of reels for this album – 'The Old Torn Petticoat', 'The Dublin Reel' and 'The Wind that Shakes the Barley'. These are three commonly known reels, the third of which was learned from the late Mrs Crotty of Kilrush, County Clare.

As with the previous two albums, Andy contributes a song of his own, 'Báneasá's Green Glade', another pastoral reminiscence. 'I remember writing it on a train somewhere between London and Holyhead. I just wanted to remember the few weeks that Muriel and I spent living in the forest in Romania. We were waiting to get news of a visa to the Soviet Union. We had gone into the tourist office and said, "We want to go to the Soviet Union, but we're unsure from their brochure whether we can stay in camping sites as train travellers, or are they only for people in cars?" The woman at the desk said, "I don't know, I will have to send a telex to Moscow. It'll cost twenty-five dollars." So we forked out twenty-five dollars. We went into town twice a week to buy provisions and visit the information place and the same girl would say, "No, there has been no answer from Moscow yet." This went on for weeks and weeks. It was towards the end of the summer. There was a big maize field near the forest. At night, we would break in to try and find reasonably ripe maize and boil it up. It was never ripe enough, though. That was the kind of life we were leading. The height of luxury was to get some lamb's liver in Bucharest. It was a good time. I wanted to record the memories of it and that song does it. Every time I sing it, I remember it so well.'

The song is followed by an adaptation of a Bulgarian dance tune called 'Mominsko Horo', which, despite suffering from the album's slightly muggy production, is an outstanding showcase of swift, rhythmic, electrifying fingerwork. Just Andy and Dónal play on this track and, despite Andy's feeling that 'it's a real shame Liam didn't play on that recording', it is acoustic music at its most devastating.

The last of the tunes are three double jigs – 'The Hare in the Corn', 'The Frost is All Over' and 'The Gander in the Pratie Hole' – with the rare occurrence of a vocal over the middle jig sung charmingly by Johnny Moynihan. The lyrics were learned from a recording by Elizabeth Cronin of County Cork and the tunes are well suited to the uilleann pipes but, as Andy explains, Liam was struggling to keep the pipes in tune. 'It was that hot day we recorded the reels and the polkas and the pipes seem to be straining to get up as high as they possibly can.'

The album closes with solemn effect as Andy sings the old emigration song 'The Green Fields of Canada' as learned from Brigid Tunney of Belleek, County Fermanagh. Despite the sparse and lonely feel of the music, lyrically the writer seems content in estrangement.

> *Farewell to the groves of shillelagh and shamrock,*
> *Farewell to the girls of Old Ireland all round.*
> *May their hearts be as merry as ever I would wish them,*
> *When far away on the ocean I'm bound.*
>
> *Oh my father is old and my mother's quite feeble,*
> *To leave their own country it grieves their hearts sore.*
> *Oh the tears in great drops down their cheeks they are*
>   *rolling,*

To think they must die upon some foreign shore.

But what matters to me where my bones may be buried,
If in peace and contentment I can spend my life.
Oh the green fields of Canada they daily are blooming,
It's there I'll put an end to my miseries and strife.

'This song came in for some criticism,' recounts Andy. 'I had a streaming cold by this time. I decided to try it anyway, because what could we do? I sang it and I asked Liam what he thought. He said, "Yes, it's good, I've heard you sing it better, but it's okay." And I thought it was okay, except you can hear that I do have a cold. Paddy Tunney was being interviewed on the radio – Johnny told me this – and he said the interviewer asked something like, "What do you think of some of the younger musicians and singers singing your songs?" And he cited my singing of this song as being outrageous and too slow and if his mother heard this she'd turn in her grave or something. I was quite upset by that because I thought his mother was a great singer, much better than him. It was a definite slight on me. They grew up with the music being played in a certain way and then suddenly here were these long-haired, bearded hippies taking their music and putting it in a different context. I can totally understand that, but what they didn't understand was the heart was in the same place. It was upsetting at the time. It's a dreadfully sad song so it didn't seem wrong for me to sing it slow. If I meet Paddy Tunney and his mother in the afterlife, I'll stand my ground!'

Compared to the fully realised vision of their debut album, or even the rooted traditional exploration of *The Well Below the Valley*, *Cold Blow and the Rainy Night* turned out to be an adventurous, if not wayward, addition to Planxty's first period. It seems the adverse circumstances facing the band's future prompted them to burrow into new avenues and subsequently generate some very interesting music. If you ask the players themselves, the recording is riddled with gremlins and mishaps; the pipes are frequently out of tune, a couple of the arrangements appear incomplete, some of the vocal takes don't quite cut the mustard, and the overall production sounds rushed. Yet there is a great spirit to this album. The inclusion of the polkas, the set of reels and 'Mominsko Horo' give the album powerful rhythmic lifts, whereas songs like 'The Lakes of Pontchartrain', "P" Stands for Paddy' and 'Báneasá's Green Glade' produce moments of delicious romance.

Cold Blow received equal amounts of scorn and praise upon its release. 'When this album came out, there was an episode of *The Long Note* presented by Mícheál O'Domhnaill, with the *éminence grise* behind him of Tony McMahon. They slated the album and they slated Liam's playing, saying something along the lines of him having spent too long in the back of a transit van. There were people who supported that view but there were others who stood up for us against those who said Planxty had gone off the boil,' recalls Andy. 'I remember James Kelly, who was a big supporter of Planxty at the time, standing up for us. I love James Kelly anyway, but I loved him more because he did that.'

The band settled on the title *Cold Blow and the Rainy Night* at the last minute. In hindsight, this is a rather suitable title that reflects the stormy mood of the musicians making the record. The album itself was packaged in a somewhat odd design. The predominantly blue cover features caricatures of Johnny, Christy, Andy and Liam with the upper halves of their body encased in a sort of snow dome-shaped window, all of which is surrounded by clouds and rain – a sort of interpretation of the title. Rai Uhlemann and Francis Drake, the two designers who had been poorly credited on the previous Planxty album, handled the artwork. 'Because of the mix-up with artwork on *The Well Below the Valley*, we decided to give them the next album to do,' explains Andy. 'Of course, by this time Dónal wasn't in the band and the band was in a state of flux and we couldn't decide upon a name. At the last minute we called it *Cold Blow and the Rainy Night*. We've always referred to that sleeve as "the artists' revenge".'

To hear the members of Planxty talk about the preparation and the making of this album, the studio bugbears, the frantic search for material, the slow, fruitless rehearsals, the all-round sense of desperation and tension, the drinking, the fights, the bitterness, the ensuing criticism from their peers – the whole, sorry story – one would assume this album was a complete write-off. 'The fact that my feelings are mixed about the album has little to do with the music,' explains Christy. 'I just recall it as being a less than happy time within the band. I was definitely drinking too much. It was an awful time. We no longer had the vital and utterly enjoyable rehearsals of yore and it was a struggle to get material together. I was no longer intoxicated by the sheer buzz of being in a band like Planxty. In fact, it is remarkable that we made an album that has aged so well.'

The English music press expressed across-the-board admiration for Planxty's new creation. 'Sheer brilliance,' said *Disc* magazine. 'Outstanding,' said the *NME*. 'This, friends, is total folk,' said *Melody Maker*. 'It's traditional Irish music played purely, and without compromise to gimmick or commercialism.' *Melody Maker* even went so far as to declare *Cold Blow and the Rainy Night* as Folk Album of the Year for 1974.

'I don't know, though, the memory plays tricks,' adds Andy. 'I wonder at the time if we felt as panic-stricken and as unhappy with the music as we remember looking back at it now. Christy always said he hated that album because he remembers it as the time when he didn't turn up in the studio and that sort of thing, and then he listened to it after about twenty years and said, "Jesus, it's really good." And I'm the same. When I listen to it I think that's really nice, but the next day if someone mentions *Cold Blow* to me I'm like, "Ah, it's fucking crap." Give a dog a bad name and you might as well hang it.'

The schizophrenic mood of Planxty was carried onto the road, playing delightful, intricate, plaintive music by night, and frequently boozing, bickering and brawling behind the scenes. 'I think it got worse,' says Christy. 'In the early days, as I remember it, there was always kind of drinking and craic, but we always made it back to Dublin. Whereas when we were abroad it was different. People would go missing. You might be in Brest or Kiel and the van was supposed to be leaving at eleven o'clock or something and we wouldn't even know where some members were.'

'I was never kind of consciously judgemental about the drinking, but I could see how it was affecting Christy,' says Liam. 'I could see how at times it just wasn't easy for him, just the sheer stress and strain of all the travel combined with the lifestyle. That isn't to say I was going to bed straight after the gig or anything like that. I remember a period of time when it seemed desperately difficult to just continue because the lifestyle was affecting everybody. But it didn't really affect performance. There was tremendous pride in the work and, for that reason, the notion of going on stage plastered was an absolute no-no.'

At the first ever L'Orient Festival in Brittany in 1974, little did the local denizens realise what they were letting themselves in for from headliners Planxty. 'We arrived over and went on the piss and disgraced ourselves gloriously,' Christy ruefully reflects. 'There was a civic reception for the band and we behaved … less than civically. There was a fight. The Lord Mayor was standing there wearing the chain, waiting to greet the band and, as we arrived, this fight started between, well, members of the band, let's say.' ('I think it was Johnny and me scrabbling on the floor!' admits Andy.)

'Later on, the fight erupted again in the van and I decided I was leaving the band, I'd had enough of this,' continues Christy. 'So I opened the door of the van and stepped out as the van was doing about forty miles an hour down the road. I vaguely remember falling out and rolling on the road, but then I became aware, "Fuck! The van didn't stop!" So I went to the side of the road, drunk and bleeding as the van disappeared over the horizon. They kept going. Five or ten minutes later, the van came back and collected me and we went back. We were billeted in this dreadful hostel and we were all staying in this dormitory and there was great hilarity and capers and fun, but then after lights out the fight started up again,' Christy recalls with a chuckle. 'But they were loving fights.'

By autumn 1974, Planxty's mood was boiling over again. The cracks were beginning to show. The pressure to make records under their demanding recording contract, the struggle to find new material and the hard slog of touring life was manifesting itself in outbursts of bad behaviour, fighting and excessive drinking. A sense of anxiety prevailed. Something was ready to pop. They had already suffered one crucial blow. The question was: could they handle another one?

Chapter 13

The Humours of Planxty

The interminable whirl of exhilarating concerts, intoxicating parties, 'loving fights' and endless drives through the night would take its toll on any band and Planxty was no different. They were victims of their own success, always in demand, always on the move, rarely able to take a breath and stop to think about the future. They had already lost one key founding member in Dónal Lunny and it seemed inevitable that someone else would scream, '*Stop*! I'm getting off.' Someone did – it was Christy Moore. Shortly after the making of *Cold Blow and the Rainy Night*, he handed in his notice. Christy did, however, agree to stay on until a replacement was broken into the band.

'I'd say my decision to leave was primarily based on repertoire,' clarifies Christy. 'I'd a pain in my hole singing the same few songs when I had a whole body of songs that I wanted to sing. I still have songs from that period that I haven't recorded thirty years later. I also missed the spontaneous combustibility of having Dónal Lunny around. He is without doubt the funniest man I know. He's a fantastic mimic and very, very sharp. He has great antennae for certain things. I got very restless once he left because I relied heavily on Dónal, perhaps too heavily at times. The band changed when Johnny came, not for the better, not for the worse. It was just a different band.'

How do you replace a singer and a personality of the calibre of Christy Moore? After all, he was the guy who put Planxty together. He was still developing his skills at this time, still finding his voice to some extent, but his talent was insuppressible. Christy isn't just a singer – he's a communicator, a healer, a comedian, a soul singer. He brings people together and makes them feel good. So the answer to the question: how do you replace Christy Moore, is very simple – you can't.

There was, however, one musician of snowballing repute. Noticeable by his thick-rimmed spectacles, fiery red hair and intense demeanour, his name was Paul Brady. Brady was a powerful young voice and an excellent musician, a man with a terrific empathy for traditional and folk music, but one with an ambition for arrangement and style beyond the parameters of convention. He once turned down the chance to join Sweeney's Men. And, although he denies any knowledge of it himself, according to Andy Irvine he also turned down the chance to join Planxty when Dónal Lunny left. This time around, though, he didn't hesitate.

Paul Brady hails from Strabane in County Tyrone on the border with the Republic. He grew up to the sound of swing and jazz and later 1950s rock 'n' roll, 1960s pop, Motown soul and rhythm 'n' blues, and healthy doses of traditional music. He learned piano by ear, and by the age of eleven he was playing guitar. He studied in UCD and was a member of various R&B

groups, covering the songs of Ray Charles, James Brown, Chuck
Berry and Muddy Waters. Andy, Johnny and Dónal all
remember Paul from his college days.

'We hooked up in the late 1960s when I was in art college and
Paul was in UCD,' says Dónal. 'Paul was playing in a rhythm 'n'
blues band called Roots Group. Then he was playing a lot of
Mose Allison songs, Georgie Fame, old R&B songs. We played
maybe a dozen or twenty times together as a duo. We played
some big gigs at that time, places like the Aula Max to six
hundred people. I didn't have a bouzouki at this stage. We both
played rhythm and Paul would play lead. He was very, very good.
Paul started playing the guitar at eleven or twelve. He was streets
ahead of me. And still is!'

It was as a member of the folk group The Johnstons that
Paul Brady first came to prominence. 'The Johnstons were
originally a family group from Slane, County Meath, two
sisters and a brother,' explains Paul. 'They were under the
tutelage of a journalist called Joe Kennedy at the time. He was
friendly with people like Liam Clancy of The Clancy Brothers
and that era of music from the late 1950s, early 1960s. The
Johnstons sang as a family at home in Slane and learned songs
like 'The Travelling People' by Ewan McColl and lots of Irish
ballads like 'Johnston's Motorcar'. They got a record deal from
an Irish-based version of the Pye label. In 1966, they had a
number one hit with 'The Travelling People'. Mick Moloney
joined the band about a year after that and, then they recorded
another big hit called 'The Curragh of Kildare', which has now
become a staple of any self-respecting ballad group from here
to New Zealand. Their brother, Michael, left and Mick
Moloney was looking to expand the group, so he asked me to
join in the summer of 1967. I was living in a flat above him in
Moyne Road, Ranelagh, at the time. I was in a blues band called

Rockhouse. We used to hear Mick rehearsing downstairs with people like Dónal Lunny.'

Paul Brady went to live in England and, later, America with the Johnstons. 'We were playing a mixture of material; contemporary cover versions of Leonard Cohen, Joni Mitchell, Jacques Brel, Ewan McColl, Gordon Lightfoot, and we were also doing hardcore traditional ballads. We released two albums in one day. One was called *The Barleycorn*, which was traditional, and the other was *Give a Damn*, which was completely contemporary. We were kind of a schizophrenic group. We were interested in trying to capture the swell of the American folk boom that was coming through people like Joan Baez and Peter, Paul and Mary and that sort of thing. We were interested in that level of song writing, but we were also interested in traditional music. It seemed to work at the time but, eventually, it split the group up because that kind of dynamic ultimately becomes controversial. The Johnstons split up during mid to late 1972. I was back in Ireland that Christmas and I went to Willie Clancy's funeral down in Miltown Malbay in January. Then I went back to the States and stayed another year.'

Andy Irvine describes Paul as 'one of the good guys' and remembers him before The Johnstons when he was at UCD studying Celtic Studies. 'A lot of students were interested in folk music at the time. The Johnstons got to Paul before Sweeney's Men. When Joe Dolan left, we asked Paul to join, but we missed him by a hair's breadth. The Johnstons were great. When Sweeney's Men were kind of big, they were equally big. In fact, they got bigger because they started to deal in contemporary music. We asked Paul to join the band when Dónal left and he told us he didn't think he could because he was still involved in The Johnstons and he felt that he was needed. We finally got him in September 1974.'

'It was a strange period when ballad groups like The Johnstons, The Ludlows, The Wolfe Tones and The Dubliners were top of the charts in Ireland from 1966 through to 1968,' Paul Brady remembers. 'We were playing on the showband circuit. We'd be playing a dance somewhere like the Town Hall in Ennis and we'd be the star attraction for twenty minutes somewhere in the middle. Down the road in Limerick, Sweeney's Men would be the star attraction. So we used to meet each other on the road all the time. And we used to meet each other in O'Donoghue's. I knew Andy and Johnny quite well. In fact, I actually played with Sweeney's Men one night in Cruise's Hotel in Limerick at a ballad session there because I think Johnny was sick. I think it was myself, Andy and Terry Woods. I had to don the Sweeney's Men uniform with the waistcoat and the striped shirt!'

All the evidence suggested Paul Brady was the correct candidate for the Planxty position. He had good musical pedigree, he already knew the guys, he played folk and traditional music, was a good live performer and a talented arranger. 'I got a letter from Liam O'Flynn asking if I would join the band, that Christy was going to leave and they needed another singer. At that time, it definitely suited me. I sort of saw Planxty as a natural progression of Sweeney's Men. Andy's interplay was well known years before that. To me, it was the addition of the pipes to the Sweeney's Men sound and, of course, Christy Moore's singing. It wasn't entirely new to me but I could see how that combination would be very new to Irish audiences. Christy's personality, in particular, was new and exciting.'

Mercifully, there were no dodgy waistcoats or striped shirts being coerced on the band by the time Paul joined in 1974. He flew back from the States and went straight home to Strabane. A few days later, he was invited to a Planxty concert in Donegal to listen to the band's repertoire and meet up with everyone.

'He came to the gig and listened to the band and we went to a pub afterwards and he took out a guitar and played 'Arthur McBride' – we were blown away, as everyone else was subsequently,' reveals Andy, completely unperturbed by this competition to his own version of 'Arthur McBride'. 'I thought, "Wow this is brilliant. This is a real upturn now." Unfortunately, he didn't actually have that many songs at the time. He had, and we sometimes did, 'Heather on the Moor', which was really good. Nonetheless, Paul gave the band a great lift. He's a dynamic performer of energy and strength. He's like a volcano. He'd have you in bits. He'd draw all your energy in the dressing room and go out on stage and explode.'

'It was a bit cheeky of me, I suppose, bringing 'Arthur McBride' to the band since Andy had already done a very good version of it,' admits Paul. 'But it was a song I was excited about singing and Andy didn't seem to mind, so it generally seemed to take the place of the previous version from the band's repertoire. The first gig I did with Planxty was in the Carlton Cinema in Dublin and that was a big concert. It was the first time I sang 'Arthur McBride' in front of an Irish audience. Then we did the Cambridge Folk Festival that year. Christy was still in the band until October 1974 and then he eventually left. I enjoyed that period with the five of us in the band.'

Liam O'Flynn and Johnny Moynihan also embraced Paul Brady into the Planxty bosom. 'I would've known Paul very well,' says Liam. 'He was a powerful force, a powerful musician. He was really into what I was doing and into the traditional tunes. He evolved his own way of accompanying. He was a great singer, a highly talented man. I looked forward hugely to his arrival on the scene. I always think it's a great shame that we never recorded with Paul, but himself and Andy made up for it afterwards anyway.'

'He was great,' agrees Johnny Moynihan. 'For a while, he laboured under the illusion that I didn't like him, which was due to a little difference of opinion we had way back in the earliest days of Sweeney's Men. When he arrived from America to join Planxty after the gig in Donegal and he took out his guitar and sang his version of 'Arthur McBride', he just blew us all away.'

The Planxty line-up of Christy Moore, Johnny Moynihan, Liam O'Flynn, Andy Irvine and Paul Brady was a short-lived one and, sadly, one that was never recorded. This line-up involved four of the finest folk singers in the country in one power-packed band. They did, however, flourish for a brief period. They received rave reviews for their appearance at the Cambridge Folk Festival. This was Planxty's second year in a row at Cambridge and, thankfully, Liam was fit to travel this time around. The ever-enthusiastic Johnny Divilly remembers the occasion. 'That was fabulous. There were about 12,000 people there. I remember carrying the old harmonium up through the crowd. It was falling apart. It was only used for one song, 'As I Roved Out' by Andy, but we brought this harmonium all over Europe.'

Planxty then moved on to Scotland for the 1974 Edinburgh Festival, where they performed a live soundtrack to the controversial play, *The Fantastical Feats of Finn McCool*, which was a modern adaptation of the story of the omnipotent warrior of Irish mythology and the magical land of youth, Tír na nÓg. This took place at the Haymarket Ice Rink for the period of a month, during which time the band squeezed in four late-night concerts after the play. 'I still know some of the actors who were involved in it,' says Christy. 'They talk about how they'd been rehearsing in Edinburgh for three weeks and the whole thing was utterly chaotic, and then when Planxty arrived and started playing it was like, "Oh, Jaysus, maybe this *will* happen." The guy who wrote it and directed it was Sean McCarthy, and he tells that story, as do many of the actors. It was like the music saved the day.

'It was based on Fionn Mac Cumhaill and Tír na nÓg and Oisín and Niamh,' continues Christy. 'I suppose scenes like Oisín and Niamh heading up to heaven on a cloud, fornicating, wouldn't have gone down too well in Ireland of the 1970s. It was a fun time. The set was amazing. The set was in the form of a huge serpent that wrapped itself right around the whole arena. The serpent's mouth opened to reveal the stage. The band was sitting in its tail. It was marvellous. There was some beautiful music too. Planxty was very good with this line-up, but very different to the original idea. Brady was a superb guitar player. He was also able to play whistle. So we had four good singers in the band at the time.'

'That was brilliant,' remarks Andy of Fantastical Feats. 'We did a couple of concerts at the time and they were excellent too. I remember doing a concert there on a Sunday and Nicky recorded it and there were pieces we did in that that we'd done especially for The Fantastical Feats of Finn McCool that were never heard again. I'd like to have a recording of that.' Even the departed Dónal regrets missing out on Fantastical Feats. 'I missed out and I'm sorry I did. Afterwards, I realised that was a productive and creative time for Planxty because Andy, Liam and Christy all talked about it many times. It seems great things happened.'

Nonetheless, The Fantastical Feats of Finn McCool caps the end of an era for Christy Moore, but also the awakening of a whole new musical and personal journey. It was time for him to pick up where he left off with his solo career, and finally get around to tackling all those songs that didn't quite fit the Planxty repertoire. Andy, Johnny, Liam and Paul Brady continued on as a four-piece. Dónal also reappeared now and again to lend a helping hand, handling the live sound for Planxty on a couple of occasions.

'One was in Castlewellan [County Down],' he says. 'My live sound wasn't great, but my heart was in the right place and we got by. During the interval of the gig a guy came up to me and said, "Do you know something, I'm from the area and I'm your fifth cousin." My father was from Enniskillen. I've forgotten the guy's name. At the end of the gig in the dressing room, which was very crowded, Paul pulled me over and said, "I want to introduce you to my fifth cousin," and he introduced me to the same guy. So it turned out I'm actually related to Paul Brady!'

Planxty toured Britain throughout the latter months of 1974, finding their feet without the massive influence of Moore and Lunny. Without Christy's big songs and on stage magnetism, this was a very different band. Nonetheless, it seems Planxty played to some of their biggest audiences ever in Britain, and were the subject of rave reviews in the press. In a review of a concert in Birmingham in November, *Melody Maker*'s Colin Irwin wrote: 'Mourn not for Planxty who have just lost their founder member and stalwart Christy Moore. For in Paul Brady, the ginger-haired former Johnston, they have somebody to broaden the scope of the band and give it a new surge of energy.' *The Guardian* wrote about a show at London University, also in November, emphasising Planxty's unerring dedication to innovative arrangements, saying: 'Horslips, the last new Irish band I discussed here, seem to be suffering a tedious pop-oriented retreat with their latest album, so I'm pleased to report another Irish band, who, so far at least, seem beyond danger of any commercial pressures.'

The band members themselves made some interesting points in an interview with Eric Winter in the *NME*, also in November 1974. In the article, which referred to three sold-out London shows, Paul Brady expresses a desire to communicate to an audience wider than that of folk fanatics. 'I must admit, we'd like a chance to get out of the folk page … We'd never tailor our music to encourage it, but there do seem to be people taking an interest who wouldn't normally have classed themselves as folk fans.' Commenting on the manner of reaction he looked for in an audience, Liam O'Flynn said, 'I tend to feel that if people are clapping and dancing they're not really listening. They're getting off on something else, I think. We tend to aim more for the ear.' 'I don't think we want to be thought of as solemn and sombre,' added Brady. 'But then we don't just want to be a boozy, good-time folk group either. What we'd like to achieve is a happy medium where we weren't expected to crack jokes in the folk-club style or cause a riot, but still put the music across in a pleasant manner.' The comment by Paul is an interesting one. It outlines one of the key differences between his more straight stage presence and that of Christy's larger than life banter.

In the same interview, Andy added, 'We like a lot of rock music, but don't have any aspirations to play it. We're interested in traditional music for its own sake, if you see what I mean. There's a whole feeling that traditional music engenders in us as four people. It's something that gets you in the gut – I can't really explain it any better.'

Paul also expressed his anxiety about not finding time to prepare new material amidst the perennial touring schedule. This, of course, has long since been one of Planxty's most damaging predicaments, and now Paul, a relatively new member, was beginning to feel the pressure. 'Speaking for myself, the basic problem is finding time to collect new material. If I was to find enough new material to keep me satisfied, I'd need to take something like a six-week holiday. Hopefully, as we get better known this is something we'll have more control over.'

Sadly, Paul Brady's dream of a more controlled schedule never became a reality. Nonetheless, great reviews in the British press continued rolling in. *Sounds* music paper reviewed a show at the New London Theatre in March and described them as 'Britain's leading traditional group ... the envy of most rock groups.' *Melody Maker* ran a large feature on the group too, including separate profiles and interviews with each band member. Andy Irvine further explained his dedication to the music. 'I enjoy singing the songs we do. I'm not a great entrenched traddie, but I'm aware of the onus of the tradition that the songs are coming from. I like doing some of my own stuff and I wish there was more of it to do, but traditional music just happens to be the music I like.'

Liam explained this version of the band's approach to tunes: 'As far as tunes are concerned, jigs and reels and so on, we tend not to arrange them, just play the tunes straight. The only way they have been arranged in the past is that instruments tended to drop in or drop out, but now we just tend to play the tunes straight.' And Johnny Moynihan typically emphasised his artistic priority over commercial ambition. 'When I remember the impact traditional music had on me, I'm not surprised by Planxty's general acceptance. I'm not really interested in whether or not it's popular. When we're doing an important concert, I do get nervous and I do try to justify the fact that it's in such a place and people are charged in on the door and so forth. But I'm more interested in it being musically good than the advancement of the group.'

The band toured Germany again in late January, early February 1975. The tour was organised by renowned promoter Karston Jhanke, and the band was joined on the road by German tour manager, Nobby. At this point, the Planxty band performance was preceded with solo sets. Liam would go on stage on his own and play solo pipes. Paul would go on, on his own, and then Andy, and then Johnny. Whoever went on last would be joined by the other members for the full Planxty experience. According to Andy's letters, the German concerts were 'an unqualified success'. In his correspondence, he sounds weary and excited at the same time; dreading the following UK leg of the tour, but satisfied enough with the band's progress to state: 'I think we could be very big by the end of the year.' However, this confidence would soon dwindle when the harsh reality of Planxty's financial affairs became evident. 'The taxman got involved and we had to get an accountant. I better not say a word against the accountant but I'm still not sure, and I don't think anybody else is, how much of the money we paid over was money the taxman was looking for or how much was for the accountant unravelling the mess, I don't know. There was that feeling in the air at the time,' ponders Andy.

The band's final British tour took place in October 1975. The driver was an Englishman called Grant Ryder. 'In September 1975, my good friend Steve Hedges called me to ask whether I would be interested in driving "a bunch of Irish folkies" on their UK tour,' explains Ryder. 'The thought of driving a band around – with no roadie duties – appealed to me. I had never heard of Planxty or to be honest any Irish folk music. I picked up the rental car, a Peugeot 405 Estate, which had a third row of seats. The support artist on this three-week tour was the folk singer Steve Ashley who also had his girlfriend Clare with him for most of that tour. The PA and a lot of the gear went by an Avis truck driven by a wonderful guy called Johnny Divilly, but often we would be carrying some of their equipment on the roof! Their tour management at the time was Michael McDonagh and Steve Hedges. Steve eventually ran his own booking agency and ended up as agent for Genesis and later as manager of Peter Gabriel for a while. It was a tight fit, but enjoyable.

'The journeys between gigs comprised of a lot of sleeping by the band interspersed with moments of anecdotal tales,' continues Ryder. 'I recall that I was driving them back from a gig in Sheffield in the early hours of the morning and was on the M1 in very dense, pea-soup fog. Everyone was exhausted, including me, and as it was such a cold night all the windows were up. My eyelids felt like they had ship's anchors tied to them. I have to say that, to this day, I have never struggled so hard against falling asleep at the wheel as I did that night. The band were oblivious to this fact but there was no way I was going to crash a car containing a band that I had come to realise were folk legends in the making!'

One one occasion, Grant got to meet one of his all-time comedy heroes, Billy Connolly. 'We were at a gig in Glasgow, which went down an absolute storm,' he recalls. 'Afterwards we were all in the dressing room and it was a tight fit. I was leaning on the door and felt a knock. I opened the door a few inches to see who was there and there was Billy Connolly asking very politely if he could come in, and Paul seeing him immediately yelled, "*Billy*!" They knew him very well and within a few minutes we were all in stitches.' Everywhere Planxty went, they were greeted with a dedicated following which included many other musicians and performers.

'Being up close to the group for three or so weeks meant that I became privy to various things that were going on,' continues Grant. 'One clear thing was that they were very annoyed with the music business and the "establishment" in general. They were, however, all extremely good company for me and I got along very well with them, in particular with Andy, who was such a gentleman. I never tired of their set and their individual talented playing. They stirred up huge responses wherever they went. They were also very kind to me at the end of the tour and thanked me individually and collectively for helping keep their spirits up in spite of the "difficulties" they were experiencing.'

This was Planxty's farewell to Britain and the press lamented their departure. Plans for a live album were discussed, but it never surfaced. The band's final tour was in France at the end of 1975 with popular French rebirth folk group Malicorne, fronted by the legendary Gabriel Yacoub. Occitan (a combination of poetry and politics) song-poet Jean-Paul Verdier was also on the bill. The tour was documented in a series of brilliant cartoon illustrations and accompanying doggerel by Johnny Moynihan, titled *The Humours of Planxty*. The schedule was a typically gruelling thirty shows in thirty-one days, but in the knowledge that this was their last tour, the mood of the band was relaxed. The tour was marked with the usual divilment and drinking and, by all accounts, much delectation in the French cuisine.

'Johnny had a woman called Dede with him on that tour. The two of them would do whatever they wanted to do. Johnny was very much into French food. He loved seafood. He loved to be in a Breton restaurant. We also had the wonderful Johnny Divilly with us,' remembers Andy. 'He tied us together a little bit. It was in a Parisian café that we told Johnny that we were going to split up. "Oh, don't, don't do that!" he said sadly. Johnny Moynihan did this fantastic cartoon of Johnny Divilly with two faces. One of them has him playing the piano, because he was a really good piano player and loved nothing more, late at night, to be playing with pretty women around him and a drink. The other was what he done before joining us, which was a butcher, so there's one of him hammering meat. And it read: "Which way will Johnny go?"'

Johnny Divilly, nicknamed Bo Divilly by the band, cherishes fond memories of this tour. 'Johnny [Moynihan] bought a red banjo in a flea market in Paris. Only Johnny would buy a *red* banjo. Anyway, that night we're playing the Paris Olympia, one of the most prestigious venues in Europe. It was sold out. There were huge queues outside and *gendarmes* with Alsatians and all this. I remember the boys were quite nervous beforehand. There was this joke going around, I can't quite remember it, something to do with a dog, probably something sexual. So I sketched out this joke on four pieces of paper and put it on stage beside the instruments. So the boys came out and the first thing they saw was this and they burst out laughing and then they lashed into the tunes and off they went.

'The following morning we were heading to a gig in Lyon or somewhere,' continues Divilly. 'It was about three hundred miles away. The van was packed and everybody was ready to go, except Johnny. Couldn't find Johnny anywhere. Jesus Christ! Where is he? I was in bits. Some French guy said there's a musician down in the Metro station. So I went down to the Metro next to the hotel and there's Johnny with the cap out in front of him with a few francs in it and the red banjo and he's playing away to his heart's content. Here was a man that was on the most prestigious stage in Europe the night before and now he's busking in a train station. Talk about eccentric! You'd always be dragging Johnny along with all his baggage. But what a great guy he is. I couldn't say a word against him.'

The band played their final gig in a small theatre in Brussels on Thursday, 5 December 1975. It was the end, for now. With the band splitting up, their recording contract was nullified by mutual consent. 'Liam called a meeting and said, "I'd like to leave the band," and everyone else said "Yes! Me too, me too,"' remembers Andy. 'When Dónal left the band, we started to slide a bit. Johnny was a lovely player, a very lyrical player, but not an engine room player. I'm not an engine room player either. We got a bit thin in sound. We no longer had the balls that we had before. Paul gave us back a lot of life, but Christy took with him everything that he had, the songs that he sang, which were really popular, and of course his presentation and the craic that he brought to the band was never replaced. So we all left the band, went over to Madigan's in Donnybrook, and got plastered. By the end of the night we were probably saying, "Oh it was a great band. Should we really do this?"'

'You just knew that it was a no-go situation,' says Liam. 'Splitting up was a good decision at that time. I knew I couldn't continue trying to make music in that sort of environment. It's pretty typical of what will and what does happen within bands. We were becoming really well known, but we weren't making any money. The financial end of it wasn't happening. It was a time when there wasn't that awareness amongst musicians that there is now about the need to get the business end of it sorted. Having said that, it was a terrifically exciting time. But when you're with the same bunch of people continuously like that, something has to give. You eventually need space. That would have been the main reason.'

Des Kelly believes that he was probably not the best person to manage the band, and describes himself as more of a fan than a manager. 'I loved them and I loved the music. When they came off stage that night, I'd just want to hug them. I'd be as high as a kite myself. When Dónal left the band, I was in the throes of recovering from a bad car accident. I was pretty low myself at this time. Things with the band were going a bit ropey. I always felt there were only four members of Planxty – the original four. Johnny Moynihan and Paul Brady came in, but it was never the same. The lads on the road were hilarious. Christy was the catalyst. Liam, in his own way, had a great sense of humour. Paul hadn't that. He was detached. Humour had a lot to do with it. There were times when that humour created havoc.'

For Paul Brady, it was a strange period in his life. He realised that the business side of things was fairly chaotic. 'There was some sort of dispute with the record company,' he recalls, 'the ins and outs of which I didn't really understand and, at the time, to be honest, I didn't really want to know. I had just come back and I was excited about being a part of the band. Obviously, it would have been lovely if we'd done an album. It was a bit of pain for me to have to work for a year and then give all the money away! We basically had to split up. This was a period in Ireland when there was no sort of infrastructure in the music industry. There weren't any big accountants. There weren't any solicitors. There was no sort of post-U2 machine that everybody in Ireland takes for granted. It was a total mess.'

It may just be a footnote to this era of the story, but the problems Planxty encountered and the obstacles that impinged upon the progression of their music stem back to their earlier rash decisions. Life on the road, financial problems, creative suffocation, a crippling contract and over indulgence of one sort or another all contributed to the band's gradual burn-out. Yet one can't help thinking it could have been so different. The general consensus in Planxty was that it was only MartinCoulter that expressed interest in recording the group. Yet, perhaps, if they'd waited a little longer before signing themselves away for a potential six albums, life could have been different.

'We wouldn't have been released in the UK only there was a guy over there in Polydor, George McManus, who understood the band,' says Christy. George McManus, born in Belleek, County Fermanagh, worked for Polydor in the UK – the label Planxty's first three albums were licensed to. 'I worked in the marketing department,' says McManus. 'Polydor had started a label called Folk Mill and they had signed a band called The Peelers that a guy called Joe Palmer was in. So they sent me along to see The Peelers and when I reported back I said forget The Peelers because there was a band called Planxty on as well. When

I saw Planxty I thought, "God almighty, what an incredible band this is." I came back to work the next day and I rang everybody in Dublin I knew. I contacted a guy called Des Kelly who was in a showband. He told me they had already signed a production deal with Phil Coulter and Bill Martin. I wanted to sign them directly, but Polydor had already turned them down, so they did the production deal with Phil Coulter and Bill Martin and consequently we did the deal with them and I did the marketing on the first three albums.'

If George McManus had reached Planxty before Phil Coulter, the story may have had a different outcome – or maybe not. One can only speculate. Either way, although unbeknownst to them at the time, this was merely the end of an era, a hiatus, a time for new adventures to be embarked upon. The band would never be the same again, but the Planxty organism was far from dead.

Excerpts from Andy Irvine's
letters from the road

August 1974, to Anglesea Road from the Edinburgh Festival

Did you see our Cambridge write-ups? Very good!
Mind you, as we only played for half an hour and
then twenty minutes, they didn't get too long to
look at us. Millions of friends old and new were
there, including a vast Galway contingent. Friends
from France, Germany, Holland, Switzerland, etc.
Stivell's outfit was very exclusive; Gabriel [Yacoub]
invited us to stay with him, René [Werneer] was
seen for one moment and Dan [Ar Bras] not at all.
Their concert got slated in the 'Melody Maker'.
Gwen [Le Gournaig] was in fine form! She refused
to talk to us, so I went up and had a very French
row with her, which caused all of the rest of the
Frenchmen much mirth! She had just punched
Stivell's wife in the nose at this point ... She is
raving.

The play is going to be great and the music is going to
be fine as well. We put together some tunes and
hunting horn/barking hounds sounds for the deer
chase scene and played it to the author, director and
assembled cast this afternoon. It was greeted by a
spontaneous burst of delighted applause! We are very
much appreciated. Paul has just learned the piece that
I wrote in Galway back in June. We are using it for the

journey to Tir na nÓg scene and it's a knockout.
It's called 'Willow Patterns'. Paul and me have
become firm friends. And feel like two old bachelors
in this kip of a flat. My bed has never been made. I
just get into it at night. The dishes lie in the sink
until needed.

Letters from English tour, October–November 1974

21 October 1974 – Postmark Northampton, to Belgrave Square

We have just done a great concert! As we only have
less than half a PA, we set it up behind us to act as a
huge monitor and the gig was a great success. There
wasn't all that much crack but the music carried the
day and we were really speeding along with no huge
silences.

We are very satisfied with ourselves!

Liam didn't arrive till about 7.45 and we were in a bit
of a panic but it all came together.

The boat trip was good, we rehearsed till midnight and
then I hit the sack.

There's a good feeling in the group tonight. A sort of
closeness that I haven't felt since the beginning. It's
almost like being in a new group.

Manchester tomorrow is sold out.

22 October 1974 – Manchester

Sunday. We are sitting in our hotel rooms in Manchester, preparatory to setting out for Leicester. Manchester last night was musically quite good but there wasn't the urgency of the night before.

We spent yesterday rehearsing in the Free Trade Hall, then gig.

Sat around last night after the gig with a glass of lemonade watching the others get pissed.

Tuesday. We hung around Leicester on Monday. Very boring. Did a radio interview for Radio Leicester and had a rehearsal. The gig was a bit nervous at first but ended in a blaze of glory and everyone was well satisfied.

Did interviews for Radio Derby and Leicester University Radio and found that the rumour after Cambridge was that Christy had been fired!

We drove down to London and arrived about 4.30am. The Irish Club is dying on its feet. Bed now costs £3 and breakfast £1. Looks like it's on the way out. It's really seedy and scruffy. I think they'll sell it soon. The night porter is new and an absolute bollox.

As we had two days off, we sat around The Irish Club and chatted in the evening. Still a nice feeling in the group and we got a nice instrumental worked out yesterday for 'Cold Blow'.

Still no albums in the shops. No wonder Christy left!

27 October 1974 – Postmark, Worcester

Yesterday we set out early for Exeter. The gig was strange. We had our horns back from the menders and thus had two stacks out front and one behind us. We all found it difficult to sing and I was a teeny bit paranoid. However, Nicky said it was the best so far. And the audience was very enthusiastic, so we haven't lost one yet.

Nicky and me had to share a double bed in one of the organiser's cottages and we only had two thin blankets. Haven't had a decent night's sleep since.

We drove back to London and did a brilliant gig in Battersea Town Hall. It was sold out two days in advance and 300 people were turned away with 800 inside. Everybody seems to have underestimated our drawing power. Next time we come, we should try and do our own gigs.

Anyway we got an incredible reception. We got little enough sleep that night and after lunch with George McManus [Polydor], we drove to Bristol.

It turned out to be the least good gig of the tour. Even so we went a bomb. It goes to show how our standards have risen...

There was a mix-up in the hotel when we finally got there and I had to sleep on the floor in a sleeping bag. Well, I offered. We made an early start as we are in Lincoln tonight.

4 November 1974 – Postmark, Newcastle, Staffs

Into the last week. Tour still going well. The two London gigs were not great but we still went a bomb and got a good review in 'The Guardian'.

Last night in Birmingham, we were back to our best and played one of our best concerts.

We hope to leave from Holyhead next Sunday morning at 3.15am which means I'll be home at 8am.

Tonight the Manchester jetset has arranged a huge party for us...

7 November 1974 – Postmark, Berwick on Tweed

One letter for the road. The jetset came to the hotel and we'd a few drinks. I'm a bit pissed. Liam is lying on the other bed, intent on raiding the larder now Bill the landlord has gone to bed.

Unfortunately, he's just fallen asleep.

We'd a very heavy night last night with the same crowd. They'd organised a party for us and I got very blasted.

Woke up this morning in a strange bed and haven't been quite the same since. Liam is well asleep now and I don't know whether to wake him or not. I think probably not...

Dede is here, mopping up Johnny Moynihan.

Letters from German Tour, January–February 1975

24 January 1975 – Hannover, to 15 Marlborough Road

We are just waiting to fly from Berlin to Hannover and thence by car to Braunschweig where we perform tonight. As you know, I missed the plane at Dublin airport which left not only on schedule but two minutes early and had to fly to Dusseldorf where I waited about three hours for the Hamburg flight. I was a bit tired when I arrived but was able to play everything and the concert was a massive success. (Note: Andy was late joining the tour because of a septic finger.) It was fuller than last time but not jammed. We went down a bomb! Afterwards Polydor was taking us out to dinner and a lot of friends tagged along.

We had a meal and a few drinks and a few more drinks and eventually went on to another place.

I decided to horseplay with Johnny and fell heavily on my face which is bruised and horrible. I also broke a bit more off my tooth and the nerves of the one next to it are very painful. Also bad bruising to my knee.

O, the joys of drink.
But ... my troubles were only just starting ...

Back at the hotel, I discovered that Des had my room
and the night porter said, 'You must pay for another
room.' I had the money but I was now so drunk and
the guy was treating me with such disdain that I got
ratty and when given the form to fill in, I wrote: 'Mr
Noise Irvi' – whatever that meant – and then got fed
up and scribbled all over the pad. The night porter
was not amused and refused me a room. I stormed
out to the railway station where Johnny and
Gabrielle came after me but I was too far gone and
wouldn't listen to reason. They went off and I had a
beer and decided to go back to the hotel and
apologise. It was no use, the bollix of a night porter
would have none of it so I leaned on the night bell
and he said he would call the police.

I decided to wait there and confront the police.
When they came, he talked to them and I can't
remember what the outcome was. I went back to
the station and had a couple more beers and then
looked for a place to lie down. I presume I found a
place because I woke up to find myself being
frogmarched into the police station. This all took the
whole night and it was 9am by now. They let me go
and I went and had coffee with a Pakistani who was
telling me about some whore he had screwed in
Copenhagen.

The police had told me, 'For you, ze Bahnhof ist
verboten!'

I went back to the hotel where the staff had changed and I had breakfast.

I was in rags, half pissed, limping, face out to here – but in good spirits!

Nobby [tour manager] brought me to a doctor who changed the bandage on my finger and then we went and did the most horrendous TV programme.

I couldn't believe it.

For three hours, we drove around in an old car. It was open and the wind was biting and it was pissing down. All for a three-minute film. We were all in fantastic form and the jokes and bons mots were hysterical. We'd a bottle of whiskey to keep out the cold. Towards the end, we all got cross! The whiskey was gone and we had to catch a plane to Berlin. Sitting up on the back of an open car playing the guitarra in the rain, miming to a tape for three hours. Fuckin stupid.

I was totally bollixed in Berlin, of course.

The audience was fantastic though and they wouldn't stop clapping at the end.

Luckily, afterwards there weren't too many people we knew and Nobby bought us a steak, a couple of beers and I finally got to bed.

This morning, I went to the dentist who told me he

thought it was just the fall and that it would get better in a couple of days.

Ah well! It's good to get the madness over on the first day!! Now for some sanity.

25 January 1975 – Gottingen, Germany

The concert in Gutersloh was a great success and I went off to bed afterwards instead of going to the Jugoslavian restaurant. I finally got out of my bad mood yesterday evening just before the concert when Paul told me I was bringing everybody down!

Tue evening. The concert was great in Gottingen last night or at least I thought so. After the ascetic life I have been living, I found myself with masses of energy and after the gig I was speeding. Paul and George Furey – the two youngest – came to the gig and I went for a few beers with them afterwards. What a pair of spoofers!

26 January 1975 – Gutersloh,
Sender: Irvine, Dreary Westphalia

I'm depressed and fed up. We are staying in a boring town and will have been here three days by the time we leave on Monday. Our gig in Braunschweig went very well – it was booked out and we had some drinks afterwards which was quite boring and yesterday came on here to Gutersloh with a day off. Had the mandatory 'Eintopf' with Nobby's mother.

Johnny's bouzouki got broken in an accident and he had to borrow a 12 string guitar for tonight's gig which we've just come home from.

More tomorrow, my heart is not in it and I am hating Planxty and all who sail in it at this moment...

Did I tell you that Johnny Divilly, Des and Liam went down the Reeperbahn on Tuesday night?

They apparently had a glass of beer, bought three floozies a glass of wine each and got bills respectively for DM598, DM462 and DM278!! That's £100, £80 and £50.

Divilly rolled his bill into a ball and tossed it back at the barman! They finally got out paying £10 between them.

I am a bit pissed off and have stopped socialising with the rest of the group.

We do solo spots before the group which is very pleasant but we're kind of bollixed by the end of a three-hour concert. We have now lost Gisena and are left with Sitta and Gabrielle (who says not a word but can always be found staring at me). I think I will spend the day practising and see if I can get the 'Lochmaben Harper' into my set before the end of the tour. I went to another dentist who said the tooth might be dead. I will have to wait and see.

My finger is better but it's badly bandaged at the

moment and I can't get it changed till tomorrow.

Both the doctors have emphasised that it's really bad for me to use it and that it may get re-poisoned so I just have to hope they are being conservative. It looks much better except that all the dying skin makes it look a bit leprous.

I wish I was at home. I must be getting old because we're really having a nice time. Good concerts and no hassles, except the one that sparked off my bad humour. We refused to go to Koln for a radio programme – Nobby was the instigator because he didn't think it was important; we all agreed. However when Nobby rang Karsten Jahnke [tour promoter], Jahnke was livid and said we must go, it was very important and he would dock £500 out of our fees. Nobby changed his tune and so did I.

Liam however was adamant and Paul sided with him because he wouldn't be able to get a decent meal before the concert. The usual impasse and argument.

I split. I'm fed up with meetings. The whole thing becomes like a High School debate.

2 February 1975 – Bremen

Sitting in a Wienerwald restaurant waiting for lunch, Johnny Divilly, Nicky and myself. We are heading off towards but not into Belgium. We can't cross till tomorrow for Customs reasons. Liam and Paul have flown straight to Brussels and Johnny and Gabby Hayes have gone to her place in Bonn. Feel kind of isolated without Nobby. We had a farewell meal last night and I wound up paying for it all!

I'm really dreading the wagon journey.

The gig last night was a gigantic success. In fact the tour, in general, has been an unqualified success. We never got less than two encores. The more I think of it, the more I consider this coming UK tour of paramount importance. We must have three or four new pieces to play. I think we could be very big by the end of the year.

It's a terrible temptation, now that the German leg of the tour is over, to think that the whole tour is over and it's quite depressing when one realises it's not.

The tour has been really tiring. Apart from the drinking and travelling, I never found the actual performing as heavy before. We do about two and three quarter hours altogether and I come off the stage bollixed. I'll be glad of a rest and can't wait for the spring this year.

Time to go back to the hotel and bid adieu to Hippo and then I'm at the mercy of Mr Vile.

Face no longer very lumpy, tooth probably in need of crowning – still painful. Hand – dispensed with the bandage last night. Peeling skin, red and stiff but I think, okay.

Neumunster gig was a great success. After the gig,
Liam and I went back to Manfred's house in the
country and drank till all hours. We had a day off
and I spent most of it groaning. In the evening, we
went to Kiel and drank draught Guinness.

Tonight we bid adieu to old Germany.

Chapter 14

Moving On

By the end of 1975, Andy Irvine, Liam O'Flynn, Johnny Moynihan and Paul Brady all faced the prospect of stepping outside the Planxty bubble and into the real world. The previous couple of years had been both exhilarating and torrid; the future was uncertain. All they really knew was that they wanted to continue making music. The question was simply: In what context? 'I had no grand plan for myself at all,' admits Liam. 'All I knew was that the folk club scene in England was great. There was reasonable money to be made and there were terrific audiences to play gigs for. And America was there. I'd sampled America in 1971 before Planxty, so I felt there was a whole world out there for me to explore and evolve in.'

Dónal Lunny and Christy Moore had both already left Planxty and had experienced varying degrees of success, as it took time for each of them to find their feet. Dónal's expeditions with Shaun Davey's experimental group Bugle in 1973 never really came to satisfactory fruition. 'A year and a half later, we were still rehearsing and I just ran out of steam,' admits Dónal. 'I know Shaun was disappointed, because we hadn't realised the potential of his work, and I regretted this very much. In retrospect, we were very idealistic, and many of the things we attempted to do were very difficult to execute. Shaun changed musical direction as soon as we broke up, and I was sorry he didn't record the material he had written in the time we were together.'

Nonetheless, exciting times beckoned. Dónal was gradually carving out a parallel career as a studio producer. His interest in the mechanics of recording and mixing music had been simmering for quite a while. 'I didn't know what a producer was because my experience of producers, which was really only Phil Coulter, didn't inform me very well. For a long time as a producer, I was just some sort of quality control, you know. "That's in tune, that's grand, are you happy with that yourself? Grand." It was only much later that I began to realise that there was actually room for a lot of creative input as well. Just, I suppose, making suggestions to people, pointing out possibilities.

'I pretty much took every job I was offered. There might have been a few things I decided not to do back then, but it would've been because they were completely outside my bag. Although what seems to contradict that is the first thing I ever purportedly produced, which was 'New Places, Old Faces' by Skid Row, but Bill Sommerville-Large did more than I did.'

Dónal undertook his first proper production assignment on the self-titled debut album by his old Emmet Spiceland buddy, Brian Byrne, in 1973. The following year, he produced a lost classic in *Celtic Folkweave*, by the duo known as Monroe, featuring Mick Hanly and Mícheál Ó Domhnaill. Ensemble groups playing traditional tunes with or without a mix of contemporary folk music were becoming increasingly in vogue in Ireland since the emergence of The Chieftains and Planxty. The Donegal-based group Clannad, formed by members of the Ó Braonáin family, created an ethereal New Age impressionism, which, over time, became massively popular on the international stage. A collective of Galway-based musicians performing under the name of Dé Danann generated serious excitement with the bouzouki-fiddle-driven chemistry of Alec Finn and Frankie Gavin.

Another noted Donegal music family, the Ó Domhnaills, formed the majority of an imaginative folk assemblage called Skara Brae. The Ó Domhnaills grew up partly in Rannafast in the Donegal Gaeltacht, and partly in Kells, County Meath, as one of the families transplanted to the area in the hope of generating an Irish-speaking community. Skara Brae featured sisters Tríona and Maighread Ní Domhnaill, their brother Mícheál, and Dáithí Sproule. The Ó Domhnaills' mother, Bríd Comber from Dublin, had been immersed in the world of Irish choral singing. Their father, Aodh Ó Domhnaill, was a collector of songs, a schoolteacher, musician and composer.

The band gelled at UCD in the late 1960s, initially influenced not just by the Donegal song tradition, but also by new groups such as Sweeney's Men, Pentangle, Joni Mitchell and even The Beatles. The style of Pentangle's two guitarists – Bert Jansch and John Renbourn – was particularly significant to the playing of Mícheál and Dáithí. This folk-style guitar and the use of an electric clavinet accompanied the harmony-style singing. Skara Brae recorded one excellent self-titled album in 1971, after which Mícheál went on to join Mick Hanly as Monroe, and Tríona joined the enigmatic and short-lived group 1691 (named for the year of the Treaty of Limerick), with Matt Molloy on flute, Peter Browne on pipes, Tommy Peoples on fiddle, and the late Liam

Weldon on vocals and bodhrán. The group recorded one album in Brittany, which remains one of the elusive treasures of Irish traditional music.

In 1974, Dónal Lunny signed up with another cast of virtuoso musicians who would captivate the youth of Ireland with an energised new treatment of traditional music. They played hard and fast, and partied even harder and faster – they were called The Bothy Band. The initial genesis of this group was called Seachtar, the Irish word meaning seven people. The line-up was cemented from a music social scene in the traditional clubs in Dublin, and first came together as the house band for the twenty-first anniversary of Gael-Linn Records. Tríona and Mícheál Ó Domhnaill had been playing with a Meath-born piper from a Travelling family, Paddy Keenan, who had been involved with blues and rock music in Europe and England. He was renowned for his fiery open-fingered style, which could be traced back to another great itinerant piper, Johnny Doran. Dónal would later dub him 'the Jimi Hendrix of the pipes'. The trio were joined next by Paddy Glackin, a Dublin-born fiddler of Donegal parents, and Matt Molloy from County Roscommon, long since considered Ireland's premier traditional flute player. Clare-born accordionist and broadcaster Tony MacMahon joined next, followed by Dónal himself.

The seven-piece formation didn't last long. MacMahon bowed out to concentrate on television and radio production, thus rendering the name Seachtar redundant. Mícheál had recently come across a photograph taken in the 1890s of a group of tattered-looking musicians called The Bothy Band. The name was in reference to the migrant Irish workers in Scotland and England who lived in stone huts known as bothies. The name stuck and the new Bothy Band made their official debut at Trinity College in Dublin on 2 February 1975.

The next casualty was Paddy Glackin, eventually defeated by the hard grind of touring life. The vacancy left behind was filled by another fine Donegal musician who was well known on the Dublin scene for his unique style of fiddling, Tommy Peoples, who had previously played with 1691 and was a member of the world-famous Kilfenora Céilí Band (in fact, he was married to Marie Linnane, daughter of Kitty, who was the leader of the Kilfenora Céilí Band). Peoples's fast, sharp Donegal style fitted perfectly with the Bothy temper.

It was with this line-up of Dónal, Tríona and Mícheál Ó Dhomhnaill, Matt Molloy, Tommy Peoples and Paddy Keenan that The Bothy Band recorded their self-titled debut album for the newly formed Mulligan label. The album is predominantly referred to as *1975* and is universally regarded as a classic. There was a fierce, almost incensed edge to The Bothy Band's execution of traditional songs and instrumentals, several of which were learned from Tríona's and Mícheál's aunt, Neíllí Ní Dhomhnaill. The Bothies recorded their second album, *Old Hag You Have Killed Me*, in Rockfield Studios in Wales in July 1976. As was the case with the previous album, the production duties were shared between Dónal and Mícheál.

The task of recording this tempestuous collective of musicians under tight time restrictions was something Dónal took in his stride. 'When we recorded *Old Hag You Have Killed Me*, I remember in the last three days for mixing I got nine hours sleep altogether. I was going to bed at 9 a.m. and getting up at 11am. Keeping everybody focused was difficult at times. Oh the euphemisms! Sometimes a "festive" atmosphere would transpire and so the clock was running because there would only be a couple of hours before people were out of order. It would be a matter of catching things before they went over the edge. And when they did, I was in there with the rest of them more often than not!'

Old Hag You Have Killed Me would prove to be the mellow counterpart to the hard-hitting energy of their debut and featured genius Sligo fiddler, Kevin Burke, who had replaced Tommy Peoples. Burke is a London-born fiddler of Sligo-born parents who had grown up playing in pub sessions and with céilí bands and, later, spent time in Europe and the US where he played with Ry Cooder and recorded with Arlo Guthrie (son of Woody). Kevin was back in Ireland on the invitation of Christy Moore. He played on several of Christy's solo albums and it was through Christy that he heard about The Bothy Band.

Another part-time member of the band was Peter Browne, who filled in for Paddy Keenan on a number of occasions. Browne is a Dublin-born piper and another student of the holy trinity of Séamus Ennis, Leo Rowsome and Willie Clancy. Today, he is the commissioning editor of music programmes in RTÉ Radio.

'The Bothy Band was quite a different animal to Planxty,' comments Dónal. 'There was a furious energy in the instrumental playing of Matt, Tommy and Paddy; it was as if they drove each other to their limits. It demanded corresponding energy from the rhythm section of Mícheál, Tríona and myself. This was contrasted with Mícheál's and Tríona's fragile renditions of slow, tender songs. Kevin Burke eventually replaced Tommy, but it didn't alter the dynamic output of the band.

'Looking back, Planxty almost seems sedate beside The Bothy Band,' continues Donal. 'It wasn't, of course, but one of the things that also spurred us to reach higher levels of energy was that we felt we were in competition with the brute power of bass and drums music generally, and Irish discos in particular. The late 1970s was when discos really began to take over from live gigs all across Ireland. The logistics were inescapable; a publican could hire a DJ and put on a disco for very little money by comparison with a live band. That the quality of people's lives was reduced was, as is usual in matters of commerce, of no concern to most of the pub owners. Although there were a few who did actually love the music, so we didn't run out of gigs altogether. Fortunately, there was a lot of interest in Irish music across Europe at that time, and The Bothy Band was out there as much as any other band on the road. We toured many times in Brittany and some of the tours were very memorable. Others were difficult to remember afterwards, no doubt due to the combination of beer and pastis we all consumed in quantity after the concerts.'

Dónal thinks that, in the many ensembles he's been involved in, a collective personality emerges, which is unique to that combination of people. 'Planxty had its own personality, which is difficult to define. It was quite sophisticated, though this didn't prevent outbreaks of complete hilarity from time to time. We took ourselves seriously, but not too much so. The Bothy Band was more of a roller coaster experience, mostly because we celebrated more wholeheartedly after our performances. So when we were touring, sometimes the adrenalin generated in the concert came from the precariousness of battling with formidable hangovers. Having said that, the band was unanimous in its pursuit of great music, and we were all highly critical of our performances. A great sense of solidarity developed in The Bothy Band as time went on.'

The Bothy Band recorded their third and final studio album – *Out of the Wind into the Sun* – in June 1977 at Lombard Sound Studios in Dublin. By now, the band had a presence in Europe, famous for their hammering live performances, and equally infamous for their wild and sometimes erratic behaviour – stories of The Bothy Band on the road would make your toes curl. Aptly so, their fourth record was a live album called *After Hours*, recorded in Paris in 1978 not long before the band finally imploded. The BBC later issued another live album of two performances, one in Paris in July 1976, and another in Kilburn in July 1978.

'Sheer exhaustion brought The Bothy Band to an end,' explains Dónal. 'We had been touring sporadically for five years, and weren't much better off at the end of it. For me, it felt like everybody needed a change. We had management difficulties – not always management's fault – because at that time, the genre of traditional music was relatively small and unfocused. In record shops, we invariably ended up in the "folk" section, which we felt didn't accurately describe what we were. Folk music at that time embraced some pretty fluffy stuff. Our unspoken crusade was to break into the wider musical categories.'

Aside from The Bothy Band, the Mulligan label's output kept Dónal busy as a producer. He recorded bands such as Pumpkinhead, an American group based in Ireland featuring Thom Moore, his wife Kathy and friends Rick Epping and Sandi Miller, and Midnight Well, another group founded by Thom Moore, featuring Jane Cribbs, Gerry O'Beirne and Máirtín O'Connor. Dónal also recorded various solo albums and combinations of The Bothy musicians such as Matt Molloy, Tommy Peoples, Kevin Burke and Mícheál Ó Domhnaill.

'The Bothy Band were looking for a record deal to record our first album, and Seamus O'Neill, who at that time worked in Gael-Linn Records, suggested we form our own label,' explains Dónal. 'So Mulligan Records came into being. Mícheál and I were directors along with Seamus O'Neill, but our frequent touring prevented us from having any real control. Some very good albums were released over the next five years. One of my favourites was the *Andy Irvine/Paul Brady* album. I got out of the company in 1983.'

Andy Irvine and Paul Brady had built up a strong chemistry

during their time together in Planxty, and so when the band called it a day, they decided to forge a duo. But Andy also had other obligations. His old friend Alec Finn invited him to join Dé Danann to replace the recently departed Dolores Keane. Andy now unwittingly found himself in two different outfits at the same time. His predicament came to a head when two Dé Danann television engagements clashed with a Breton tour booked with Liam and Paul. After some consideration, Andy made the decision to leave Dé Danann and pursue the avenue of music that was closest to his heart. He suggested Johnny Moynihan as a possible replacement, as he was a free agent since the dissolution of Planxty. Johnny stepped in and Andy was free to continue with Paul Brady. The music that followed would suggest he made the right decision.

Andy Irvine/Paul Brady is widely recognised as one of the great Irish albums of any genre, and one of the great folk albums of any place. It was recorded in August 1976, again in Rockfield Studios in Wales. Dónal produced and Kevin Burke accompanied on fiddle. This album in some way compensates for the fact that Paul never had the opportunity to record with Planxty, as it features some of the music that they probably would have recorded together had the band lasted a little longer. A case in point is the stunning Paul Brady version of 'Arthur McBride'. Where with Planxty it had taken the shape of a hearty singalong with a rich arrangement, Paul transformed it into a slowed-down, jaw-droppingly poignant ballad. "Arthur McBride' is a gigantic construct, a masterpiece on Paul's part,' reckons Dónal. 'It's a wonderful version,' agrees Liam. 'Paul had made such a super job of it himself. He devised his arrangement and accompaniment to it and sang it in his own style. It was very complete. But it never really worked in a band context.'

The album also features Andy's scorching version of the great horse-racing classic, 'The Plains of Kildare', Brady's soulful performance of 'Lough Erne Shore' learned from the singing of Paddy Tunney, and Andy's original composition 'Autumn Gold', another soul-searching jewel, which is described in the album's sleeve-notes by the late Frank Harte as 'the final song in a quartet written by Andy during his sojourn in Eastern Europe ...'

'I think I can speak for Paul as well when I say that we are very proud of this album. It takes a long time to reach a distance from something you recorded and to listen to it dispassionately. It's almost as if one can take no credit for such things. It was the period of evolution that we had reached at that point and it's great that it was captured,' states Andy.

'If Planxty had stayed together it would have been that album,' suggests Paul. 'It would have been the *Planxty MK 3* album. Andy and I were quite focused at the time, musically. We thought it would make sense and it would be economically viable to start working as a duo. We then started touring all over Europe, in France, Belgium, Germany, Holland. We went to America. We did a concert in March 1977 in The Town Hall in New York. And we made this album. I think it's great, I love it. It was magical making it. We didn't have any notion whatsoever that people would still be talking about it thirty years later. We were just doing the songs we had been touring with for years. It's amazed me ever since how popular it has become, not even among folk people. Everywhere in the world I go, people from the strangest disciplines of music come up to me and tell me how much they love that album, from punks to people involved in mainstream pop. It just had something. I don't know what.'

Dónal says that he realised the music was going to be of a very high standard because of the calibre of Andy's playing, his concentration and his focus. 'And exactly the same for Paul,' he explains. 'Paul, I feel, would probably have been the most important person in the traditional scene if he had persevered. I was in awe of his take on traditional music and what it had hidden in it, which is always what I look for. It's the idea of taking a simple tune and just checking out what hidden root there is in it, harmonically. Sometimes, traditional tunes have the most charming configurations of harmonies that are unspoken because the traditional tune is unaccompanied, but the potential is there. Paul is great at finding very elegant solutions to the accompaniments.

'The material was superb,' continues Dónal. 'I felt, not out of my depth, but I suppose I didn't feel I had the authority I normally would have as a producer. I felt very challenged in trying to get the best out of the mixes. You could spend hours and hours getting a take right. If it was a mandolin overdub or a guitar overdub or backing vocals, if you didn't actually make this work in the mix, it was all in vain. It was intense work – long days and long nights, seventeen-or-eighteen hour days. And then when you get to the mix, it's twenty-hour days.'

Andy Irvine/Paul Brady was a formative record for many music fans growing up during this era. One such enamoured youth was Fermanagh's future influential broadcaster, John Kelly. 'I knew this album before I knew Planxty,' says Kelly. 'I remember my father, who never passed any remarks on music I liked, saying, "That guy Brady's got an interesting voice." When I discovered that Paul Brady and Dónal Lunny both had cousins that lived near me, I found this extraordinary because, as far as I was concerned, I was in a backwater that had no connection whatsoever to the outside world. This was somebody who made records and was on telly and was in a band. I always thought these people came from another planet.

'I think it's such an extraordinary record that I still haven't heard it properly. When I put that record on now it's still a strange, odd thing. The way Brady was singing was odd. I knew singers from Fermanagh like Paddy Tunney, but in very formal circumstances. The music in my head was associated with school and *slogadhs* and competitions. But probably the first time I heard Paddy Tunney, to me he was just some aul guy singing. It's much later in life when you appreciate something like that, but when I heard Brady he was singing like Paddy Tunney in this voice and this accent. He could sing Paddy Tunney and he could sing Little Richard, Ray Charles, Lightnin' Hopkins, he could do it all. He's really not a simple guy. He's quite a mellow and relaxed man nowadays, but he was edgy. He was a ball of energy in those days.

'The songs themselves were bizarre,' continues Kelly. 'Where I grew up, Irish music was parlour music, it was John McCormack or Frank Patterson or Percy French. And suddenly you hear this stuff. In hindsight, I know now the reason I like it is the same reason I like John Lee Hooker or Will Oldham or the material on the Harry Smith box-set. It's raw folk music. It's music of that scale and magnitude, big, big songs full of real people. So it was the voice, the songs, the strangeness of the songs, but also the way it was put together.

'I could understand that Brady was a brilliant guitar player. I could play three chords and I knew the enormous gulf between someone playing three chords and what Paul Brady did. I could understand that. But the stuff that Andy was doing I couldn't comprehend. I couldn't work out what he was doing. I couldn't even in my head see his hands move. How does he do that? Where is it coming from? What informs what he's doing there? I just found it extraordinary.'

For John Kelly, hearing Planxty and The Bothy Band was 'as big as hearing John Coltrane or Howlin' Wolf'. When he first heard The Chieftains, he thought they were incredible in terms of the arrangements. He loved The Bothy Band for the same reason he loved Jimi Hendrix and The Sex Pistols – for their sheer power. 'They were like a rock band. But Planxty I loved for their delicacy. I remember interviewing Liam one time and he described Andy's playing to me as being like "a filigree".'

Kelly describes Planxty as crucial in terms of informing him about music and what he should be listening to. 'I was reliant absolutely on *Top of the Pops* and, from 1979 on, 2FM,' he explains. 'I was fortunate in that from early on I got into Rory Gallagher and Van Morrison and people like that and they were always name-checking people so you became aware of Leadbelly and Bobby Bland and Hank Williams and Muddy Waters. And, from Planxty, you heard about Woody Guthrie and various Irish musicians. You read these names on sleeve-notes. I still find that the fun element of music.'

Apart from their tours in Europe and a highly successful concert in New York, Andy and Paul recorded a six-part BBC television series in Belfast called *The Gig in the Round*. In the end, just one timeless album and a couple of years touring was enough for Andy Irvine and Paul Brady. 'Paul got married about that time,' recalls Andy. 'It wasn't his desire to go travelling the world, which I'd kind of gotten into after the Balkans. So I might do four or five gigs in Germany with Paul, but he wouldn't want to do any more than that. I was doing quite long tours with Mick Hanly, which was great too because Mick was brilliant on the road.'

Paul Brady enjoyed his time performing with Andy, but their partnership eventually ran its natural course 'We played pretty much from late 1975 through to early 1978. I began to feel I wanted to get off the road for a while. My wife and I had just had our first child in 1977. I suppose I was never going to be the touring animal Andy was. I kind of needed to get off the road and have time to myself to figure out what I wanted to do next. I'm the sort of person who needs to sit down and reflect.

So I split up the partnership simply because I couldn't keep going the way Andy was going. Again, there was no problem or no animosity. Musically, I was still very interested in playing with Andy. These things just happen. I suppose I was also trying to see if I could make an album on my own and see what that would sound like. So then I made *Welcome Here Kind Stranger* in 1978. Andy played on it, Dónal played on it, and Tommy Peoples and Noel Hill played on it. That was fun. Everybody was doing their own albums at that time.'

Dónal was back in the producer's chair for *Welcome Here Kind Stranger*, which became the *Melody Maker* Folk Album of the Year in 1978. Although Paul did record a number of collaborative albums with people such as Tommy Peoples and Matt Molloy, *Welcome Here Kind Stranger* is his folk swansong. 'I always thought his instincts were unerring in his treatment of traditional songs and tunes,' states Dónal. 'His departure from the traditional field is regrettable, because he had so much to offer to the development of contemporary Irish music. He started singing his own songs and rock music. He wanted to make a break from the traditional thing. I remember at least one occasion when the audience was just baying for 'Arthur McBride', and Paul was practically reduced to tears refusing to sing it. But he had to do that to move on and to go where he wanted to go, which is brilliant.'

Andy, Paul and Dónal all contributed to another, now rare, album in 1977 entitled *The Gathering*. 'It was an American woman called Diane Meek who put this album together,' explains Andy. 'She was a distant Guggenheim inheritor. She settled in Dublin for a few years and her house became a kind of party house. She lent Mulligan Records money in the early days, so she was kind of important. She had a label for traditional music called Sruthán [a stream or small stretch of water].

There was Paul, Dónal, Matt Molloy, Leo Rowsome, Peter Browne and myself – not all playing together. She had an artist friend in Florence who would come over and draw us for the cover. We all felt indebted to her to some extent, we couldn't refuse. But we really didn't want to put our best things on it. We all did two pieces. It didn't come out on Srutháin in the end, it finally came out after Diane had died on Green Haze, which is a label connected to Rounder Records in America. All the credits, which I presume Diane Meek had written down years before, were wrong. Paul did 'Heather on the Moor', which is classic Brady. I did 'There's Sure to Be a Row', a song learned from Willie Clancy that I like a lot. Dónal's stuff is really good also.'

Andy performed in a number of television shows at the time, either solo or with various formations. One particularly memorable performance was for *Live at the Embankment*, which catches him in dazzling form flanked by Dónal and Paul. 'That TV show Paul said he'd do it with me if I played on his one, which showed the beginning of a slight drift between us. We were playing as a duo up to that point, but we decided to do the two shows separately. I was really nervous. I'd be thinking, "Oh God, that TV show next week, what am I going to do?" I asked Dónal if he'd be on it but he was going to Canada with The Bothy Band the day before. He gave me a ring later and said that he'd changed his flight and he could do it, which I thought was a great loyal thing to do.'

Perhaps Andy was still developing his own confidence as a solo singer minus the backing of a band like Planxty or as one half of a duo with musicians like Paul Brady, Dónal Lunny and Mick Hanly, but he was susceptible to extreme performance nerves around this time.

'When I was relaxed, I was good, and when I wasn't relaxed, I wasn't very good,' he openly admits. 'I decided I'd try hypnotism to combat my nervousness. At the time, I didn't know any-thing about it. I thought it would be like the theatrical hypnotists and somebody would say [in a deep voice], "On Tuesday the twelfth, you will be very relaxed." I looked up hypnotists in the phone directory. I didn't find any hypnotists but I found a hypnotherapist in Clontarf, so I gave him a go. I got off to a really bad start because he opened the door in his bedroom slippers. I thought pseudo doctors who open the door in their bedroom slippers *can't* be any good. He brought me in and for everything he said, my confidence in him evaporated a bit further. He said, "I'm going to give you some cards with colours on the back. I'm going to go out of the room and I want you to put them in the order that you like the colours best." They were all grey and dull brown and dirty yellow colours. I didn't like *any* of the colours. By this point, I thought this was a dead loss so I put them in any order. He continued on but I wasn't listening after that so I paid him his twenty quid and thought, well that's that.'

But Andy still wasn't done with the idea, so he looked up the phonebook again and found someone else, who used to advertise in *The Irish Times*. 'I called him and I had a long conversation on the phone with him and I made an appointment. He opened the door himself too. Once again, there was no nurse in a white apron or anything like that. He said, "I want you to read my book while I'm in here with another patient." I was looking to be hypnotised and had no interest in reading this guy's book. He brought me in half an hour later and I lay down on the couch and I said, "Look, I have an early gig tonight and I have to be out of here at six o'clock." I had a gig in The Meeting Place on Dorset Street.

'He said he was going to take me through the twenty-two stages of serenity. He said, "I want you to imagine you're sitting on a cloud and looking down," so I did that. The second one was, "I want you to imagine you're sitting on a cloud and feeling really good." Right. I managed that one. The third was, "I want you to imagine that you're sitting on cloud looking down and feeling really happy because the happiness is coming from within you." So I thought, "How the fuck do you imagine that?" So I began to lose it. The fourth one was even more difficult and they went on to twenty-two different stages and I don't remember any of them after that. I couldn't get the hang of it at all. At the end of it he said, "Now, I want you to scan forward twenty-four hours. Just think of leaving here and going to the gig, it's a good gig. You're leaving for Wales tomorrow I believe, so just imagine doing that. It should only take you a couple of minutes." So I lay back – this sounds ridiculous but it's true – and I imagined myself paying him, going down the stairs and not being able to find my car. I'm walking around the streets in my imagination looking for my car.

'After a couple of minutes he said, "Are you finished?" I said, "No, I can't find my car." He said, "What! I told you if you have any problems to let me know. This could do you irreparable damage!" I'm thinking, "Oh, fuck off." He looked at his watch and said, "Right, the time in the real world is half past six." I said, "What! I told you I had be out of here by six!" "Oh, yes," he says, "we'll just do the scan." So I close my eyes. My heart is beating rapidly and my temples are throbbing with panic and I couldn't do anything, so after about thirty seconds I paid him and went off and drove home to get my instruments and drove to The Meeting Place. I was about half an hour late. The place was crowded and I'd missed the sound check. The first thing I did when I got in there, I was so nervous, was I knocked over one of the waitresses with a tray of drinks in the middle of a really quiet song. I played the gig and I was so nervous it was one of the worst gigs I ever played. So that was the end of hypnotherapy for me.'

By 1972, Christy Moore had garnered a very loyal following in the folk clubs of northern England, but the formation of Planxty that year pretty much jettisoned his solo career and, three years later, he found himself back ploughing his original furrow. 'The year after I left the band was very difficult,' explains Christy. 'Part of the reason it was difficult was because Coulter made it very, very difficult for me to work. The deal was if any of us ever left Planxty, we'd be released from the contract. Polydor were prepared to record me, but Coulter wouldn't release me. I had no profile in Ireland as a solo singer, so I had to start from scratch, literally. I had some very lean times. I really had to scrape the bottom of the barrel. I remember doing cabaret gigs, some dreadful places, and being treated really badly, or just not being able to get any gigs. But I have to accept responsibility for that myself as well in that I would have been drinking a lot.'

Christy got back on the horse, so to speak, in 1975 with an album titled *Whatever Tickles Your Fancy*. It was recorded in Ashling Studios in Rathgar, Dublin, and featured a rock rhythm section. 'Through Nicky Ryan I had befriended Jimmy Faulkner and Declan McNelis. I phoned Kevin Burke in London and invited him over for some rehearsals. He came and stayed. With Jimmy and Declan, we began a residency in The Meeting Place in Dorset Street. Initially, we played Monday nights, but soon began Saturdays as well and we were beginning to sound like a band. Robbie Brennan joined us on drums. I was a bit out of my depth playing with a bass and drums rhythm section and I could not offer much direction.'

The following year, a self-titled album adorned with the bearded head of Christy himself appeared on the record shelves. Amongst the standout tracks is the brilliant and epic 'Little Musgrave', the words of which he discovered on pages scattered on the floor of an auctioneer's in Dublin. (This song would be recorded again with beautiful results on the Planxty album *The Woman I Loved So Well*.) Jimmy Faulkner, Declan McNelis, Kevin Burke and Dónal Lunny made up the band, and Mícheál Ó Domhnaill and Barney McKenna contributed too. After Kevin left to join The Bothy Band, Christy started touring with Faulkner in Germany, France, the UK, Austria, Holland, and all around Ireland in a Peugeot 404 diesel pick-up.

1978 was his busiest year yet with the release of three albums. Christy was living in County Carlow and performing good gigs around the country. The first of these three albums, *The Iron Behind the Velvet*, was recorded in Keystone Studios in Harcourt Street, Dublin, and features Andy Irvine, Christy's brother Barry (Luka Bloom), Jimmy Faulkner, Gabriel McKeon, Tony Linnane and Noel Hill. 'The music was fun to play. I was trying to get a band together, but it was not happening – fellows had day jobs and others had their own projects and gigs to prioritise, so it just faded away once we had her down on wax.'

From here, Christy went straight into his first live album, *Live in Dublin*, where he was reunited with Dónal and with Planxty's soundman, Nicky Ryan. With Jimmy Faulkner in tow, they recorded gigs, mostly around Dublin, including the Grapevine Arts Centre, Trinity College, The Meeting Place and Nicky Ryan's parlour, but they also returned to Pat Dowling's in Prosperous. Finally, Christy completed the triumvirate with an album titled *H-Block* in support of the men and women 'on the blanket' in the H-Blocks and Armagh jails. Dónal, Declan Sinnott, Mick Hanly, Matt Molloy, piper Dan Dowd, Frances Brolly, Noel Hill and Tony Linnane all played on the album. Actor Stephen Rea read two works by Bobby Sands and one by Brian Ua Baoill. The political and civil rights themes contained in the album stirred controversy.

The launch of the record was even raided by Special Branch, fortuitously affording the album even more publicity.

Despite the culmination of their activities in 1975, Planxty's music remained vivid in the public consciousness. George McManus of Polydor UK compiled an album from the three Polydor albums plus the single version of 'The Cliffs of Dooneen', his own personal favourite. He released it in 1976 as *The Planxty Collection*. A review of the album in September of that year in *Melody Maker* was an affectionate obituary to the great band of the 1970s that offered so much insight and celebration of Irish music culture. But, touching as they were, the sentiments were somewhat premature: 'One of the saddest days for folkies all over Europe must have been when Planxty announced their split a year ago, but this album, with its intelligent cross-section of material spanning the Irish group's history, will serve as a reminder of just how brilliant they were.'

Chapter 15

After the Break

In hindsight, it appears that the original version of Planxty started and ended in a flash. Three albums, a variety of line-ups and many miles of touring were condensed into three short years. It was an intense and fertile vacuum of time. No wonder the band self-combusted so quickly. In fact, it seems almost like frozen time – a wild, blurry and slightly implausible dream. Yet the resonance of those years abides; the memories of their concerts and recordings are carved elegantly, magically into the Irish music firmament.

The continued presence of each individual member compounded the effect. Throughout the mid-1970s, Liam, Andy, Dónal and Christy remained friends and frequent collaborators, often appearing on the same festival bill, and encountering each other in the studio and onstage. Christy had gradually re-emerged in the public consciousness as a solo artist of considerable presence. Andy returned to the guise of a rambling romanticist of yonder plains, an authoritative ambassador of international folk. Liam remained the untouchable master musician whose abilities revelled both in the bosom of the tradition and the unfettered territory of mixed-cultural experiments. Dónal survived The Bothy Band, and continued to blaze a trail as a studio producer, while remaining the perennial conduit for so many other musicians.

Whereas Paul Brady shed his folk persona for new songwriting pastures and Johnny Moynihan gradually retreated to a folk hinterland away from the spotlight, the four original Planxty players never strayed far from the public's field of vision. It seems for all its self-destructive properties, Planxty remained a magnetic concept.

Throughout this period, all four musicians had come into contact with Kevin Flynn, a well-known impresario from County Sligo. The fast-talking Flynn, a roguish yet lovable singer and promoter, had initiated the first Boys of Ballisodare Festival in 1977. Andy Irvine describes him as 'a man with a quick brain and a quicker tongue', adding that 'he was not a man to hide his light under a bushel'. The Boys of Ballisodare was a folk and traditional music festival that featured soloists and groups of various styles and ages. 'It was the first festival of its kind in Ireland,' states Flynn proudly. 'We started in 1977 with The Bothy Band, Clannad, Tom Paxton, a who's who of Irish music and some guys from America as well. We went all the way to 1983. I tried to keep the line-up as folky as possible, but also tried to mix a bit of blues with it because I thought they could lie well together.'

Kevin Flynn was also friendly with Planxty's old sound engineer, Nicky Ryan, who was now serving the same role with Clannad (and would later become their manager). Flynn had set up Ogham Records with The Chieftains' manager, Maurice

Cassidy, and released Clannad's 1978 live album, *Clannad in Concert*.

In 1978, The Bothy Band played the Ballisodare Festival for the second year running, on a bill that featured key contemporary groups such as Oisin, Clannad and Boys of the Lough, alongside traditional players such as Josie McDermott, the duo of Fred Finn and Peter Horan, Packie Duignan and *sean-nós* singer Nicholas Toibin. Christy, Liam and Andy all performed solo that year and, despite a noticeable buzz of anticipation and vocal pleas from the attending audience, the temptation of an impromptu Planxty reunion was resisted.

'At the first Ballisodare Festival, Kevin Flynn paid me double my fee, which is something that never happened to me anywhere, and I know he paid a lot of people double their fees as well,' recounts Christy. 'That's the sort of guy he was. Kevin was also running gigs in The National in Kilburn in London. As well as being a kind of an Irish dancehall, kind of madhouse, Kevin put on these gigs of folk music that he liked. He was bringing different combinations of people over and I played a few of them.'

Flynn explains that he used to organise the festival like an old traditional concert, with a main act and maybe four or five support acts in the first half. 'I might have Joe Burke and Tommy Peoples over separately and then have The Bothy Band finish up the concert. I was able to pay the boys double what they were getting in Ireland at the time. I knew Karl Dallas who was a highly regarded journalist for *Melody Maker*. He also founded a paper called *Folk News*. He needed backing and he came to me, so I backed it and I used to get good publicity out of that.'

Under the umbrella of *Folk News*, Karl Dallas, organised a concert with Doc Watson and Merle Watson in the State Cinema in Kilburn. The tickets were selling slow so he asked Kevin Flynn to pull in a few favours. 'The Planxty boys had all played for me individually previously, so I asked Christy, Andy, Liam and Dónal – all four of them – to come over and do separate sets for the first half of the Doc Watson concert,' Flynn explains. 'So the way it worked was Liam could play with Dónal, and Dónal could play with Andy and it would all be mixed around, but they wouldn't all be on stage at the same time. Colin Irwin from *Melody Maker* was a friend of mine at the time and he put a headline down in the paper hinting that Planxty would all be in the same place at the same time, you know, a will-they-won't-they type of thing. And that sold out the concert and everyone started talking about it. Donovan and all the big English folkies came along. Planxty didn't actually play together that night, but it got everyone talking about them again.'

'I believe that Kevin Flynn went to great lengths to actually put Planxty back together,' declares Christy. 'It just didn't make sense for him to have the four of us individually booked to play support to Doc Watson. I remember the gig as being quite bizarre. It was great to get an opportunity to hear Doc Watson. But there was a lot of drinking and smoking going on and I'm quite hazy about it all.'

Once again, Planxty had teased their audience with the possibility of a comeback, albeit unwittingly. Nevertheless, their rebirth was in the stars and their paths were crossing with such regularity that it seemed inevitable that they would converge again. Furthermore, Kevin Flynn was going out of his way to encourage a reunion. Flynn was a long-time Planxty fan who had sung in his own early 1970s Sligo group, Geantraí. 'The Clancy Brothers were the first people to introduce me to it. I remember going to see them in the Albert Hall back in 1966 or 1967 when they came back from America. When I was in college, we had a priest from America who started a glee club [a singing group] and he had Clancy Brothers records from back in 1961 and he had us learning those things off.'

Christy is cited as the protagonist that put Planxty together at the very genesis of the group, and he assumed that role once again in 1978. 'From early on, and this still exists to this day, I do have a fire in my belly for pushing things,' he says. 'I am the one who makes things happen. That has been my history. In between gigs and rehearsals, I'd be the one who would spend a lot more time thinking about things and hopping balls. I went from being in Planxty to a bit of an abyss, really. The time between the two Planxty bands was difficult enough. I longed for the excitement of the band again, so I canvassed everybody and everybody was available, and we went for it.'

'Christy got an inkling that The Bothy Band was about to pull to pieces,' explains Andy. 'The band members, I hope they wouldn't mind me saying it, but they were a volatile bunch of people. So when they split up, it wasn't a great surprise.' Dónal concedes that, although The Bothy Band hadn't quite finished, their break-up was inevitable. 'We were wrecked. It's what usually finishes bands off, gigging for two years without making any real money. Christy sort of spotted a good moment.'

In the autumn of 1978, Andy Irvine had just returned from a tour. 'My partner, Marina, told me that Dónal had phoned,' he recalls: 'And, for a moment, it looked like I was going to be invited to join The Bothy Band, and I would've loved to be in The Bothy Band but I'm not quite sure I could have afforded it! Before that ever happened though, Christy stepped in and said why don't we get the original Planxty back together? I think Liam and myself both said, "Yesss!" But Dónal had some misgivings on account of the fact that The Bothy Band hadn't quite broken up. Dónal felt a certain amount of responsibility. In fact, there was a ludicrous moment where Planxty was Christy, Dónal, Liam, myself, Matt Molloy, Paddy Keenan, Tríona ...!'

In the end, the original Planxty reformed with the addition of just one new member, flute player extraordinaire, Matt Molloy. 'There was a genuine desire to just open things up and bring in different voices,' says Dónal. 'Matt Molloy is an incredible musician and I've had great nights with him and I've been so happy to play bodhrán with him,' remarks Christy. 'He's a one off. I love his albums. He has to be the main man on the flute.'

All four original members embraced the idea of Matt joining the ranks, but it was of particular significance to Liam O'Flynn. 'Obviously, it was a huge thrill for me personally to have another musician in the group with the same sort of traditional roots, particularly one with whom I had already built this fantastic musical relationship since the early days of playing in the Old Sheiling. We had been making music together long before any of these groups ever formed.'

Matt Molloy from Ballaghdereen, County Roscommon, is another true master musician of the Irish tradition. Following in the footsteps of his father, grandfather and uncle, he soaked up the influences of the flute and fiddle music of the north Roscommon–south Sligo area, and graduated through his Christian Brothers school marching band to the fife-and-drum band. He also attended local *scoraíocht* (from the Irish word *scor*: to share) gatherings of traditional musicians to exchange tunes and discuss techniques. By the age of eighteen, Matt had won the All-Ireland Flute Championship and had a string of successes in national fleadh cheoils and Oireactas events.

Liam O'Flynn was one of the first musicians Matt met when he moved to Dublin when he was eighteen. 'We hit it off and started playing together,' he says. 'We played together at the Old Sheiling in between the ballad sets. We did that for a couple of years and had a great old time. I also got to know Dónal and Christy to some extent. The 1960s scene in Dublin was quite small, it was probably more personable than it is now. I used to meet people like Dónal and Christy and Liam and Seán Keane at the sessions in Dowling's in Prosperous.'

Molloy's musical relationship with Dónal prospered during their time as band-mates in The Bothy Band. 'It was fairly informal to begin with,' recalls Matt. 'We'd go down the country at the weekend and play a concert in Clare or somewhere, divide the profits and drink them before the weekend was over. I was an aircraft mechanic technician for Aer Lingus and had studied engineering in Bolton Street for four years. When we went professional with The Bothy Band, I got leave of absence. The group was very powerful. We gelled very well in spite of all the pundits and critics who said it was going to blow apart at any given moment. It lasted four or five years in the end, though we never really got ourselves organised from a managerial point of view. Everything was in disarray except for the music. We were too busy having a good time. I was new to the whole thing, fresh out of a secure pensionable job and I didn't know what hit me. I thought I was on permanent holidays for the first two years.'

When approached by Planxty, Molloy jumped at the chance to play with the era's *other* great folk ensemble. 'The word "reform" wasn't really used,' he's careful to point out. 'It was more like a project that was suggested, to get an album together, record it and tour the album in Ireland, England and Europe with the original Planxty members. That was it. The focus was just to do that. I was a great admirer of all four of them, so the idea totally appealed to me.'

With the musicians in place, Planxty now needed a manager to steer them into their second phase of existence. After considering a number of candidates, they eventually settled on the man who had already played a role in their re-emergence, Kevin Flynn. 'He was mad,' laughs Christy in reflection. 'He was a very intelligent guy with great vision. For Kevin, it was enough to be associated with the band. I think all he wanted was to be out on the road with us. Of course, he was supposed to be looking after the business end of things – alas, the business end of it wasn't great.'

Matt Molloy was also familiar with the incorrigible Mr Flynn. 'I met Kevin Flynn in London when he was running The National. The Bothy Band had just decided to take a break for six months and see what happened. I was playing at a show in The National with Paul Brady and some other people, something to do with Mulligan Records, I think. I was having a drink with Kevin and telling him the sad story of The Bothy Band. I quoted fees that we were getting for gigs and he was shocked and he said, "Jaysus, I know I could do ten times better than that." So he did some costings and booked a tour. The Bothy Band ended the break after four months and, true to his promise, financially it was the best tour of Ireland and England that we ever did. That was our last ever tour. I think that impressed Dónal as well.

'I got to know Kevin pretty well because he actually released a solo album for me on his record label,' continues Matt. 'He was good fun. He never seemed to need any sleep. He was ready to party all night. You'd be hoping for six or eight hours' sleep, but two hours later he'd be banging on your door, "Come on, get up! We're on the way."'

Planxty began rehearsals on Tuesday, 19 September 1978. 'We met in Matt's house to try and get a repertoire together,' recollects Andy. 'But then it largely became that frustrating thing that often happens with traditional musicians when they're trying to get sets of tunes together. "Oh, this is a nice one" and "That's a nice one" and you're writing down all these titles but they never go together. Then you finally have three tunes and then they think of another tune that might be better. There's too much choice, basically. But we had those rehearsals and then we all went off and did our own things.'

It wasn't until the following year that work began in earnest. Kevin Flynn had booked a mammoth European tour for the boys. It seemed Planxty were coming back with a splash. 'At the time, I thought it was fantastic that Planxty was finally going to do the kind of tour that we always felt we could do,' says Christy. They prepared themselves with three days' rehearsal in St Mullins in Carlow by the banks of the River Barrow. 'We did two warm-up gigs in The Meeting Place on Dorset Street,' adds Liam. 'They were very enjoyable. There was a great buzz and excitement attached to those gigs.'

From a sixty-capacity pub in Dublin, Planxty stepped straight into the deep end by headlining the 3,000-capacity Hammersmith Odeon in London on Easter Sunday, 15 April – a terrifying way to begin a tour! In hindsight, it may not have been the wisest decision. 'It was not good,' admits Andy. 'Everything was slow. The concert went on for about two and a half hours. And we got possibly our only ever bad live review. Karl *fucking* Dallas in the *Melody-fucking-Maker*. I didn't read it. It was kept from me and I've never read it.'

'It's just one breath in the life of a newspaper, but the emotional blow of a bad review can stay with you for a long time,' confesses Dónal. 'I agree,' says Andy. 'Without even reading it, it still dented my confidence. The gig was a bad move. We weren't ready. The music itself was ready, but the tuning and the continuity and all that would have been chaotic. I remember the moment when I realised I was very nervous. Van Morrison had played the same venue a few days or a week before and somebody shouted up out of the audience, "You're not as good as Van Morrison." I looked to Christy, thinking, "That guy's just crucified himself," and Christy just stood there tuning up and didn't say anything and I thought, "Oh dear, we're knocked out." That sounds very unfair to Christy, but one did look to Christy's personality in a situation like that to get a laugh out of the crowd. He's great for getting a crowd on side and had he crushed this guy it would have given us a big lift. But maybe he was feeling nervous himself or maybe he agreed with what the guy said. Either way, the comment went unanswered.'

'I wasn't able to talk!' pleads Christy. By his own admission, Planxty's European marathon in 1979 marked a period of hard partying and immoderate consumption of drink and drugs for Christy Moore. 'The wildest times I ever had on the road were on that tour. Crazy, crazy stuff. I can remember times being onstage feeling very rubbery, very woolly because there was an awful lot of up-all-night stuff. I remember one night in Frankfurt I thought I was going to die. It was a very scary night. I took stuff that I thought was something else. It was really horrible. The two hours every night when we were onstage were pretty much always good, but the other twenty-two were difficult. I remember arriving back in Ireland with mouth ulcers and my body was in really bad shape.'

After the Hammersmith Odeon, the band played Newcastle, Edinburgh, Liverpool, Manchester, Birmingham, Ipswich and Leeds. They took the boat from Harwich to Bremerhaven, Germany to begin their German tour, later moving on to Switzerland, Austria, Belgium, France and Holland. On 29 May, they took the ferry from Cherbourg to Rosslare and completed the tour with nine Irish shows' culminating with a concert at The Stadium in Dublin on 11 June. In total, Planxty played forty-seven concerts in fifty-eight days.

'We were very optimistic about how the tour would go,' reveals Andy. 'We thought we could play anywhere. We were fantasising about touring the whole of Europe. We did play

Holland, Belgium and Germany, but none of those gigs was nearly as successful as they would have been four or five years earlier. The only places we really made any money were Ireland and Brittany. It was a long tour in the end.'

Having recovered from their gruelling European schedule, Planxty settled into a more relaxed pace of life. They were, of course, now freed from the strangling constraints of their previous recording contract. They had the time and space to record under their own terms and, furthermore, they now had a producer in Dónal Lunny who had an infinitely deeper under-standing of the music than any previous technician who recorded them.

'The second time Planxty came around was when I realised I had a métier, I had a place, which is traditional music, which I love and I see loads of possibilities in it, enough to keep me going for the rest of my life,' proclaims Dónal.

From 18 to 30 June, the band convened at the newly opened Windmill Lane Studios in Dublin to make their fourth album – first of a second wind of recordings from Planxty – accordingly titled *After the Break*. A new recording deal was struck with John Cook of Tara Records, the label that released Christy's *Prosperous* album all those years earlier. 'Tara put up the money,' explains Dónal. 'John Cook knew that if he got a Planxty album on Tara, it would sell endlessly.'

'When Tara initially acquired *Prosperous* it was more to manufacture the LP in Ireland and satisfy the sales demand rather than with any intention to start a record label,' explains John Cook. 'However, after the Polydor contract had expired and the band had taken a respite, the reforming of Planxty seemed an ideal situation to jump-start a label. With the *Prosperous* conn-ection and the high profile generated by three album releases, it seemed a good proposition to record Planxty and thus establish a record label in a relatively short space of time. However, the investment for that time was substantial and Tara was also competing against other record companies to re-sign the band. However, Tara won the day and *After the Break* was recorded.'

The engineer on the album was Brian Masterson, a musician well known to the band from his days playing with the group Supply, Demand & Curve, who were favourites of Dónal's and Andy's from back in the days of The Mugs Gig. Masterson was one of the founders and directors of the studio. 'Having bands like Planxty was great because, before then, a band who were that good generally had to go to London to record, which had its own set of problems.'

'I'd known Brian for forever because he lived opposite me on Marlborough Road,' informs Andy. 'I was into progressive rock at the time, like Pink Floyd and Soft Machine. Brian turned me on to Terry Riley, who was a kind of hippie from California who played minimalist music. He also turned me on to Stockhausen. Brian was way out there and I was trustily following along. He was always great.'

Dónal agrees that Brian was an important figure in the life of Planxty the second time around. 'I had this recording that he made of The Chieftains playing 'Cotton Eye Joe'. At the time, I thought this was the best recording of an acoustic performance I'd heard. There was such activity in the air around the music coming out of the speakers at you. I thought, "How did he manage to do this?" Also, he has a brilliant way of putting the musicians at ease in the studio. This is very important. It's like horses lining up for the Grand National. If you can't actually soothe them down enough to get them into the box, then there's no race. Brian was brilliant at that, at relaxing people and making them feel that they're not being examined or criticised.'

Naturally, Dónal himself was assigned the role of producer. 'After The Bothy Band, I had a much clearer idea of where the rhythm section sat and what the potential power of each instrument was. There was a lot more focus on the tonality of instruments. On the earlier records, the guitar sounds might be too bass-y, the pipes might be too harsh, and it's amazing the difference it makes. You're painting a picture. And by the second time around, I'd done a lot of painting. Not to say that I would take credit for all of that. But the whole recording industry was growing up and we were in a better situation.'

'I was just in awe of him,' admits Brian Masterson. 'He was just so insightful. His instinct was unerringly right. It was a great album, but it certainly took time to get it that good. We were all young then and the crazy hours were part of it. Dónal was the guy steering the boat. People relied on him. And it was all done with such subtlety. He wasn't one of these guys who came in and said, "We have to do this" or "We have to do it my way" or any-thing like that. You just knew he was right.'

Masterson remembers the atmosphere in the studio as being excellent. 'It was a combination of very hard work, in terms of their perfectionism, interspersed with just complete muck, having great fun, breaking up laughing. And you needed that fun aspect because you couldn't actually go on at that level for twenty-four hours.'

After the Break has a shimmering eloquence, a sense of control and detail that reflects the breathing space the band, and the repertoire, had found by 1979. It doesn't have the edge-of-your-pants feel of the second and third albums, or the infectious, unstoppable zeal of their debut, but it has an assured, measured finish that perhaps those albums lack. It opens with 'The Good Ship Kangaroo' – a jollily relayed tale full of wonderful, silly language and turns of phrase about a man who leaves his one

true love for a life of seafarin' across foreign waters. He finally
returns bearing a bounty of exotic, if not potentially inapp-
ropriate, gifts: 'tortoises from Tenerife and toys from Timbuktu/
A China rat, a Bengal cat and a Bombay Cockatoo.' Alas, the
sailing man is too late, as his washerwoman has since absconded
'with a smart young man that drives the van for Chaplin, Son &
Co.'. The jilted sailor subsequently resigns himself to life without love: 'I'll go unto some foreign shore, no longer can I
stay/And with some China hottentot, I'll throw my life away.'
The album's original sleeve-notes suggest that the word
'hottentot' probably meant opium, but in actual fact it is a
reference to the Khoikhoi ethnic group of southwestern Africa.
(The word 'hottentot' is nowadays considered offensive by the
Oxford Dictionary of South African English.)

'The Good Ship Kangeroo' was learned from the late Mrs
Elizabeth Cronin of Macroom, County Cork, and since its
introduction into Planxty's repertoire, featuring a stunning
instrumental break towards the end, it has remained a firm
favourite among live audiences. 'It actually has the same melody
for every verse and chorus,' explains Dónal. 'That's about fifteen
repeats, which I varied by coming up with two different chord
accompaniments for the verses, and a third one for the chorus.
Then I wrote the instrumental, which Liam plays and Andy put
his own parts together for each section. It really does work –
Christy himself only realised recently that it was the same
melody all the time!'

The first set of tunes features three double jigs – 'East at
Glendart'/'Brian O'Lynn'/'Pay the Reckoning' – and, instantly,
we hear the sound of Molloy's flute crystallising beautifully into
the Planxty bedrock. The sparring of Molloy's flute and
O'Flynn's pipes gives these jigs an impressive lift, and with all five
musicians playing together – Andy on bouzouki, Dónal on

blarge (standing for 'bouzouki, large') and Christy on bodhrán – the sound is pure, classic Planxty.

The next song is 'You Rambling Boys of Pleasure', one of Christy's favourite Andy-sung songs. It marks a drop in mood from the buoyant opening. This is sad and sorrowful – a classic folk song template of precious love fouled by the temptation of gold. It's total Andy Irvine territory. The song was learned from the singing of Len Graham and Joe Holmes from County Antrim, and also from Ian Stevenson of Derry. The sleeve-notes also state that the song was 'half remembered by W.B. Yeats and rewritten by him as 'Down by the Sally Gardens'.' The final verse frames the rambler's lost fantasy:

> And I wish I was in Belfast town and my true love along
>   with me
> And money in my pocket to keep us in good company
> Liquor to be plenty, a flowing glass on every side
> Hard fortune would ne'er daunt me, for I am young and
>   the world is wide.

The second set of tunes is three reels, 'The Blackberry Blossom'/ 'Lucky in Love'/'The Dairy Maid'. The second and third reels were learned from the playing of Willie Clancy, his influence still firmly engraved in Planxty's music, and as much with Matt's playing as with Liam's.

The rambling theme continues with Andy's second song, 'The Rambling Siúler'. The song is not dissimilar to 'The Jolly Beggar' in theme, depicting a colonel disguised as a beggar for the purposes of preying on the virtues of farmers' daughters. It was collected in the north of Ireland by Sam Henry, but is of Scottish origin. The album's second set of reels include 'The Lady on the Island'/'The Gatehouse Maid'/'The Virginia/Callaghan's'. The first two reels were popularised by the great Sligo fiddlers of the

1940s, Michael Coleman and Paddy Kiloran. For Matt himself, this music ran deep. 'Paddy Kiloran was a family friend. Himself and my father went to America together in the 1920s so I have a special *grá* for his music. It's where my music comes from, from these people.' 'The Virginia' is another reel learned from Clancy, and 'Callaghan's' hails from the Kerry fiddle tradition, particularly the playing of Denis Murphy.

The next song is the album's glittering centrepiece, 'The Pursuit of Farmer Michael Hayes'. This six-minute epic identifies one of Christy Moore's finest vocal performances. It comes to Planxty via a number of sources. Christy heard versions of it sung by John Lyons, Tom Lenihan, and an unknown singer on Donncha Ó Dulaing's *Highways and Byways*. Christy also received written versions from Mike Flynn and Seamus MacMathúna. The air comes from a song that Andy used to sing in early Planxty days called 'All Around My Hat'.

The lyrics portray the glorious flight of a man self-described as 'a bold undaunted fox'. With a reward posted for his capture for the slaughter of a cruel landlord, he leads his pursuers in a merry dance up and down Ireland. Christy sings the words with great urgency as a raspy concoction of blarge, mandolin, flute, bodhrán, uilleann pipes and two whistles tumble along with him. 'He killed a cruel landlord who was destroying the lives of tenants and their families, who was taking food from the mouths of children and squeezing the life from their parents,' explains Christy. 'This monster's trade was protected by English law and by an army of occupation. I see Michael Hayes as a freedom fighter.'

> They searched the rocks, the gulfs, the quays, the ships,
>   the liners in the bays
> The ferryboats and steamers as they were goin' to sea

> *Around the coast they made a steer from Poolbeg*
> *   Lighthouse to Cape Clear*
> *Killarney town and sweet Tralee, they then crossed into*
> *   Clare.*
>
> *When they landed on the shore they searched Kilrush*
> *   from tip to toe*
> *They searched the baths at sweet Lisdoon, likewise*
> *   Miltown Malbay*
> *Galway bein' a place of fame, they thought 'twas there I*
> *   might remain*
> *Still their search was all in vain for I gave them all leg*
> *   bail.*

In the final verse, the epic chase ends as Farmer Michael Hayes finally leaves the country in triumphant and arrogant exile.

> *As the moon began to shine I thought I'd make a foreign*
> *   clime*
> *Leave them all to search away for Farmer Michael Hayes*
> *To Dublin town I made my way and then to Cobh and*
> *   Americay*
> *Now I'm in the land of liberty, a fig for all my foes.*

Two more tunes, 'Lord McDonald'/'The Chattering Magpie', lead us into the final song of the album, 'The Bonny Light Horseman', an Andy Irvine-led number that had mysteriously mutated in its translation from the versions he heard from Dolores Keane and John Faulkner. 'By this time we were doing backing tracks and the voices went on last and we were all three of us standing around the mic and it became a bit of a Welsh male choir,' he quips.

The album closes in spectacular form with a Bulgarian dance tune in 9/16 time called 'Smeceno Horo'. 'When I said, "I've got this Bulgarian piece of music, would you fancy doing it?" I'm sure they all thought, "Oooh, what's this?" ' reflects Andy. 'But they did it and it was fantastic. To me that was one of the great successes, that Liam and Matt Molloy took this piece of music that they didn't understand, took the phrases and kind of engorged it, and when it came out it was played like Irish music would be played if it was an Irish tune. It was the closest I ever got to melding two traditions together.'

The *After the Break* artwork was put together by Pat Musick, a Colorado-born artist who was living in the UK in the mid-1970s on a student visa. 'Planxty's music embodied a spirit that reached me directly,' says Musick. 'It was sort of a distillation of everything I liked best across what I then knew of the spectrum of Irish music – from purist traditional to The Chieftains to The Clancy Brothers – all integrated together. The incorporation of non-traditional instruments and rhythms gave further voice to the spirit, soul, melodies, complexities and heart that were already there. With Planxty, the integrity of the music is the bedrock. Their tremendous skill and craftsmanship with their instruments, songs and arrangements goes without saying, as does their spirit and enthusiasm – always coming across as spontaneous, however tight the arrangement.'

In art college in Portland, Oregon, Musick specialised in calligraphy and was enamoured with the ornate work contained in the Book of Kells, as well as harbouring an interest in Irish music and folklore. She developed two 'modern' typefaces based on original early sixth-to-ninth-century manuscripts. One of those typefaces provided the lettering for the new Planxty logo. The logo appeared along the top of the *After the Break* album sleeve in warm woodcut lettering.

The body of the sleeve sees the band photographed live onstage, framed in a wooden window and viewed from the perspective of what looks like a backstage dressing room. The back sleeve features an overhead view of the five musicians onstage in the throes of performance and within the album sleeve was contained a lyric and information insert. Musick had the difficult task of collating the words. 'It was not easy to get hold of them,' she explains. 'I was living in England; they were all over the place, involved in individual gigs and in performing with others, as well as the Planxty reunion. Again, this was long before e-mail and getting lyrics over the phone from England was out of the question. I was on one of my extended visits to Ireland and I remember meeting with Andy in a chipper in Ranelagh. I believe he dictated the lyrics to 'You Rambling Boys of Pleasure', 'The Rambling Siúler' and 'The Bonny Light Horseman' to me on the spot.

'I hadn't been able to get hold of Christy but was told he was performing at a benefit rally against the proposed nuclear power plant at Carnsore Point in County Wexford,' continues Musick. 'Since that seemed to be the only way to catch up with him – and I was interested in the issue as well – I got myself down there somehow. I remember lying on the grass in the sun, somebody playing onstage in the background, Christy sitting there on the grass dictating the song lyrics to me, me scribbling them down as fast as I could. There were a couple of points where Christy pointed out something delightful in the poetry of the words – imagery, alliterations, almost tongue-twisters when sung at high speed; explanations of pronunciations or terms.

'Of course it's obvious from Christy's repertoire, his performances and his own songwriting that he loves the poetry and sounds of words, but it was pretty cool witnessing his digressions of delight about particular phrases as he recited the lyrics to me,' continues Musick. 'Especially, maybe, considering the setting: a large rally about a major environmental issue that also embodied, as these things do, the issue of the people/down-to-earth values versus powerful government and economic forces. And also, that was the time when the situation of the detainees in the H-Block in Northern Ireland was quite intense. I remember that the pen I was using to take down the lyrics was one of those Rotring graphic-design pens with an extremely fine point, Christy commented on how much a hunger striker in the H-Block would be able to write on a sheet of toilet paper (to be smuggled out) with a pen like that. Maybe this epitomises Christy, in a way: committed to issues, never forgetting struggles and injustices, yet also able to give time, and to take and express delight in things like words and music – his sensitivity and awareness, embrace of the small wonders, beauties and humour in life, along with the great issues, inequities and frustrations.'

After the recording of the new album, Planxty were back on the road in July, but now the touring was more sporadic. They played The National in Kilburn, and a handful of dates in Belgium and France. In Ireland, they headlined the third Ballisodare Festival, which meant a busy weekend for both Dónal and Matt, considering The Bothy Band was also on the bill!

Matt Molloy's spell with Planxty was now coming to an end. He began performing with The Chieftains and, before long, they co-opted him as full-time member to replace the departed Michael Tubridy. As vital as his contribution was to *After the Break*, everyone agreed his move to The Chieftains was a wise one. 'Matt wanted more tunes, and also The Chieftains played melody, exclusively,' explains Dónal. 'They play unison. It was a good career move for him and none of us begrudged him.'

Molloy joined The Chieftains during a period of great success for the band. His first recording with the group in 1979 was The Chieftains' ninth album, *Boil the Breakfast Early*, which duly received a Grammy nomination upon its release. That year he also played with The Chieftains at the Phoenix Park to a vast audience of some 1.35 million people. Alas, they were just the warm-up act. Headlining that show was Pope John Paul II. After sampling the transitory delights of both The Bothy Band and Planxty, Molloy finally had his long-term home with The Chieftains and he remains a member to this day.

His former colleagues in Planxty were enjoying the plaudits bestowed on *After the Break*. Colin Irwin of *Melody Maker* picked up on the Planxty revival with the same fervour he held for their previous incarnation. He began his review cautiously, saying: 'The gravest danger in the resurrection of Planxty was always that, in attempting to recreate the extraordinary verve and majesty of their original incarnation, they neglected natural current instincts and succeeded only in becoming a parody of their selves. That they've managed with ease to avoid this considerable pitfall alone makes this a great record.' Irwin also remarks: 'Liam O'Flynn has become an even more accomplished piper than he was before.' He summarises his thoughts by describing *After the Break* as 'an essential album'.

In the same issue of *Melody Maker*, Irwin travelled to the west of Ireland to catch Planxty's re-emergence in full flow. Planxty's manager, Kevin Flynn, had acquired The Hill Bar, once a crumbling western stronghold of traditional music in the surfing hotspot of Strandhill in County Sligo, now reinvented as The Venue – Planxty were billed surreptitiously as 'mystery guests', or as some posters mischievously read: 'Clad'.

In Irwin's article, Andy talks giddily about the success of the tour: 'It's just like the first tour we did together. Just like the old days. It's amazing. We can barely believe how well it's going at the moment.' In one of the most insightful Planxty write-ups in the UK press, Irwin observes with golden detail the habitual nuances of their personalities and their interaction; the way

Christy scribbles out a set-list of initials on the back of his hand 'and the others look at it and copy on their own hands' or even how Liam O'Flynn spent considerable time writing a notice appealing to 'those who feel unable to remain quiet while musicians are playing are requested to go to the front bar', seemingly to little avail.

He depicts Dónal in his role of musical director: 'If Christy is the flamboyant front of Planxty, Irvine the engaging romanticist and Liam O'Flynn the virtuoso, then Lunny is the withdrawn catalyst. Many hours later, he gets mellowed off his box and falls over in Kevin Flynn's kitchen, but that's another story.'

From Irwin's account, predictably enough, the performance was distracted by the party-like atmosphere of the occasion. The great Paddy Glackin, present to tape the event for his *Long Note* radio show, joined the band onstage at the end of the night. And manager Kevin Flynn even got in on the act with a reportedly impressive shot at 'The Flying Cloud' after much cajoling from Christy. Irwin also details the following night's concert in Galway's Leisureland venue. It was the last night of the tour and a combination of high emotions, nerves and vodka conspired to render it an erratic performance. The night culminated with American singer-songwriter and tour support Jim Page joining them on stage for a shambolic attempt of his own anti-nuclear anthem, 'Hiroshima Nagasaki Russian Roulette'.

The *NME* didn't get around to reviewing *After the Break* until February 1980. Nonetheless, they wrote of it with similar excited tones. 'The return of Planxty is, in folk circles, roughly akin to a Beatles reunion,' begins Fred Dellar. He concludes the review with: 'What is important is that Planxty are back and making good use of vinyl once more. Spread the news quickly.'

Chapter 16

The Woman I Loved So Well

Back in 1972, Planxty were four young men swept along by a wave of fresh, revolutionary and highly emotional music. Yet it became apparent throughout 1979 that the second coming of Planxty was never going to replicate that nascent energy. There were now families and mortgages to consider, real-world responsibilities, and also a reluctance to dedicate time solely to one musical project. Once *After the Break* was released, Planxty wasn't so much a band as a collective of respected doyens who regularly returned to each other to make music in a way only they could – but each had aspirations and ambitions beyond Planxty.

Dónal Lunny was a man driven to forge new connections and apply fresh contemporary ideas to Irish music. Likewise, Liam O'Flynn was ready to take the piping tradition into pastures never dreamt of before. Christy Moore could no longer restrain his, some might say, God-given vocation to become a folk singer with a unique voice and an iconic presence. He had *other* songs he needed to sing. Andy Irvine simply couldn't stand still for very long. His romantic vision manifested itself as an ongoing journey that engaged all the different music and musicians that he met along the way.

In between the Planxty activity of 1979, Andy managed to squeeze in tours in Europe with both Dónal, Mick Hanly and Gerry O'Beirne. He also recorded his debut solo album, *Rainy Sundays...Windy Dreams* with Dónal producing, Liam contributing, and many old associates, such as Paul Brady and Frankie Gavin of Dé Danann, guesting on various songs. In mid-December, Planxty had a rehearsal with a view to beginning afresh in the New Year and, once again, new influences penetrated the band's substratum. For as much as they were aware of the magic of the original four-piece, Planxty also had the capacity to become a viscous, morphing entity that absorbed additional musical personalities.

On 28 February 1980, Planxty headlined the Sense of Ireland concert at the Royal Albert Hall in London to a capacity audience. When they returned to Ireland they recorded two programmes for RTÉ television at the Pavillion in Dún Laoghaire, and settled down to rehearsals in Kilkea Castle in Castledermott, County Kildare. 'Noel Hill and Tony Linnane, "the twins", came down for the second bit,' recalls Andy.

Tony Linnane and Noel Hill were one of the great double acts in traditional Irish music and another two creative sons of County Clare. Noel Hill is a master of the concertina, an instrument of such cultural resonance in that part of the world that it is nicknamed 'the Clareman's trumpet'. Hill was compelled towards the instrument from a young age, sneaking practices on his older brother's concertina when no one was looking. Séamus Ennis once declared him 'Ireland's greatest concertina player' –

no mean accolade. Tony Linnane, also from Clare (Corofin), is one of the most mysterious and revered fiddlers in the country. He is described as a mild-mannered man, a great tutor and an electrifying player. In 1979, the duo came together to record an eponymous album for Tara Records, which is now considered by many to be one of the best albums of traditional Irish music ever made. Although they weren't adopted as full-time members, 'the twins' helped expand the traditional elements of the Planxty sound to great effect.

'I was living in Havelock Square in Sandymount and I opened the door one morning and Andy Irvine was standing outside,' recollects Noel Hill. 'He said, "I've come to ask would you be interested in working with Planxty." And I said, "Hold on now, I'll think about that and I'll get back to you in a few days." [Laughing] And then I said, "Fuck off! Come in and I'll make you a cup of tea. When do you want me to start?"'

'We knew them all very well,' remarks Tony Linnane. 'Dónal Lunny and Liam O'Flynn used to come down to Clare a lot at that time. My opinion always was that Planxty was great. To be honest, I thought, of what was around, they were the best. You couldn't fault them. To be asked to play with Planxty was great for us at the time. We were young and it gave us a lift.'

'There's never a dull moment with Planxty,' confirms Noel. 'I have a great *grá* for all of those boys. When you're onstage with Christy Moore, absolutely nothing can go wrong. Even when things *do* go wrong, it's still perfect. He has such a stagecraft. He's so brilliant. If a microphone went off or the whole sound system went haywire, or whatever might befall the people onstage, you couldn't have a better man there than Christy because he'd turn the situation into something better again. He's a great storyteller through song. Dónal and Andy are both brilliant arrangers. And as a melody player, I love playing with

Liam O'Flynn because I have a piping slant to my own playing. We were in good company.'

After rehearsals, the six-piece band embarked on a nineteen-date Irish tour, once again concluding with a Dublin concert in The Stadium. 'I remember we started off doing a "dry" tour and Lofty [manager Kevin Flynn had by now acquired the nickname "Lofty"] fell on the second night,' giggles Andy. 'On the third night, I encountered Liam having a meal with a bottle of wine. And then Christy fell off. We played on St Patrick's Night in Enniskillen where Dónal has a lot of relatives and he came back about seven o'clock in the morning in rags. I was left as the token non-drinker.'

In July 1980, Planxty returned to Windmill Lane Studios in Dublin to record their fifth album, *The Woman I Loved So Well*. This new recording, once again, signposts another shift in the Planxty sound. *The Woman I Loved So Well* is a gentle compendium of songs and tunes. The musical emphasis is on intricate, decorative and plaintive moods, tempos and arrangements, rather than the lusty pace of the early recordings.

The other new addition to the fold was Bill Whelan, a pianist/keyboardist and arranger from Limerick who had graduated through law school and was involved in film music and stage musicals. He had scored the main title music for the film *Bloomfield*, starring fellow Limerick man Richard Harris. Prior to joining Planxty, his mainstay was touring Andrew Lloyd Webber and Tim Rice musicals around Ireland. Whelan was also becoming a session keyboardist of note. In the spirit of Planxty's current predilection for expansion, he was invited to bring his Fender Rhodes piano into the studio.

'From a very early age, I had been very interested in the whole idea of interacting with traditional music and bringing other influences and other musical tastes that I might have had myself into it,' explains Whelan. 'What really attracted me was Andy specifically bringing in all the Eastern European times and odd rhythms against the music and Dónal's extraordinary musical sensitivity when it came to accompanying tunes.'

Whelan recalls entering into the situation with a mixture of fear and excitement. 'I remember coming in and feeling delighted to be asked and then sitting down behind the keyboard and having to come up with an accompaniment that sat in with what was already quite ornate music. I had to find the space to do things that didn't clutter the music but also added a little. Their whole approach to recording, the "filigree" approach, to my musical sensibility was fantastic. I felt at home, even though I was worried about what I was doing. Planxty was already four very significant figures in Irish traditional music and you felt you had to be careful where you walked.'

The album was recorded over two periods – 23–29 April and 16–19 May. Matt Molloy joined the boys in the studio again and, with Noel Hill and Tony Linnane in tow, Planxty nailed some of their finest ever recordings of traditional dance tunes. The Clare duo kick off the first set, a pair of double jigs, 'Out On the Ocean'/'Tiocfaidh Tú Abhaile Liom', strongly associated with their home county, the latter of which, like so many other Planxty dance arrangements, was learned from Willie Clancy. About forty seconds in, you can hear the tentative presence of the strings, and gradually the music takes on an almost baroque feel. Yet again, Planxty had managed to create something mellifluous from what would be an experimental cacophony in someone else's hands.

Liam takes centre stage on two hornpipes, 'The Tailor's Twist', first heard from the fiddler Joe Ryan, and an untitled hornpipe learned from Junior Crehan. 'Junior tells me he heard the tune from the late Denis Murphy, who brought it back from

America,' says Liam in the sleeve-notes. This is a sprightly set, which employs prominent use of regulators, expertly played by a musician at the height of his powers. The final set of tunes is three reels, 'The Woman I Never Forgot'/'The Pullet'/'The Ladies Pantalettes', featuring the note-perfect interplay of Tony Linnane and Noel Hill alongside the patented Planxty strings, which are at the same time delicate and rhythmic. Bill Whelan's Rhodes provides a delicious glisten over the traditional instruments, and the final flourish of pipes and bodhrán going head to head with concertina and fiddle is truly fine music to behold. 'The twins' learned the first reel from the great Tulla fiddler Paddy Canny, who Tony describes as one of the greatest Clare musicians. 'He's eighty-five or eighty-six now and he still plays music. I heard him play in Miltown just last July.' The second reel Tony learned from his good friend, the Miltown Malbay flautist Jim O'Connor, and the final reel Liam picked up from his first tutor, Leo Rowsome.

Songwise, Christy sets the pace with the album's opener, 'True Love Knows No Season'. 'In December 1979, I met Noel Shine in the Phoenix Pub in Cork, where he sang this song for me. It was written by Norman Blake and it's special in that it's the first cowboy song I've heard in a Cork City pub,' writes Christy in the sleeve-notes. A multi-instrumentalist most famed for his acoustic guitar playing in the bluegrass style, Norman Blake also made significant forays into folk and country, touring with June Carter and Johnny Cash in the 1960s, playing on Dylan's country-rock opus *Nashville Skyline* in 1969 and on various albums by Kris Kristofferson and Joan Baez. By 1979, his reputation had spread to such far (out) reaches of the world as Cork City. Planxty do him proud on this pacific version of his tale of the ill-fated outlaw Billy Gray.

Andy's first offering is a very old song extracted from the *Sam*

Henry Collection. 'Roger O'Hehir' tells the story of a boy from Eight Mile Bridge in County Down from 'honest parents of fame and renown'. Roger, however, fails to remain on the straight and narrow. Love-turned-sour prompts a life of pilfering, on the run from the law and morbidly concludes with our hapless anti-hero swinging from the rope. 'Roger never amounted to much, we fear,' writes Andy in the sleeve-notes. The words are set to delicately plucked strings and whispering flute. In a sense, Roger seems like an unworthy and incongruous subject matter for such refined, pastoral folk music, but such was Planxty's wicked juxtaposition of moods and themes.

Andy's next undertaking is an outstanding highlight in his singing career, 'Kellswater'. It's another diamond culled from the *Sam Henry Collection*, courtesy of John Moulden's book, *Songs of the People*. According to the sleeve-notes: 'It appears to have come originally from one Jim Carmichael of Ballymena, County Antrim.' Like much of Planxty's repertoire, the song is alive with smitten young couples, angry fathers, rocky boat trips and the menacing threat of the gallows. Although, unlike several other songs here, this one doesn't brandish a bloody ending. On the sleeve-notes, Andy even goes so far as to congratulate the hero and heroine for being the only surviving characters on this entire album!

His third and final song on *The Woman I Loved So Well* is the famous Scots ballad 'Johnny of Brady's Lea', which features yet another outlaw central character. In this particularly violent tale, our central character's weakness is poaching. Ignoring his mother's warning, he sets off with his two grey dogs to hunt deer. After a successful hunt, he and the dogs gorge themselves on venison and deer blood until they become heavy with sleep. The seven resident foresters get wind of the theft and attack Johnny in his slumber, wounding him mortally. The words are graphic in detail:

> *And the buttons that were on his coat were of the gold*
> *   so good,*
> *And the two grey dogs that he lay between, their mouths*
> *   were dyed with blood.*
>
> *And the very first shot that the foresters fired, it*
> *   wounded him in the thigh,*
> *And the very next shot that the foresters fired, his heart's*
> *   blood blinded his eye.*

Despite being ambushed, Johnny somehow manages to kill six of the seven foresters, leaving the seventh man with seven broken ribs, a broken arm and collarbone, but well enough to ride off to tell this gory tale. The song has been sung to numerous titles through the years – and dates from at least the early seventeenth century. It is listed in the *Child Ballads* as 'Johnnie Cock'. Ewan McColl sang 'Johnnie O'Breadisley' and also 'Johnny O'Braides-Lee', and June Tabor recorded 'Johnny O'Bredislee'. According to Andy, 'Johnny Moynihan sings a version called 'Johnny O'Cocklesmuir' where the hero kills six, wounds one and rides off unscathed.'

The Woman I Loved So Well ends in grandiloquent style. Christy Moore sings an eleven-minute-plus, twenty-eight-verse ballad that is universally deemed one of the epic sagas of the folk stratosphere, 'Little Musgrave', a song he had previously recorded for his self-titled 1976 album. It takes a special voice to sing such a poetically sewn monolith of folklore. The story follows the forbidden love of a gallant knight referred to as Little Musgrave and the wife of his lordship, Lady Barnard.

> *It fell upon a holy day as many's in the year,*
> *Musgrave to the church did go to see fine ladies there.*
> *And some were dressed in velvet red and some in velvet*
> *   pale,*

> *And then came in Lord Barnard's wife, the fairest among*
> *   them all.*

Having exchanged twinkling love-struck glances at church, a furtive love blossoms. The couple flee to a secret retreat, but Lady Barnard's foot-page, loyal to his Lord, is compelled to blow the whistle on this adulterous act.

> *'I have loved you fair lady, full on and many's the day.'*

> *'And I have loved you Little Musgrave, and never a word*
> *   did say.'*

> *'I've a bower in Bucklesfordbury, it's my heart's delight.*
> *I'll take you back there with me, if you lie in my arms*
> *   tonight.'*

Lord Barnard spends many verses trailing the betraying couple, and when he finally catches up with them, swords are raised, blows are exchanged and blood is spilled. It is Musgrave's blood, but the killing doesn't stop there.

> *'How do you like his cheeks?' he said. 'How do you like*
> *   his chin?*
> *How do you like his dead body, now there's no life*
> *   within?'*

> *'It's more I like his cheeks,' she cried. 'And more I want his*
> *   chin.*
> *It's more I love that dead body, than all thy kith and kin.'*

> *He's taken out his long long sword, to strike that mortal*
> *   blow,*
> *Through and through the lady's heart, the cold steel it did*
> *   go.*

> 'A grave, a grave,' Lord Barnard cried, 'to put these lovers
> in,
> With me lady on the upper hand. She came from better
> kin.'
>
> 'For I've just killed the finest knight that ever rode a steed.
> And I've just killed the finest lady that ever did a woman's
> deed.'

People all over the world continue to speculate on the origin of this song. Some have suggested that these noble characters did actually exist. Others believe the words are based on a stage play. Maybe it's a combination of the two. It clearly has travelled and has been modified along the folk process. The song has been performed and recorded by countless artists including Joan Baez, Fairport Convention, Doc Watson, Peggy Seeger and Ewan MacColl.

As he famously explains when introducing this song on stage, Christy first found the lyrics on pieces of paper scattered on the floor of an auctioneer's in Dublin. On the album sleeve he explains: 'I was lucky enough to collect a tune from a Nic Jones album on a field trip through Liam O'Flynn's flat.'

Whatever of its colourful, meandering history, Christy makes the song his own with this diction-perfect narration. The accompanying strings sparkle with a sequined constellation of notes. Liam's pipes are a vital second voice in the song, illustrating the key moments such as the shrill of the warning horns and the sorrowful lament for the murdered lovers.

Matt Molloy leads an elegiac outro of 'Paddy Fahy's Reel' on the flute as the album fades out. 'I first heard the adjoining tune in a dressing room in Germany when, having just died the death, Matt played to us and made me forget where I was for three minutes, twenty-three seconds,' wrote Christy. And so ends *The Woman I Loved So Well*, leaving the listener with an enchanting sense of displacement, tingling with snapshots of other worlds, ancient times, fantastic fairytales and sinister fables.

The Woman I Loved So Well was wrapped up with a reception at Windmill Lane on 9 June 1980. 'The next band in was Status Quo,' continues Noel. 'They overlapped our session. There was an unreal amount of champagne in the studio as we finished the album, so we ended up having this almighty party with the four lads from Status Quo. We'd a great hooley altogether. The album got well washed down. I was nearly going to say, I'll never forget it, but I forget most of it.'

Pat Musick was invited to tackle the artwork once again. She responded with her finest work for Planxty, creating a dreamlike woodland portrait, like an illustration from an old children's storybook with intricately detailed Celtic framework. 'I was in London, finally writing my postgraduate thesis,' explains Musick. 'Tara sent me a cassette tape of the album, and I played it over and over and over, listening and absorbing the music, the "feel" of it, the images in the lyrics. The overall feel of this album has always had, for me, a tremendous crystalline and delicate strength. All the songs are poignant. Even the ones where issues of injustice are raised, or the hero is a likeable outlaw. The instrumental subtexts involve a lot of countermelodies, intricate finger-picking, counterpoint, musical illustration or augmentation to the words. All this is quintessential Planxty, of course – it's just that these qualities are particularly apparent to me on this album, and this particular album as a whole has a flavour that, to me, suggested the intricacy, beauty, and gem-like quality of Persian manuscript illumination.

'Just about every image in it is taken from one of the songs – the "badlands that lie to the north of New Mexico" [from 'True Love Knows No Season'] is in the background, with the figure riding in on a grey horse because Roger O'Hehir recounts "I stole a grey horse"; the roses on either side of the central picture refer to "the rose of the morning, the pale flower of dawning" as well as "among wild roses we'll sing" [from 'Kellswater']. In bands above and below the central picture are the horn and sword from 'Little Musgrave', the bow from 'Johnny of Brady's Lea' and flames from 'Kellswater'.

'The interlace border is a reference to ancient Irish tradition motifs, and also, being a sort of chain-link design, it's an oblique suggestion of "may the chains of old Ireland bind around them" [from 'Kellswater']. The girl represents all the heroines in all the songs. Her gentle interaction with the deer was to emphasise the mood of innocence that later becomes tragedy in just about every one of the songs: on the back of the album I had an image of a deer struck by an arrow ("Johnny shot and the dun deer leapt/He's wounded her in the side"), symbolising the turn of events in most of the songs. Also on the back, the woman's reflected image in the stream was shown – without the woman sitting on the bank above it – meant to suggest the memory that lingers; "the woman I never forgot". The intricacy of detail, pattern, colour, and imagery in the art overall was meant to represent those qualities in the music.'

From the evidence of fine music recorded on *The Woman I Loved So Well* and the accompanying tours and performances, it appeared Planxty were engaged in a creative reverie. But it was an intermittent reverie. 'It couldn't last,' states Andy. 'From 1979 onwards we weren't always doing Planxty. We didn't go to the office once a week to see what the gigs were coming up. We did tours. Between tours, we didn't play together. It was different.'

The summer of 1980 was dotted with spurts of activity. In July, the pared-back original four-piece Planxty played a tour of Italian castles. Everyone remembers this tour with hazy satisfaction. Back in Ireland, they returned to The Boys of

Ballisodare festival on 9 August. Kevin Flynn was in his fourth year running the festival, and Marcus Connaughton, formerly of Polydor Records, was the publicist for Ballisodare. 'I was their Dublin office, so when Chuck Berry or Diz Dizzley or Ramblin' Jack Elliot or any of those guys came in, I'd meet them in Dublin and get some press set up,' explains Connaughton. 'Lofty was a rogue, but a very likeable rogue. He was like something out of a movie because he wore white suits. He was also quite generous. He was a sort of an Arthur Daly of the promoting world. You might describe him as mercurial.'

Bill Whelan was now performing live with the group and he was joined by another new addition to the line-up in the form of a young Cork fiddler by the name of Nollaig Casey. Casey, who is nowadays considered one of Ireland's greatest fiddlers, hails from a well-known West Cork music family. Her prodigious aptitude for music – both traditional and classical – at a young age propelled her into the limelight. She was proficient not just with the bow, but also on piano, tin whistle, uilleann pipes and as a singer. She won several All-Ireland titles for her fiddle-playing, and best all-round performer in 1972. She left University College Cork with a music degree and became a professional player with the RTÉ Symphony Orchestra, and later became one of the leading freelance musicians in the country. She was right at home with the master multi-instrumentalists of Planxty.

'I knew Dónal quite well at that stage,' reveals Nollaig. 'I also knew Andy. I was in Dublin playing with the RTÉ Symphony Orchestra at the time. Dónal was working on the music for a film called *Shadows of our Skin*, based on the Jennifer Johnston book. He asked me to play on this. I was very young at the time, twenty-one maybe. We rehearsed the music in Andy's house and Dónal and Andy obviously decided they liked my playing. So some time after Planxty re-formed, Dónal got in touch and asked would I play with them. It was a huge honour.'

Both Nollaig and Bill Whelan joined the band in the second half of the Planxty live set. It was an opportunity for the public to witness both sides of Planxty – the steadfast correlation of the core four-piece and their visions of a more expansive music.

'I'll never forget the Ballisodare Festival,' comments Bill Whelan with fond amusement. 'I drove up from Limerick. I had the tape on in the car and I was listening to the tunes and feverishly trying to remember everything. I arrived and I discovered that Dónal was producing everybody, so he was off working on other stages and in other tents as is Dónal's wont. Andy was somewhere else with a friend. There was no sign of Christy, no sign of Nollaig Casey. So I found myself alone on the stage for the rehearsal with Liam O'Flynn, who I had hardly spoken to because he wasn't really around for the early rehearsals. He came in looking resplendent, so tidy. He put down the pipes and opened up *The Irish Times* and sat down on the stage in his position while I set up my Fender Rhodes.

'People kind of arrived and looked around and went away,' continues Whelan. 'Eventually everybody seemed to sneak up on the rehearsal and then suddenly we were all together and off we went. And then, at the end of it, everyone had to go off and do other things. Dónal went off to produce the world, Andy went off to meet a friend, Christy had a meeting with someone or other and there I was left looking at Liam again, who I still hadn't really talked to. He said to me, "What are you doing?" "Well," I said, "we're not on until eleven." It was about two o'clock in the afternoon. He said, "Sure we'll go out to Lofty's for a pint." And we went out to Strandhill and we had several pints and lunch. We had a great time. I began to meet all Liam's friends, these people who sort of appeared occasionally. We had a fantastic afternoon, went to bed, got up in the evening and played a great gig.

'It was at Ballisodare that I met all kinds of other people for the first time. I met Tommy Hayes and Steve Cooney hanging around with Stockton's Wing and there was a kind of electricity in the air there. There was a great sense that there was a lot happening and there was a lot of cross-play of musicians and a lot of openness musically, which was terrific.'

Planxty were back in rehearsal just two days after Ballisodare to prepare a set for a week of shows scheduled in the Olympia Theatre in Dublin from 18–23 August 1980. It was to be another milestone in their career, but also one with controversial repercussions years later. Each of the Olympia concerts was recorded seemingly for the purpose of a future release. Seven years later, the tapes became the subject of dispute when Kevin Flynn – by now Planxty's *former* manager – compiled a double cassette release entitled *The Best of Planxty Live*. 'We taped everything every night and I waded through every tape and I made a shortlist of the best recordings,' explains Flynn.

In 1987, the tapes were released without the band being consulted. Mattie Fox, at this time Christy's manager, stepped in to assist the band in their obstruction of the release. 'We managed to get it stopped, but it was actually released and there are copies floating around,' continues Christy. 'It's okay. I'm drunk on it, which is fuckin' terrible. I'm very embarrassed about it. I do all these long introductions. I would still squirm if I happen to hear it.'

The credits on the original tape-sleeve read: 'Produced by Kevin Flynn and Michael Germaine, and Engineered and edited by Brian Masterson.' Although John Cook released the album, there is no mention of Tara Records. In fact, no record company is credited. The sleeve also had the catalogue number printed on it – PLANX MC01.

'What happened was Lofty Flynn had paid the band money for a French tour and he never got it from the French promoter,' explains Andy. 'He decided to recoup it by putting out the Olympia tapes. We must have recorded all the gigs with a thought to doing something with them. The next thing was he brought out this double cassette with the help of John Cook.

'I don't blame anybody really individually for doing that,' continues Andy. 'An injunction was taken against printing the thing, but they're all out there. I think it's very good, actually. I didn't know Christy was drunk. He doesn't sound drunk to me, he sounds great. I think the other three felt it was a bit warts 'n' all and, I must admit, I didn't agree with that. It was a live album! I wasn't ashamed at all. If there was a bit of glitch or something not quite right, fuck it, that's the way it was. I didn't feel as precious about it as the others. But I certainly agreed to go ahead and stop it being printed. Kevin was okay. He obviously did it because he knew if he'd asked us we'd have said no. So he just went ahead and did it. He was like that.'

The first anyone knew about the Olympia tapes being on sale was when Christy saw them in HMV in Grafton Street. 'As with all things of this nature, it had far more impact because we weren't consulted on the idea.' explains Dónal. 'So it felt a bit like having something stolen from us. Worse again, we'd already decided these performances weren't good enough to be offered for sale. I have to say it was gratifying for us to be able to stop the sales and retrieve all copies and masters; often in these situations once things get this far, nothing can be done.'

The intriguing 1980 Olympia tapes are sequenced like a live performance with the first half, second half after the interval and the encore. It begins with Andy and Dónal playing 'The Plains of Kildare'. The song doesn't exist on any official

Planxty album, although an excellent version of the song opens Andy's 1976 album with Paul Brady. Liam and Christy enter the stage and instantly a mood of giddiness prevails. Christy says, 'I'd like to thank Andy and Dónal for a very fine set they did there ... best support band me and Liam played with for a long time.'

The band continues as a four-piece for the first part of these concerts, while Bill Whelan and Nollaig Casey wait in the wings. When they do enter the stage, Nollaig kick-starts a set of jigs in fine style and, once again, the addition of another traditional musician on the tunes really gives Planxty that extra depth.

Throughout it all, Christy continues to joke and mess around with the between-song banter, sometimes quite surreally. He jibes the other band members for the length of time it takes to tune their instruments: 'Give us a shout when you're in tune and we'll start. Y'see Dónal and Andy played in the Artane Boys' Band and if you played out of tune, you got a dig, y'know, so they're afraid to play out of tune. There's a big Christian Brother behind the curtain with a leather!'

The Olympia tapes include several more titles never officially recorded by the band: 'The Emigrant's Farewell', Liam's solo piece, the double jig 'The Gold Ring', Barney Rush's 'Nancy Spain' and Bill Caddick's 'John O'Dreams' – two songs more indelibly associated with Christy's solo repertoire. They also perform a lovely rendition of Jack Warshaw's protest classic 'No Time for Love', although this song would later become more synonymous with the group Moving Hearts, which featured both Dónal and Christy.

Bill Whelan's lasting memories of the Olympia shows are of standing ovations and a pervasive sense of warmth and appreciation from the audiences. 'In those days, people didn't do standing ovations. Nowadays, they do them all the time but, in those days, you really had to work hard to get a standing ovation. The audience were with the band the whole way from the first note. You could feel that fantastic rush that came from the audience when you changed from one tune to another tune and move off in a different key and there's always an energy to the build-up of the arrangement and each time there was another wave of recognition from the audience.'

Bill had entered the Planxty fold with great respect for the musicianship of Dónal Lunny, Andy Irvine and Liam O'Flynn, but now he had first-hand awareness of Christy Moore's invaluable presence. 'He was extraordinary,' exclaims Whelan. 'He was exactly as we all think he is. In those days, things were a little more chaotic than they are now. It was wild. Christy just had that thing where he could just walk out there and the whole band came in behind him like this large engine, but he led it. And yet everybody felt they had their place and he was deferential to everybody's particular input. Nevertheless, there was no mistaking that it was Christy who was relating to the audience. It was his particular brand of humour they connected with. He was the focus. He had an absolutely common touch and could reach out to an enormous number of people. I think it was through Christy's conduit that the filigree of Andy and Liam's piping and the slightly more detailed approach to music was introduced to audiences. It was because Christy was there that all of a sudden he was able to turn a spotlight on these individuals and deliver them to the public in a way that they may not have done in another outfit.'

Throughout this period, the make-up of Planxty was going through continual changes, but one factor remained constant: the humour. As the most recent new members, Nollaig Casey and Bill Whelan witnessed this in its full effect, sometimes with painful results.

'One story that I'll never forget is when on tour in France and we were staying in this place in Rennes, I think it was actually a boarding school,' recalls Nollaig. 'There were these long stone corridors and we were having relay races up and down the corridors and somebody came up with the bright idea of throwing a pillow out the window and there would be a prize for the person who got the pillow first, which was down in the yard, about three floors down.'

Bill also remembers this incident in detail. 'There was a bit of tour cabin fever going on. There was some sort of mad game invented. Christy, at the time, was being very good, and didn't approve of any of this carry-on. Andy mischievously introduced another refinement to the game where on the way down you had to bang on Christy's door. I was a bit of a new boy, so I was nervous about getting fully involved. I remember standing in the hall and the door of Christy's room opened and he stood there wrapped in a blanket like a ghost and he walked down to the van and banged the van door and that was the end of it.'

'I was quite a good runner and I ran like the hammers of hell down the three flights of stairs and literally jumped out the front door,' continues Nollaig. 'It was two o'clock in the morning and pitch dark. I'd forgotten there were about ten steps leading up to the front door, so I literally sailed out into the air, landed with a thud. I broke my foot but I didn't realise it at the time so I kept running for another fifty yards with a broken foot to get the pillow.'

Bill remembers the frosty atmosphere the following day because Christy had been kept awake by the rest of the band's carry-on. 'So that night on stage in Paris, when he was introducing everyone to a surprised Parisian audience, he'd introduce me and then he said, "And then beside him we have a young woman on the fiddle, and well, last night, as you can see, she got plastered in Paris and plastered in Paris!"'

'It was hilarious stuff,' continues Bill. 'I enjoyed touring with them very much. There was great camaraderie with the band and the crew, Norman Verso and Jimmy Hickey and all those guys. Also my memory of Lofty was great. For one thing, we always got paid. He had a certain style. I remember arriving at one of the gigs in Brittany in a rainstorm. It was raining so heavily you could actually see the rain dripping down along the wires of the lights inside the marquee. Lofty walked in and said, "Okay, we're certainly not playing here," and he had a big row with the promoter, got some money and left. And afterwards he said, "I couldn't expose the band to that sort of danger." I had a very good feeling about Lofty.'

Fun as they were, the tours and the accompanying craic became less common for Planxty as other quests were calling each individual member. Just as Christy, Andy and Dónal were branching out with new projects, bands and collaborations, Liam O'Flynn, the quiet man of Planxty, was engaged in other visions of his own. By 1981, he was involved in a project called *The Brendan Voyage* – his collaboration with composer Shaun Davey (Dónal's old comrade from Bugle), which became a huge success. The theme of Davey's work is based on the epic voyage of Tim Severin who, in 1976, set sail in a small leather-covered boat to retrace the voyage undertaken by St Brendan, Abbot of Clonfert in 500 AD. Many scholars believe that St Brendan and his team of missionaries actually made it to the New World in this meagre boat, and it was Severin's mission to put this legend to the test. Led by Severin's written account of his remarkable journey, Davey musically portrayed the expedition from Brandon Creek, County Kerry, past the Faroe Islands, the Cliffs of Mykines, Iceland, and the icy waters of Labrador, before finally docking safely in Newfoundland.

'Shaun Davey initially came to me with the idea of composing one tune for the uilleann pipes based on Tim Severin's account,' explains Liam. 'That went quite well, so we did another one, and then another one and he eventually decided we should tell the story of the whole voyage through music. The pipes represent the small leather boat. The next thing was to figure out what instruments could represent the wind and the storms and the rocky seas. Shaun decided an orchestra was the only thing that could do it, and at the time the idea of traditional instrumentation and classical instrumentation was very new. It became something that I did regularly from then on. It turned out the uilleann pipes really worked in this context as a sort of central instrument.'

As these new horizons opened up, the activities of Planxty became more and more disjointed. A natural evolution was challenging Liam, Christy, Dónal and Andy to take their abilities to new pastures and new heights. In the coming years, they were set to encounter orchestras, rock groups and musicians of all disciplines.

But there was life in the old dog yet; festivals, tours, recordings, television and even more new members entered the fray, as the Planxty revolving door began to creak into action once again.

Chapter 17

Words & Music

Some music groups are formed around the vision of one artist, and some are equal creative collaborations between two or more artists. Planxty very much sits in the latter category and has, for the most part, featured four musicians who each make an equally essential contribution to the group. Bands such as these are rare entities and generally only come together in fortuitous circumstances. When you consider the singular ability of each musician involved, one cannot reasonably expect a group such as Planxty to stay together indefinitely. Artists of this high calibre will inevitably face new challenges in their individual journeys, and those challenges won't necessarily correspond to those of their colleagues.

By 1981, Christy Moore and Dónal Lunny were faced with this exact dilemma – they discovered creative challenges that Planxty simply couldn't cater for. For Christy, it was a matter of repertoire once again. New songs were entering his conscious-ness, songs that addressed social issues, some of which were long-standing, some of which were directly related to Ireland's bleak mood at the start of the 1980s. Christy's need to change gear coincided with Dónal's desire to explore new rhythmic possibilities within the music. Again, Dónal couldn't quite find what he was looking for within the Planxty framework. This problem partly inspired the formation of a new group, Moving Hearts.

'I wanted to put wheels on Planxty at that stage with bass and percussion and I was tardy about it,' explains Dónal. 'I was just talking. I did go into the studio and record something, but it actually went sideways on me. Also, there was the eternal problem that once you bring in the bass and the drums they become locked together in a certain way, which is very difficult to avoid. It's down to the musicians, the drummer and the bass player, and what their experience of music is – and usually it's rock. Trying to sort of circumvent that was a huge problem. It was just too hard to make them take on different roles. In hindsight, I think what we needed wasn't a drum kit, but percussion. It could've been managed that way maybe.'

'I had been banging on about it for a while and Christy came to me one day and said, "Look, that idea that you had, why don't we take that forward?" So the next person we contacted was Declan Sinnott and out came Moving Hearts, singing all the songs that didn't fit into the Planxty repertoire. That was really where Moving Hearts came from. That became the platform and the outlet for what Christy wanted to say. But, way back in the earlier days, it didn't feel right to sing songs that were outright political. 'Only Our Rivers Run Free' was maybe the only one.'

The Moving Hearts line-up fluctuated initially. Bill Whelan left after one rehearsal, and renowned musicians such as Richie

Buckley and Tommy Moore quickly came and went. But soon this unusual new band started to take shape. Brian Calnan from Cork was drafted as drummer. Eoghan O'Neill joined on bass. Davy Spillane, an exciting young uilleann piper from Dublin, also signed up, as did jazz saxophonist Keith Donald. Here was a collective from a variety of musical backgrounds – rock, folk, blues, jazz and traditional – somehow finding common ground.

On their self-titled debut album, Moving Hearts spoke with a free poetry, with the songs of Philip Chevron, Joe Gibbs, Jim Page, Jack Warshaw and Jackson Browne. The songs are universal protest songs and Irish songs that lamented a bloody, brooding history, yet also celebrate the common people who struggled, fought and evolved throughout. Outside of their heterogeneous music, Moving Hearts had an egalitarian feeling that wasn't commonplace in the star-driven rock business.

Musically, Moving Hearts was a million miles from Planxty's layered acoustic sound. Where Planxty had turned the page for Irish music at the start of the 1970s, Moving Hearts heralded in the 1980s with this new amalgam of electric and traditional instrumentation.

'A more modern approach was deemed to be something that a band had to do at that time,' ponders Andy Irvine. 'Planxty was a bit stagnant by that point. I think people were moving in different directions. Everything has its season. Also, Christy was getting very heavily into political songs at this time and Planxty had never been a vehicle for that and I think Christy saw this too. I don't know. I think I would have been more malleable than Liam, but I don't know.'

Moving Hearts and Planxty ran parallel for maybe a couple of years, but Moving Hearts took off pretty quickly. Andy says that he and Liam felt a little sidelined at the time. 'Christy sent a note saying that he felt he couldn't play with Planxty any more and one took it that Dónal was in the same boat, although no note has ever surfaced yet [laughing]!'

'At that stage, Dónal wanted to move in other musical directions with Planxty if possible, but if not, then in some other form,' says Liam. 'It wasn't happening for them musically with Planxty. I remember, at one stage, he said he wanted brass. Dónal was going somewhere that I really didn't have any interest in going. I knew that. Instinct tells you these things.'

For Christy Moore, Moving Hearts was an adrenalising, if brief, period of his life. They played all over the country with ferocious, intense live sets, including a legendary series of shows at the Baggot Inn in Dublin. But Christy only made it as far as album two, *Dark End of the Street* in 1982, before bailing out.

'We just lost the fuckin' plot completely,' says Christy. 'It became a whole chord game and fellas trying to outdo each other with how brilliant they were. There were very good times in the early days, but it would never have had the cohesiveness, musically, that Planxty had. I think the difference was that, in Planxty, there was four people focused on the music and in Moving Hearts it was never that way.'

Dónal continued with the group, making a live album before disbanding and later reforming for the acclaimed instrumental album *The Storm* in 1985. 'When Christy left the band, Mick Hanly joined. I had been making efforts to move the musical centre of Moving Hearts towards Irish music, and away from the mix of rock 'n' roll/jazz/Irish music that we were playing, and I hadn't succeeded in doing that. We were a sort of a rock band with traces of Irish music, and I felt it could have been a lot more.'

It became a tradition of its own that when any members of Planxty handed in their resignation, it was never quite clear-cut as to when they'd actually be leaving. In 1981, Planxty and

Moving Hearts operated concurrently. The end was inevitably drawing near for Planxty, and the consistency of the group's activities was splintered, but they still had time for a series of interesting one-off events. They faced their demons in March 1981 by returning to the scene of their disastrous comeback show in 1979 at the Hammersmith Odeon in London. Colin Irwin from *Melody Maker* was on hand to review the event and he emphasised the inherent pitfalls in introducing additional musicians into a group with such a close partisan following: 'There's a unique bond there which makes it difficult for new members to be accepted. So, the new Planxty line-up with Dónal Lunny, Andy Irvine, Christy Moore and Liam O'Flynn augmented by keyboard-player Bill Whelan and fiddler Casey took a long time to win confidence.'

Irwin also notes several developments in the live set: 'They now have a more modern, contemporary feel, which even embraces Ewan McColl's 'Go Move Shift' and a political Irish song 'No Time for Love' to climax the set; Whelan's keyboards giving them a harder edge, and Casey's classically flavoured fiddle stretching them in another direction entirely.'

He concludes the review with a positive and respectful tone: 'And they still prove that when O'Flynn lets loose on the pipes, Lunny sets the fire beneath him on bouzouki, Irvine drives along on mandolin, and Moore soars above it in that extraordinary sensitive voice, there's nothing on earth to touch them.'

Back in Ireland, the Ballisodare Festival in Sligo wasn't the only major folk event in the late 1970s. The Lisdoonvarna Folk Festival in County Clare got under way in 1978 and remained one of the biggest events on the cultural calendar for six years. Planxty, all its individual members and Moving Hearts all performed at Lisdoonvarna, but it was Christy Moore who became most synonymous with the festival in 1983 when he unveiled a brilliantly witty snapshot portrait of this great gathering of personalities in his song about the festival 'Lisdoonvarna'.

> *A 747 for Jackson Browne,*
> *They had to build a special runway just to get him down.*
> *Before The Chieftains could start to play,*
> *Seven creamy pints came out on a tray.*
> *Shergar was ridden by Lord Lucan,*
> *Seán Cannon did the backstage cookin'.*
> *Clannad were playin' 'Harry's Game',*
> *Christy was singin' 'Nancy Spain'.*
> *Mary O'Hara and Brush Shiels,*
> *Together singin' 'The Four Green Fields'.*
> *Van the Man and Emmylou,*
> *Moving Hearts and Planxty too!*

Lisdoonvarna was founded and promoted by Paddy Doherty and Jim Shannon. Paddy Doherty was born in Kilshanny, County Clare. As a youth, he frequented the musical mecca of Doolin and embryonic visions of a unique music festival flickered in his mind from an early age.

'I was still in school when I thought of putting on an outdoor festival,' recalls Doherty. 'I remember going to see *Woodstock* the movie. I think I went to see it three or four times in the one week. I was just blown away by the whole idea. I was obviously very young and had no involvement in the music business at that time, but it stuck with me. When I left school, I didn't do anything too serious. I went to England for a year. I was so consumed by this idea of the festival that I felt that whatever I was doing was just a temporary situation. I was totally obsessed with it. I was trying to convince different people to listen to me.

'Eventually, my partner Jim Shannon came on board. Jim was

a friend of mine who was going to college in Galway. We hung around together. I mentioned the idea to him and he just thought it was brilliant. We originally tried to start in 1977 but it didn't happen. We then decided to go a different route. The Ballisodare Festival was under a tent and we decided to have it outdoors and to bring in all different types of music. We wanted to place traditional music on a rock-style stage. It was like a mix of traditional, rock and all sorts of world music, if you like. We also had this idea, which we did over several years, to have Irish step-dancing on a rock stage. So we had this mix and, from the very first year, the mix worked really well.'

Setting up a major outdoor music festival in the late 1970s in Ireland was a fairly unprecedented and politically messy venture, as Paddy Doherty and Jim Shannon soon discovered. 'There was a huge amount of controversy around this event. Some local people objected. At that time, there wasn't a licensing system in process. The only licence that we required was to sell drink, which was very important for this kind of event, and we were turned down. A certain number of people objected in the local court, including the parish priest, who stood up in front of the judge and said he had a moral obligation to come down and object to a licence being granted for this event. Eventually, we went to the circuit court and we got the licence and we won the case. It was all over the papers. You've no idea how that felt.

'We needed a headline act in 1978 and we wanted The Chieftains,' continues Doherty. 'We were summoned to Dublin to meet them in The Clarence Hotel. It was like a big corporate-type room. They were all sitting around a big table and us at one end. We were quizzed up and down about all this controversy. Will it happen? Or won't it happen? But we knew we needed them confirmed. We'd convinced a bank manager down here to give us enough money to pay a deposit on their fee, which we did at the meeting, to seal the deal. It was a battle all the way, but we were young and there was nothing going to stop us. Christy also played the first Lisdoonvarna. For months before the festival, I hounded him. We had this number for him in Kilkenny, where he was living at the time, but he was never there. Obviously, there were no mobile phones in those days so we would physically have to go to Dublin to find him. At that particular time, he tended to hang out in folk venues in Dublin like The Meeting Place in Dorset Street. We would go in there in the hope we would meet him and, eventually, we did. We talked to him and we described what we were doing. Christy was always a great listener. I don't think he really committed to it then though. So we went to Dublin again to a place called The Grapevine Arts Centre where there was an old folk club. We met him again there and we had a chat and he decided to do it.'

Over six years, Lisdoonvarna became a huge cultural event. As Paddy Doherty explained, their vision of presenting traditional Irish arts and music with international folk stars such as Roy Harper and Richard and Linda Thompson, and big rock, blues and country acts such as Thin Lizzy, Rory Gallagher, Van Morrison and Emmylou Harris, was a great success.

Christy remembers the excitement of 1981. 'Planxty was third on the bill after Chris De Burgh and Paul Brady. History has it that this was the biggest crowd at Lisdoonvarna. De Burgh was huge at the time.'

Paddy Doherty remembers Planxty playing Lisdoonvarna in 1981 too. 'Mattie Fox was managing them. I remember meeting him in the Old Ground Hotel in Ennis. We were very new to the business. We had this vision of what everybody in the business looked like. Mattie looked very different in the sense that he was very conservatively dressed. We found him very approachable. I don't know what he really thought of us. We had a strange mix that particular year. We had bands like Steel Pulse, The Beat, John Sebastian, John Martyn, Roy Harper, Dr Feelgood; it was amazing. The first year we had about 15,000 people there. We gradually worked up to 40,000 by the end.'

One member of Planxty who was particularly busy at Lisdoonvarna was Dónal Lunny. He manned the festival sound desk for the three years from 1981. In 1981, he performed with Planxty and Moving Hearts, while fulfilling his soundman duties over the same frantic weekend.

'I ran away from the sound desk, changed my trousers, and ran up to play with Planxty,' laughs Dónal, recalling his hectic schedule. 'Paddy Doherty and Jim Shannon were brilliant. They were fighting enormous obstacles to get it together. There was local resistance, there was the weather, and there was the whole business of hiring stuff and getting people in and the risk involved, but they made it happen. It was a fantastic achievement. I loved being on board. I have to say, though, when I was doing the sound for Lisdoon, I wasn't qualified. There were aspects of the technicalities that I didn't understand that I needed to understand, so it should have been better. One of the standout performances for me was Emmylou Harris. I can still see her singing 'Queen of the Silver Dollar'. It was just beautiful, massive, like an ocean liner coming at you.'

Just as it reads in Christy's song, everyone flocked to Lisdoonvarna – rock stars, politicians and celebrities from all walks of life – celebrating Irish music culture with international friends. But, for many people, the abiding memory of Lisdoonvara was a lone, gaunt piper seated in the middle of the stage, playing dark, ancient music to the assembled folkies, hippies, liggers, luvvies and rockers.

'Séamus Ennis was amazing,' states Paddy Doherty. 'We both got very close to him. We always treated him very, very well. He'd come down a few days beforehand and go to the Willie Clancy Summer School. We'd pick him up and take him to the festival. He loved the outdoors. I remember one year he followed a punk band and just went up there on his own and played the pipes and they just loved him.'

Liam O'Flynn also harbours similar memories of seeing one of his mentors on the big stage. 'My abiding memory of all the Lisdoonvarnas was seeing Séamus up there on that huge stage. It's amazing to think that this guy sitting in the middle of the stage playing slow airs on a set of uilleann pipes could hold his own in a line-up of big folk and rock acts. The audience stood there listening, totally appreciating the significance of it all.'

1981 saw more unforeseen Planxty activity. Bill Whelan had produced Johnny Logan's winning Eurovision Song Contest entry 'What's Another Year' in 1980. This meant the Eurovision would be staged in Ireland the following year. Producer Ian McGarry invited Whelan to write something for the centrepiece of the programme, which would be performed during the interval of the competition.

'I thought about it and then I suggested getting Planxty and Dónal involved,' explains Whelan. 'It seemed to me to be an opportunity to present the band internationally in the way that the Eurovision can do. Also, we had the lucky position of not being in the competition and not dragged into all that stuff. Instead, we had our own little special position, which, of course, was subsequently to happen with *Riverdance* some years later. I met with Dónal and we talked about it and we went back to Ian McGarry with the plan that Planxty would do it and I would write something for it and Dónal and myself would write something jointly for it. I was very much excited by the work that I was doing with Dónal at that stage and wanted to continue the marriage.'

Timedance was a three-part suite of elegant baroque-influenced traditional music, later released as a Planxty single on seven-inch and twelve-inch formats. The line-up also included Nollaig Casey on fiddle, a rock rhythm section of drums and electric bass, and a five-piece brass section. The first piece was a traditional arrangement by Dónal, Liam and Bill of a tune learned from Junior Crehan called 'The Humours of Barrack Street' and the second and third parts, 'Isercleran' and 'Ballymun Regatta', were co-written by Bill and Dónal. The single version of *Timedance* was released on WEA with a version of Barney Rush's 'Nancy Spain' on the 'B' side. 'Nancy Spain' was a song Planxty played live, but it later became more associated with Christy's repertoire. Planxty's presence at the Eurovision Song Contest was nothing short of surreal. Picture them playing this elegant, crafted music amongst this onslaught of slightly ridiculous pop exhibitionists from around Europe. The winners that year, incidentally, were Bucks Fizz, a sort of smiling, day-glo British replication of the successful formula of the two-guys-and-two-girls singing quartet as mastered by the hugely successful Swedish act, ABBA. They weren't exactly typical of the sort of acts Planxty were used to sharing the bill with. The Planxty performance was rendered even more phantasmagoric by the addition of contemporary ballet dancers cavorting on the stage in front of the musicians. How Christy Moore kept a straight face remains a mystery.

When later asked for his recollections on the *Timedance* episode, Christy wrote:

This was the time of the Fender Rhodes and ballerinas with legs as long as wet weeks. How could a fellow concentrate on his humble bodhrán with such shenanigans? The Irish Ballet Company, no less, and poor

Liam trying to keep the reed cool in his chanter while Andy was batin' out some auld whoro in 19/17 time, and Dónal was in his element winking at dancing divas and laying it all down at the same time as Steely-Dan Whelan was reverberating the auld ivories like a barrister on acid, whilst the Cork wan Casey was laying loving lines of pure music over the top of us all. There were ballerinas and men kicking legs in all directions as we rehearsed for the interval spot of the 1981 Eurovision Song Contest. Our manager, Baron Von Rise 'n' Shine, told us that this was our big chance to be megalithic. There would be 680 million people watching the shite and every one of them would want to see Planxty in The Baggot thereafter ... My hole!

But no one got hurt or arrested and, as memory serves me, there was a night of champagne and capers. There is a twelve-inch of it kicking about and, doubtless, it is a fine piece of work. I had no input into its creation apart from a few taps on the riddle rim and plenty of encouragement to Liam who was sitting beside me. 'The Ballymun Regatta' will never be forgotten. The main men in the writing of Timedance were Dónal Lunny, Andy Irvine and Bill Whelan. Liam provided the principal sounds and I hung around for the craic doing my utmost not to compromise the shebang. After that version of Planxty ran its course, Bill Whelan went with it on into Riverdance and achieved world domination with Son-of-Timedance. More power to him, although I've always felt personally that more acknowledgement was due to his erstwhile cohorts in Planxty; Dónal Lunny and Andy Irvine. That is a personal view and I've never heard either of them voice a similar view. If only Flatley and Jean Butler had been around a few years earlier we'd all be fartin' through silk.

'We all used to get great entertainment from watching the Eurovision Song Contest, but definitely not in the way the presenters intended,' chuckles Dónal in retrospect. 'It was an unusual context for Planxty, to say the least, but as we weren't part of the actual circus, it felt okay – and somewhat exciting. It's interesting ... Because my notion of adding bass and percussion to Planxty was greeted with unease by the other three, *Timedance* afforded me an opportunity to at least briefly swim in different musical waters. My contribution to the triptych, 'Ballymun Regatta', was arranged for orchestra by Bill. And though I wasn't happy with aspects of it, being out of my depth in the realm of orchestration, I think Bill did a great job.'

Bill Whelan explains that he wrote 'Isercleran' in a house called St Cleran in Galway. 'The older name was Isercleran and I wrote it literally as a planxty for the place. I did all the orchestral arrangements and Dónal and I did the rhythm-section arrangements between us. At that stage, I had started working with Paul McAteer as a drummer on other projects, so we brought him in. Ian McGarry got this choreographer called Ailish McCourtney-Baldwin. It was very balletic. It was contemporary ballet rather than traditional dance. I suppose there was an attempt to be contemporary rather than traditional.

'I remember doing a plane trip with Dónal,' recalls Bill. 'We had the first Sony Walkman machines and we were swapping Steely Dan tapes. We both had that real fascination with – you would have to call it – jazz sensibilities, syncopated rhythm sensibilities. Dónal can never do anything without being rhythmically interesting, and he has an extraordinary harmonic sense as well. Dónal and I had a lot of common interests.

'When we performed *Timedance* live it always got a fantastic response from the way the whole thing builds and comes together. It's an exciting piece of music for a live performance.

We knew that 'The Humours of Barrack Street' was an important thing to have there to satisfy Liam's desire to keep that connection to the tradition. Liam was always standing on some rock to do with the tradition and that was great. Those kind of energies have a real value.'

As it transpired, *Timedance* pre-empted a grander manifestation of Bill Whelan's vision for a contemporary Irish music composition and performance. In 1994, Dublin was host to the Eurovision Song Contest for the fourth time and Bill Whelan was, once again, invited to contribute to the interval entertainment. *Riverdance* was an extravaganza of furious Irish dance choreography and sweeping, orchestrated Irish music that proved to be the most spectacular half-time show the Eurovision, or any event of its ilk, had ever seen. The music was composed entirely by Whelan and performed by the Irish choral group Anúna, the RTÉ Concert Orchestra and an assortment of traditional musicians. The performance made instant stars of the lead dancers, Jean Butler and Michael Flatley. The single went straight to number one in Ireland and remained there for eighteen weeks. The show quickly became a huge hit in the theatres of London's West End, Broadway and all over the world, reaching its 5,000th performance in March 2002. Undoubtedly, *Riverdance* was one of Ireland's biggest cultural exports of the last decade. Many musicians and commentators see a direct link from *Timedance* to *Riverdance*.

'It was no mistake of mine to call it *Riverdance* because it connected absolutely to *Timedance*. It was a nod in a direction of where I believed it came from. My time in Planxty was at a time in my life when I was picking up many of my skills and finding my own voice in terms of my musical expression,' explains Whelan. 'It was very important and influential. I picked up other skills along the way. I learned to orchestrate and *The*

Seville Suite and *The Spirit of Mayo*, and all that. I had begun to work on a much larger scale and understand how an orchestra works and that's kind of a lot of what I do now in that area. But the seminal engine of that came from my association with Planxty and my association with Andy Irvine and Eastern European music, my own adventures with Spanish music and Brazilian music. They all form part of what I do, but are no less important in their individual position. For me, Planxty was essential.'

There was a strong feeling of uncertainty to Planxty in the early 1980s. They were making beautiful music together, but they were playing by and large to the same audience. The distractions of solo careers, new groups and collaborations prevented the band from making any real headway. If Planxty had taken the leap and toured the United States, circumstances may have been different. It had been touted in the music press on several occasions that they would take their music to America. In hindsight, it seems like an obvious move to make, and could well have been the making of the band on the international stage. But it never happened. Liam O'Flynn had already tasted life and music in America and was eager to return.

'At one point it was all set up to go,' states Liam. 'But Dónal and Christy decided they didn't want to do it. This must have been around the early 1980s. They had obviously talked about it together and then one day they announced that they couldn't visualise going to America. I was disappointed because I'd been to the States and I'd seen the sort of audiences that were out there and they absolutely would have gone bananas for Planxty. And I think it caused a lot of disappointment out there as well.'

Christy, Dónal and Andy remain hazy about plans of bringing Planxty to America, however. 'America is such a vast place that one can have so many different attitudes towards it,' says Christy. 'I love America. I love Americans. But one has difficulty with different aspects of the American dream or the American psyche. I've no recollection of what happened. But if Liam remembers it, it probably happened.'

Dónal doesn't remember this very well either, but acknowledges that they probably didn't want to go to America just to do the 'Irish thing'. 'There was that whole romantic thing, which probably still exists in the States. You have people who left during the Troubles and that's the last snapshot they have of the country, so this is how they still see it. Back then the same thing applied. Not just in politics, but the sentimentality and the distillation of that, which would end up in the shillelagh and shamrocks department, souvenirs of Ireland. "Give us 'Danny Boy', give us..." It all boiled down to the lowest common denominator. No harm to the people who saw it that way. It's just that's not what we were about. It's always an easy trap to fall into, to sort of reinforce the stereotype. We were always determined to try and avoid that and play to a broader public, to be musicians to play music that's worth listening to and not because it's Irish.

'I did go there with The Bothy Band and we did a few profoundly Irish gigs and they were exactly what I would have been afraid of if Planxty had gone out. But we also played to American people, 'open gigs', if you like. That was a really great experience and I've been to America loads of times since. My views are now a little broader than they used to be.'

A slightly puzzled Andy Irvine has no memory of any conversations about touring America. 'I think there was a period in 1982 when I was a little distanced from everybody else. I was down in a cottage in Wicklow getting new material together. I remember being very surprised to get a telegram from Liam saying: "Plan to proceed" or something really ambiguous. I'd no idea what it meant. And it was a plan to make the next album. I may have been a little out of the loop at that time. Liam might have known something I didn't.'

Planxty's 'plan to proceed' manifested itself in the shape of *Words & Music*, their sixth and final studio album. It seems odd now that Planxty went ahead with this recording given the fact that both Christy and Dónal had expressed their desire to leave. Andy Irvine's diaries even reveal that, in January 1982, himself, Liam and Bill Whelan had a meeting with popular English folk singer-songwriter Ralph McTell with a view to forging an alliance. Clearly nothing came of it because in March 1982, Planxty was rehearsing again, meeting with manager Mattie Fox and planning an eleven-date Irish tour in July. On 24 August, the band played the National Stadium in Dublin in a concert that was recorded by RTÉ. It would turn out to be the last concert the original four-piece played together.

Nonetheless, in October they began rehearsing for the album and, in late October and early November, they recorded *Words & Music* in Windmill Lane Studios in Dublin for the WEA label.

The album opens in fine style with a set of jigs, the famed double jig 'The Queen of the Rushes' and 'Paddy Fahy's Jig', named after the Galway fiddler of the same name. Andy sings the moving emigration ballad 'Thousands are Sailing', which details with lucid pathos the emigrant's last night at home, packing his bags, saying farewell, catching the train and departing from the shores. Andy also sings 'Accidentals'/'Aragon Mill'. 'Accidentals' is a self-penned instrumental, and 'Aragon Mill' was learned from the North Carolina singer Si Kahn, in which he applies his sensitive touch to another sad theme, that of the closing of a cotton mill and the subsequent termination of a way of life.

Christy tackles some big songs, Bob Dylan's 'I Pity the Poor Immigrant' from his 1967 album *John Wesley Harding*, and 'Lord Baker', another epic learned from the mouth of John Reilly.

Christy admits that *Words & Music* was the only Planxty album he felt disappointed with. 'Well, I was disappointed with certain things. I was disappointed listening back to 'I Pity the Poor Immigrant'. It's not a particularly good Planxty performance. It is a huge song and we never quite did it justice. Maybe some day the real band will have a go at it. Dylan should do it with us. I'd even forego my lead-vocal status for that one! I understand this song so well that I can almost imagine having written it myself. I think Liam really gets it too.'

Christy also feels that 'Lord Baker' never achieved what it could have achieved. 'I'd like to record it again too. 'Lord Baker' is the greatest song I've ever sung. It can't be sung at will. The setting has to be suitable and it needs the ears of at least one person who understands. Everything worth singing about is here in John Reilly's adaptation of this masterpiece. I've done a lot of work on it, but not many would notice. This song removes me from my reality. Many songs do, but none to this extent. It can almost break my heart with loneliness or raise it with joy. Planxty have yet to do the definitive version.'

Liam chose some interesting music for this album also, including 'Táimse Im' Chodladh' ('I'm Asleep'), an ancient *aisling* performed on the pipes. 'Séamus had just died and there was something going on inside me because of that. I remember recording the slow air 'Táimse Im' Chodladh' and feeling a strong sense of Ennis, who he was, what I'd got from him, and the fact that he wasn't going to be around any more,' explains Liam. 'Dónal Lunny produced this beautifully sympathetic accompaniment to the tune. That track is very powerful.'

''Táimse Im' Chodladh' is great,' says Andy. 'We tried to put bouzouki and hurdy-gurdy on that. I played the hurdy for hours to fit in with it until Christy came in with a sorrowful face and said, "Andy, it's really great, but we actually feel it's too much."

And they were right. It actually holds up much better on its own. It's lovely. I love it.'

Liam also contributed 'The Irish Marche', a sixteenth-century piece from composer William Byrd sourced from *My Ladye Nevell's Book of Virginal Music*, and it is one of a suite of twelve pieces entitled *The Battell*. On the album sleeve-notes, Liam suggests it might be inspired by an Irish clan march because 'it certainly has that feel about it'.

Words & Music was produced by Dónal and engineered by Andrew Boland. The sleeve-notes also credit Dónal with an array of obscure instruments, from ancient devices such as the spinnet (a small harpsichord-type instrument), the dulcimer (from the zither family), and the bowed psaltery (Greek instrument from the harp family), to the Prophet synthesizer. With Dónal's synthesizer, Bill Whelan's keyboards and bass guitarist Eoghan O'Neill on loan from Moving Hearts, this album has a strong contemporary feel, at least more so than any previous Planxty album. Nollaig Casey plays fiddle, as does James Kelly, consi-dered to be one of the greatest Irish fiddlers of his generation. Kelly is the Dublin-born son of the late John Kelly, the Clare fiddler and concertina player and one of the founding members of Seán Ó Riada's Ceoltóirí Chualann.

Words & Music suffers from being the least remembered and least celebrated of all the Planxty albums, due in no small part to the fact that the group had practically disbanded before they even started to record it. It was also the least satisfying recording for all members of Planxty.

'The thing I remember mainly about *Words & Music* was the band were hardly ever in the studio together,' ponders Christy. 'I remember Dónal and I being in the studio a lot. I remember a lot of overdubs. At the time, I thought it was quite good, but I don't remember it being a band vibe.'

By 1983, Christy Moore and Dónal Lunny had finally closed the door on Planxty, leaving original members Andy Irvine and Liam O'Flynn with additional member Bill Whelan pondering the future. After numerous meetings, they decided to keep the Planxty name and build a new group around these core members. They enlisted James Kelly on fiddle, Arty McGlynn on guitar and singer Dolores Keane, with Mattie Fox once again handling the role of manager.

Arty McGlynn is from Omagh, County Tyrone. His family's background is in traditional music; his mother played fiddle and his father played accordion. Arty himself was playing accordion from a young age, but it was the guitar that captured his enthusiasm as he grew up listening to jazz players such as Wes Montgomery and Barney Kessel. By the time he turned fifteen, he was playing professionally. After years playing in dance bands, travelling around the UK and the US, sometimes playing pedal steel, Arty was eventually drawn back towards the world of traditional Irish music. He made the album *McGlynn's Fancy* in 1979, hailed as a classic and considered the first real recording of guitar played in a true traditional style. By the time he teamed up with Planxty in 1983, he was an in-demand player.

Dolores Keane, from Caherlistrane, County Galway, is a singer and multi-instrumentalist who can play concertina, flute, whistle, hurdy-gurdy and bodhrán. Ciarán MacMathúna recorded her singing when she was just five years old. Prior to joining Planxty, she collaborated with her husband, John Faulkner, on several albums and was a member of one of the other great trad/folk ensembles, Dé Danann, for their self-titled debut album (produced by Dónal Lunny) before being replaced by Andy Irvine.

'We were looking for somebody who could play an instrument and sing and nobody came to mind,' explains Andy.

'And then I suddenly thought, "Dolores Keane plays the flute!" That was the band: Arty, Dolores, James Kelly, Bill, Liam and myself, which is a great line-up. Nollaig was very upset, and quite rightly too. She, in her inimitable way, rounded on me in the car once in Donnybrook and said, "Why am I not in the band?" I was very embarrassed and I had to lay it off on Liam, which was not totally fair.'

Andy Irvine later nicknamed this incarnation of the band as Planxty-Too-Far, as it seemed doomed to failure and perhaps not a good idea in the first place, given the fact that it was far removed from what Planxty actually was. 'History will tell you it was a mistake to call it Planxty, but it wasn't a huge mistake because it didn't do very well and no one remembers it, so that's okay. But it was interesting music. I don't think Liam was too into it. Liam often didn't turn up to rehearsal. It was very "Bill-influenced". If you work with Bill you will find yourself playing "Bill-influenced" music, which is fine because I like a lot of his music. Arty was up to that. We played chords that we would never even have heard of at the beginning of Planxty. A lot of it was really nice. It's never been heard before or since. There's about half a concert on tape. I liked it a lot but it never really settled in.'

Liam believes that the new formation didn't have the same force as the original Planxty. His feeling is that although the 'other' Planxtys were really exciting musically, they never made the impact of the original band.

Bill Whelan recalls that rehearsals didn't go too well, either. 'Planxty rehearsals were hard in the best of times. It was hard to assemble the people. "Planxty-Too-Far" rehearsals were *really* difficult. Many of them took place in my house in Ranelagh. People could arrive anything from on time to several hours later to the next day. It was a lovely group, but it was doomed in some ways. Andy, Liam and I wanted to keep going. You do invest emotionally in all of this. It's not just a gig. At the time, we were intent on keeping things going but, in hindsight, it probably wasn't the best judgement call and we would have been better to just let things go. Nevertheless it was a nice band, a great group of players. 'Moorlough Shore' was a fantastic piece and Dolores delivered it absolutely brilliantly. It had real promise, musically. But was it Planxty? That's the question.'

An ill-fated tour of Britain was the final straw for the Planxty-Too-Far project. They began at the Edinburgh Playhouse on Friday, 1 April 1983. 'We did a gig in Glasgow on the Sunday. The gig wasn't a great success. There didn't seem to have been much advertising for it. It wasn't until after that gig that we discovered the next gig on the Monday was not in the northeast – as we had been told – it was in Norfolk. Mattie didn't know the gig was not in the northeast until Sunday evening when there was no possibility of getting down to Aldeburgh to the Benjamin Britten Posthouse, a magnificent gig for a band like us. The band could not get there in time. It couldn't be done. We decided we had to pull that gig. So we went and had a few drinks thinking tomorrow would be a day off.

'In the early morning, I was rudely awakened by phone calls from various friends of the promoter, Liam got a couple of calls, and probably Dolores Keane did as well. Most of us did, except Bill Whelan, who was not really a folkie, as it were. All the phone calls were like, "Andy, the promoter is absolutely heart-broken, the place is sold out, he's asked me to ring you to beg you to reconsider and come down to the gig." Of course, old pros that we are, we shrugged off the hangover, got up, had the breakfast and everybody agreed that we were morally bound to do it, except Bill who was outraged that we had reneged on our decision of the previous night. Mattie rented a plane. Bill refused to go on the plane. He said he didn't go on small planes. He said he would go directly to Glasgow airport, fly to London and would catch a train down to Aldeburgh and that he probably wouldn't be there in time for the first half, but he would be there before the end of the gig. So we said okay. We set off on a little plane piloted by some Australian guy. It was freezing cold. We were all in rags from the night before. Dolores told me that I was sitting there and my whole beard was actually frozen up with ice. Eventually, we got somewhere close to Aldeburgh and got picked up and did the first half of the gig to great acclaim. We extended the interval a little bit hoping Bill would arrive. He didn't.'

'I left the tour because I really felt we were being fucked around,' explains Bill. 'No advertising, nothing done, tiny audiences ... But there's no use in pointing the finger anyway. I just think it was kind of one of those projects that was not going to happen.'

Bill, however, did return to the group to play a very successful concert at the Dominion Theatre in London. Although disorganisation prevailed, Andy firmly believes that on musical terms the tour was a success.

After the UK tour Planxty-Too-Far retreated to Ireland for the final round of live engagements, making a *Late Late Show* appearance and playing some eight shows including the Stadium in Dublin on 27 April. Christy Moore was in attendance. 'They played some beautiful music, but it was no more Planxty than ...'

'We did a tour in Ireland. It was so forgettable that I've actually forgotten it,' states Andy. 'That was the end of Planxty-Too-Far. It's a shame because it was good music. I left on a long tour and travelled to the Balkans two days later and was in contact with Bill by phone once or twice. We had agreed to do more gigs in the autumn. I didn't get back till the middle of June and I found, to my surprise, that the band hadn't exactly split up, it had just fallen asunder. An unfortunate ending to the second coming …'

This was surely, finally, the end. For a band that had achieved so much, it seemed like a somewhat lugubrious way to finish up.

Chapter 18

The Third Coming

Allow me, as author, to introduce this chapter in the first person. In late 2002, while working as a presenter and researcher for the RTÉ Cork music television series *No Disco*, I had the notion of making a one-off programme about Planxty. I had become completely entranced by the band's music in the preceding years – not just Planxty, but the enlivening feel of Irish folk and traditional music from the late 1960s, through the 1970s. The *No Disco* series was rigidly structured around new music videos of a 'left field' persuasion, cut with snippets of interviews and somewhat monotonous studio links. I thought it would be rewarding to adjust the format, try to create something with more narrative, history and depth. Planxty seemed like the perfect subject.

Rory Cobbe, the programme editor, as he was credited, agreed this was a good idea and explained that it would require a lot more time and energy than was normally budgeted for a show in this series. I was lucky to be working with someone receptive to the idea and who was prepared to allow that extra yard of freedom.

For older generations, Planxty was already a fondly celebrated legacy. But for me, the excitement was still fresh, the music roused something in me. There was a definite dichotomy at play, a deep sense of heritage and, at the same time, a strong feeling of something that was new and exciting. At the time, it was over thirty years since Planxty had first come together and over twenty since they last performed publicly, yet the music had maintained its relevance and vitality.

Having spotted some wonderful live footage on Nicholas Carolan's *Come West Along the Road* (a series dedicated to the traditional Irish arts), I set about delving into the RTÉ archive for more Planxty footage. When I started looking, I found there was plenty to be found.

Although it had been over twenty years since they had performed as a group, my hope was that at least one member would be willing to talk on camera. Andy Irvine was the only one I knew at that time. I had met him a couple of years earlier when I invited him to play a guest spot in Whelan's in Dublin on behalf of the American cult songwriter Will Oldham. He seemed like a very affable and talkative character, so my hopes were largely pinned on his contribution.

The only idea I had for contacting Christy Moore was via Bren Berry, a respected booker at Aiken Promotions and the Vicar Street venue who had been personally handling many of Christy's shows in Ireland. Without guaranteeing any results, Bren was happy to help and promised to pass on the request to Christy. Despite Bren's best intentions, I genuinely didn't expect to hear back from him. Christy is a national icon, and was, at the time, slowly easing back into public performance after a long hiatus.

I was therefore completely taken aback to receive a call from him out of the blue. For a moment I paused, convinced it was one of my friends impersonating his familiar voice. But I soon realised it was actually Christy. He was lovely. He told me he watched *No Disco*, which surprised me. He also told me that Planxty music was still very important to him, and he would be happy to help out and contribute to the documentary. He said to contact him whenever I was ready. It was a huge boost.

Andy Irvine, as I had hoped, was also disposed to talking on camera. In fact, he turned out to be quite the historian and one of the most impressive speakers and storytellers in front of the television camera I have ever witnessed. I remember thinking it was a pity all my interviewees weren't as lucid and enlightening. He has a strong sense of gesture when he is talking, which I guess stems from his acting experience. When we first met him, he peered over the rim of his spectacles at us, 'almost like an Edwardian schoolteacher', Rory noted.

Dónal Lunny, it turned out, was living in Japan and not available to talk on camera. Because I was so excited by the results we were having with the other members, I accepted Dónal's unavailability. Later, after getting to know the man and becoming accustomed to his fantastic manner and insight, I regretted this.

Christy gave me Liam O'Flynn's phone number. I met Liam on a sunny and crisp winter's day in St Stephen's Green in Dublin. I remember him standing at the park gates as he inhaled a hearty breath and pronounced something on the lines of, 'Stephen's Green is a wonderful place. It's like the lungs of the city.' I strolled around the park with him, as he chatted about old times. He was very polite and softly spoken. He had an other-worldly aura about him, distant and quiescent.

Myself and Rory shot links at key landmarks from the Planxty history – O'Donoghue's pub on Merrion Row, Dublin; outside Downings house and inside Dowling's pub in Prosperous, County Kildare; at Windmill Lane Studios; and at Madigan's pub in Donnybrook. It was great fun.

I was most nervous about the interview with Christy, as he had caught me off-guard with his response. I bought my first Christy Moore record in 1989, a vinyl copy of *The Voyage*. I wasn't aware of his Planxty history at the time, but he's had a perennial influence on Irish culture right throughout my life. He requested we meet in the Cup O'Coin coffee shop in the Blackrock Market where a lovely man by the name of Denis allowed us to film the interview as his customers came and went. I remember Christy's son Pádraic was present. He told me he was interested in observing and learning about his father from a different perspective. The interview was quite a revelation. Christy spoke with great fondness of the first two years of Planxty, about the excitement of witnessing a generation of people being turned on to this music that connected them with their Irishness, their roots and their heritage.

But Christy didn't hold back from discussing the negative aspects of the business music either. 'If I remember correctly no record companies were interested – Phil Coulter was the first to become interested. He recorded the band and he sold them on. I think the scene we emerged from didn't have any business acumen in it. It was the folk scene, basically. It was the ballad scene. There weren't businesspeople involved in it so we didn't have any knowledge of all that. But, that said, none of the record companies, be they the independents or the nationals or internationals, were interested initially. It was only when Coulter recorded us that they became interested.'

Andy Irvine didn't hesitate in expressing his disappointment with what happened to the band's back catalogue either, particularly the albums sold on to Shanachie Records who reissued them with misspelled song titles and incorrect details on the sleeves.

'The first three albums are owned by Shanachie Records, and they put them out in a really scrubby way with the wrong pictures that were taken later on earlier albums, and misprints ... you know, 'The West Coast of Clare'... c-l-a-i-r-e.'

In the course of the documentary, Christy's opinions became even more explicit. 'Basically, there are things going on with Planxty material that really pisses me off. Anybody who wants to seems to be able to get hold of those old Planxty tracks and put them out on any fucking old crap compilation they want to. And that pisses me off. I don't like that. I don't like arseholes having total access to my work. So certainly that was one lesson that I would've learned.'

Christy explained that the band no longer had any control over their recordings. 'None whatsoever. Phil Coulter sold it to some crowd in America called Shanachie, who I don't know.'

He went on to add, 'I'm glad that people have access to the music. But, y'know, they do real tacky things like the way they reproduce the sleeves and they don't put in the sleeve-notes and they just try and cut corners all the time. And as for where the money goes that's another ... again I'm not lying awake over it. But I suppose if I had the chance to do it all again, the music would stay the same but other bits and pieces I'd do differently.'

Andy had more to add as well. 'I was always the treasurer of Planxty until Paul Brady came into it, but I'm still the person who writes to Shanachie and says, "Listen, you owe us money." It's like trying to draw teeth. But I persist. I get angry. I get furious too. I get furious with record companies because you have to ask them for money, always. They never send you a cheque, as they should, twice a year … not in my experience.'

Andy and Christy's comments took us completely by surprise. This was an aspect of the Planxty story that we really weren't aware of at the time.

We met Phil Coulter at the Helix Theatre, where he was filming as a judge on RTÉ's *You're a Star* music talent show with pop impresario Louis Walsh and former Eurovision Song Contest winner, Linda Martin. We gave him a transcript of the comments that had been made and gave him the opportunity to express his opinions and experiences of working with Planxty on camera.

Coulter emphasised his regard for the Planxty members and the esteem with which he held the music. 'One thing I would like to make very clear, I am immensely proud of what I did with Planxty, and I think that at that time it was something very, very special, and continues to be something very, very special. In point of fact, with my hand on my heart, I would say that I have heard nothing since Planxty that gives me the same excitement. I have nothing that moves the goalposts the way Planxty did. I have heard nothing that has the same dynamic as Planxty, nothing that has the same energy, that same originality, that same fusion of things. I was very proud to be part of it, and I still sign off on it when I look back on my thirty-five years in the music business, that's one of the things that gives me great, great pleasure. And I still play the Planxty albums.

'Now, whatever about the other stuff, that's unfortunate. I don't feel that I have in any way acted in bad faith with Planxty. I still have a huge respect for all of the guys and for their music. And I wouldn't want to be perceived as somebody who exploited that situation, who didn't care about it, or who was cavalier about it. I was none of those things and it's still very important to me.'

He went on to defend his decision to sell the Planxty albums to Shanachie Records. 'Well, in terms of the control and in terms of the fact that Shanachie now own the product, in the early 1990s we were restructuring, I had split with my ex-partner Bill Martin, we were restructuring the company and, in fact, the masters were offered to Christy. It was a situation where it was one of the assets of the company. Shanachie had been asking about acquiring the masters. We offered it to Christy and we couldn't strike a deal because, well, what was offered by the record label was assessed by them and indeed on the basis of royalties etcetera and potential. We couldn't come to a deal but the offer was there. It was maybe a year or so later when the Shanachie deal was signed off on and Shanachie got the control of the albums.

'The reality of the record industry is such that, again, when you go back to the early days of Planxty trying to get the albums released in the United States I can tell you there wasn't a queue of major labels looking for the band. And the one label who got it, the one label who appreciated Planxty, one label who themselves were very keen on the whole acoustic world and world music, they were a couple of guys who had signed The Chieftains and Ladysmith Black Mambazo. These were guys who were doing things in music that no other American record label were doing and they were very keen on Planxty. So we were glad to get a deal, albeit on a small and independent label. No label is perfect. They certainly made mistakes. I wasn't thrilled with some of the artworks and things, etcetera. But you know that's the chance that you take. Every artist, every producer, every songwriter would love to have ultimate control over his product. That's a luxury that very few of us actually ever have.'

In a later interview, Christy was keen to make it known that, despite his misgivings, he wasn't losing any sleep over previous record company dealings. 'On one hand, it's a complete fuck-up, but on the other hand the music is out there. There's a rip-off going on somewhere, but the music is out there. It's still in existence. It's still being sold out there on Grafton Street this morning. There are people buying it, bringing it home, and playing it, so fuckin' great, good work. If I had the choice in my life of having whatever money all these people made out of the band or being able to play the music, I'd much rather be able to play the music. We all have our health. We have this life in music, and I wouldn't swap it with any of them. I certainly wouldn't swap it with Phil Coulter or Shanachie.'

Despite the misgivings expressed by Andy and Christy, the overall mood of the documentary was positive. We were determined that first and foremost this was going to be a celebration of Planxty's music. I think that was achieved through the electrifying footage and the passion with which the musicians spoke of their work. It was also achieved, I suppose in the context of the *No Disco* series, through the thoughts of younger musicians from the fields of rock and experimental music, who expressed their inspiration and admiration for Planxty.

We featured contributions from young Irish songwriters such as David Kitt, Richie Egan from instrumental rock band The Redneck Manifesto and Colm Mac Con Iomaire, fiddler with The Frames. The programme was broadcast on 3 March 2003 and was the subject of much debate and excitement. The feedback was phenomenal, particularly from younger viewers who hadn't previously been aware of Planxty's music. The Planxty members watched the programme themselves and gave us positive feedback, which was thrilling.

One of the big talking points of the programme related to a comment Christy made right at the end regarding the constant speculation of the original line-up regrouping. 'There's nobody longs for it more than myself and the other three guys. Definitely the time is right. Let's go for it,' he proclaimed.

But did the other members really feel this way? Certainly, no one else had said so. Dónal wasn't present. Liam remained 'mysterious' as always. And Andy expressed an interest in remixing or re-recording the first three albums, but revealed little else about a reformation.

The elusive Planxty reunion had been a key talking point of the Irish folk world for many years. 'We all met in Christy's house seven or eight years ago,' recalls Liam. 'We all sat down and had a play. But it just wasn't the time. It's hard to say why. It could be a combination of all sorts of things. I suppose it would be to do with what was going on in people's lives at that time.'

Nonetheless, they have come tantalisingly close on a few occasions. At an Andy Irvine gig in Whelan's in Dublin some years ago, he was joined onstage by Christy Moore and Dónal Lunny as surprise guests. The rumour at the time was that Liam O'Flynn was stranded on one of the Aran Islands and unable to complete the Planxty line-up, but Liam confirms that that wasn't the case at all. 'I certainly wasn't on the Aran Islands or any other feckin' island. I was at home. It was sort of like "if you feel like coming along, or if you don't…". I remember thinking this was something that could be great on the surface, but the more I thought about it I realised it could be fuckin' awful. It could be a terrible disaster. It could've been an awful jumble and a mess, and I certainly didn't want that to happen. I knew that Dónal and Andy and Christy would know plenty of stuff they could do together. That could happen fine between the three of them. But once you get the fourth in you're into Planxty and that's something else altogether.'

On 1 July 2002, Christy Moore played a low-key show at Whelan's, accompanied by Dónal Lunny. Liam O'Flynn joined them for the final third of the set and raised the roof, but there was no Andy Irvine in sight.

In October 2001, during his twenty-three-night stint at the Vicar Street venue in Dublin, Paul Brady assembled what he calls the Liberty Belles for six of the nights. It's a group that features himself, Andy Irvine, Dónal Lunny, Liam O'Flynn, Noel Hill and Paddy Glackin. He was revisiting a 1978 concert with the same line-up, the recording of which had recently surfaced and was released as *The Liberty Tapes*. Still, though, it wasn't Planxty by any means.

After revealing his aspirations for a Planxty get-together on *No Disco*, I questioned Christy further on the matter. 'For me it hasn't come to an end,' he said. 'We may not have played for twenty years, but it hasn't come to an end. And it won't as long as we're around. Even though we don't get up on stage and do it and we don't record, we're still living it, really. When we get together we just sit down and fall straight back into it. The hilarity sets in. We're all still playing. We're all still recording. We're all still doing it. We're very much alive.'

A mysterious postcard from Christy Moore arrived for me on Tuesday, 7 October 2003. It had a list of names and phone numbers, good people to talk to regarding the Planxty biography. It also read: 'There might be something of interest happening on Saturday. I'll be in touch.'

The Royal Spa is owned by Paddy Doherty, one of the founders of the Lisdoonvarna Festival and who was also now looking after Christy's own live bookings. The venue has a great reputation on the traditional and folk music circuit. This place is very much all about the music. It was here that Liam, Andy, Christy and Dónal finally got down to the business of playing together again and they were doing so in private, testing the water, so to speak. 'We have an old dining room in the hotel that

I set up for them to rehearse in,' explains Paddy. 'I remember going in there and hearing those tunes coming back together and it was unbelievable to be there and experience that for the first time after all those years.'

There were no guarantees or commitments going into these rehearsals, but they instantly clicked and within days a poster advertising The Mugs Gig and the names Andy Irvine, Dónal Lunny, Christy Moore and Liam O'Flynn was tacked to the door of The Royal Spa. Could it be that the long-awaited re-emergence of Planxty was about to happen? It may have been twenty years since they last played together but, once these four gentlemen began playing, the Planxty magic crystallised once again.

Just over 200 lucky people crammed into The Royal Spa on Saturday, 11 October. It was a night of high emotion, hilarious banter and soaring music. Christy mentioned onstage that the band had watched the programme we made and that had given them the push to finally get back together. To have some sort of inclusion or recognition in this process was truly one of the highlights of my life. To be sitting five or six rows away from the stage, watching my heroes and soaking up this glorious, singular sound was mind-blowing. And without getting too flowery in relaying the experience, let's just say there were tears.

There were very few differences from the footage we had pored over on the programme and the Planxty of 2003. The band were all seated this time around, understandably. There was less hair on show, also understandably. And Christy played keyboards on a number of songs – with pleasant results. Other than that, it was everything you could dream for; rolling, tumbling, swerving, jubilant music, strings galore, thumping drums, walloping voices, whispering ballads, a whistle from heaven, elbows and arms and fingers, and drones and chanters and jigs and reels and jokes galore.

After the show, I was almost too overwhelmed to even speak to any of the band. I did say hello to Dónal Lunny for the first time ever that night as he made his way over to a corner of the pub to tap up an aul fella who he said had a huge repertoire of tunes. To see a musician of his stature still so excited to pick up new tunes and to revel in the company of elderly players was amazing to see. Christy was in conference with the writer and producer P.J. Curtis. Andy and Liam were mingling amongst the audience who had heard about this surreptitious gathering strictly by word of mouth.

I retired to my bed as the music raged on.

'If ever there was a band to get back together, this was the one,' Paddy Doherty told me afterwards. 'When they decided to come to my place in Lisdoonvarna to rehearse, I remember the first day they arrived down. During the early meetings there was no plan to do any gigs. It was a case of coming down to Lisdoonvarna and rehearse for a week and maybe do a little gig at the end of it. I think whatever was going to happen in the future hung on that week.'

Andy, Dónal, Christy and Liam all obviously felt the week went well because, not long after the Lisdoonvarna gig, Planxty announced a series of concerts in Dublin and Clare beginning with two at the Glór venue in Ennis and six at the excellent Vicar Street venue in Dublin in January and February 2004.

It was a huge announcement. Liam O'Flynn appeared on the news. It was a national event. Tickets disappeared in days and before long Aiken Promotions added another batch of dates at Vicar Street to the schedule – twelve concerts in total. The Ennis concerts were special, as they drew many fellow musicians, doyens of the traditional world, the sort of audience that recognised a good thing was happening. The shows sold out fast. Coffee and donuts was served to those queuing for tickets in the

cold air outside Glór. The concerts were beautiful. Des Kelly and
his wife attended one and the band paid a fitting tribute to an old
friend. Christy told the story of their former manager's rejected
showband suits and giggles rippled the venue. Observing the
sound check the following day, it was fascinating to see how
Planxty ironed out the glitches of the previous night with careful
rehearsal and intelligent communication. Dónal revelled in the
role as problem solver.

Paddy Doherty had now come on board as the band's official
manager. Paddy's presence ensured that each and every one of
these planned performances would go off with maximum
musical impact. The crew was mostly the same crew of
technicians and engineers that look after Christy's own concerts,
including Dikon Whitehead, Davy Meade, Johnny Meade, Geoff
Ryan and Christy's trusted tour manager, Mick Devine, who will
personally transport the band to and from the shows. The venues
had to be perfect, the sound pristine.

Peter Aiken of Aiken Promotions initially suggested the band
play The Point, but Planxty felt more comfortable at Vicar Street,
a venue renowned for its perfect balance of space and intimacy.
'We agreed to do a certain number of shows,' explains Peter. 'We
played it very cautious. The boys were very realistic in the way
that they'd do a couple of shows and if the demand is there
they'll do a few more. We put it out, and as everybody knows, we
put it out low-key. But it went massive. The number of enquiries
we received from overseas was incredible. The media interest in
Europe was massive. So what started out as what I thought
would be quite a straightforward thing rollercoastered into a
massive undertaking. And very enjoyable it was too.'

Bren Berry, the man who books Vicar Street for Aiken
Promotions, was ecstatic to be working with Planxty. Berry had
already built a strong working relationship with Christy and

booking Planxty for him was a sensation akin to booking The Beatles. 'Rumblings of a Planxty reunion started up as a result of the documentary and Christy kept me in the loop regarding rehearsals,' says Berry. 'This was like having inside knowledge on the Secrets of Fatima! Here was the band that we all wanted to see but never quite believed it would happen. It was a first chance for many of us devotees who were not there the first time and a dream come true for those who were.

'The rehearsals at Vicar Street leading up to the shows were so exciting for me. To hear, for the first time, four masters, the legendary Planxty, start to play live in the venue that I booked was just spine-tingling and I have to admit I had my mobile phone on for a few mates to hear it.'

People from all over the country and from all over the world travelled to Ireland for these concerts. Many of them brought albums, photographs and precious old posters from the 1970s to be autographed. Other people brought their children and their grandchildren, uniting several generations in appreciation of this timeless music. Christy, Andy, Dónal and Liam mingled back-stage with old friends and family. It was the first opportunity for their own children to see playing Planxty live and, for that reason alone, this was a thrilling experience for them.

The set they chose was well considered. The emphasis was largely on compositions from the first two records. The 'Raggle Taggle Gypsy'/'Tabhair Dom Do Lámh' segue was a huge hit, as always. It was thrilling for people of my generation and younger to finally witness that fantastic bridge from song to tune and to be part of the roar that heralds it in. 'Sí Bheag Sí Mhór' was breathtaking. To hear something so delicate, something you've only ever known as a frozen recording, to hear it live was a moment. 'Arthur McBride' turned out to be the raucous singa-long I had always imagined it to be and 'The West Coast of

Clare' sent audiences into sad, nostalgic contemplation. It was amazing to observe the effects of music so potent and hypnotising, how they could switch mood from raucous celebration to perfect solemn reflection.

'The Blacksmith', with its extended 'Blacksmithereens' outro, was another showstopper, as exhilarating and intense and climaxing as any rock band. On 'Little Musgrave', Liam's pipes act as a sort of instrumental narrative to the twenty-something verses. Almost every night, Liam commented in reference to Christy, 'I think that's what you call a man on form.' He wasn't wrong either. Christy's diction is outstanding on this long and difficult epic.

There were new additions too. The opening instrumental 'The Starting Gate' is a reworking of a set of reels from *The Woman I Loved So Well* album, but this was better, more delicate, beginning with Sean Ryan's 'The Glens of Aherlow' on an elegant solo whistle intro. Liam's choice of 'An Buachaill Caol Dubh' as the customary slow air solo piece proved to be an awesome showcase of his piping ability, as he shaped notes and drones and chords into a deep, sombre tapestry of sound and each night a thousand or so people stared at the stage with pin-drop concentration. Translated into English, the title means 'Dark Slender Boy', and, of course, Liam explained how speculation of this title has often suggested the dark, slender boy to be a bottle of stout.

On other nights, though, his slow air was 'The Death of Staker Wallace', named after Patrick Wallace, a member of the United Irishmen who was tortured and executed for his part in the 1798 Rebellion. Wallace's head was placed on a stake outside the Kilfinnane Gaol in Limerick, hence the title of the slow air. 'A grim tale, but a lovely tune!' commented Liam.

For his jigs Liam chose to play 'The Clare Jig'/'Nora Críona', never recorded on any Planxty album, but interestingly featuring both Christy and Dónal on bodhrán in what Liam jokingly described as a bodhrán sandwich – 'Quite a reassuring place to be!' he said one night.

'My Heart's Tonight Ireland' is a song written by Andy Irvine from his *Rain on the Roof* album. It sounded spectacular with the Planxty arrangement. It's also a lovely poem to days of Sweeney's Men and trips to Miltown Malbay to worship at the feet of Willie Clancy. The others members of the band seemed to revel in this articulation of Andy's tender memoirs.

Everyone flocked to these shows; musicians, politicians, painters, journalists, writers, figureheads of the tradition, teenagers, pensioners... This wasn't just about music. It was about finding a commonality. It was about us all feeling like family, for once. It was about life. About finding something timeless amidst all the stress and noise and danger of the world outside.

Broadcaster John Kelly was one of the people feeling the love at Vicar Street. 'It was hard to describe how I felt that night. It wasn't just like, "Oh this is Planxty. Finally I've seen Planxty." It wasn't that. It was more like everything's all right with the world. Everything was in its place. It happens occasionally with exceptional musicians. I would get that feeling more so with jazz. The music does what the music was capable of doing. And there are no questions in your head.

'Timeless is the right word. They just started and I thought, "This is it! This is the thing." And for me they just wiped out everything that has happened in the intervening years. There are a whole lot more bands around now and a lot more music available, loads of groups and loads of CDs, but none of them mean much to me, to be quite honest. I remember saying to Liam years ago, "If you guys got back together you'd just blow everybody out of the water." And he more or less said, "Aye, I know." I suppose since the moment they broke up they've been watching to see who would take over the mantle, but nobody has. I find a lot of the contemporary groups, good and all as they are, I'm still thinking, "Yeah, but not as good as Planxty, not as good as The Bothy Band.'"

Every night at these concerts, Christy would explain why the band finally decided to get back together, commenting on the impact of the *No Disco* programme. One night, he joked that the band watched the show and thought they better get back together before they're dead. It's typical of Christy's generosity to make these comments.

'Planxty 2004 would have not have happened without your programme,' he said to me at a later date. 'I know it wouldn't. It took for me to sit down and see Andy talking about the band and to see Liam talking about the band. And all the other people you chose, The Frames and David Kitt and those other kids … to hear them talking about it – fuckin' hell that was great. That's really encouraging for us.'

Planxty recorded each night at Vicar Street and Glór and compiled an album of the best recordings entitled *Planxty Live 2004.* It was released by Sony and sat at the number one spot in the album charts for many weeks in Ireland. The band also invited an old comrade of theirs, Philip King, to film a number of the Vicar Street concerts. He captured some beautiful live footage with insightful close-ups of the musicians, their virtu-osity and concentration but also their nods, winks and gestures and incredible musical telepathy. The DVD also features interviews with the four band members and various commentators throw in their tuppenceworth too. But the real gold is the live performances and hilarious and educational on-stage introductions that teeter on collapsing into uncontrollable laughter.

It also features some lovely extras, including Liam and Dónal's impromptu whistle and guitar combination on 'Sean O'Duibhir a' Ghleanna' that they had literally worked out back-stage before one show in Vicar Street. The DVD became a must-have item for the thousands of people who attended these milestone concerts and also for the unlucky ones who didn't get a ticket. It seemed to be glued to the number one spot in the DVD charts for months on end.

For producer Philip King, who claims you can mark his life out as Planxty-referenced segments, the DVD was another massive achievement. 'The filming was on and off and on. I was talking to Christy and talking to Dónal. And they didn't really know. It might be too much pressure. I was sort of saying, "If we never even put it out, just do it, run a camera over it. Just do it, just make a document of it." But then, eventually, I suppose because we have a good trusting relationship, it happened.

'I remember going to Lisdoon to the hotel and walking into the room and Christy giving me a big hug and just saying, "There we are, part of the team." It was such a privilege for me after all of those years and having known them all in different guises and different ways all of my life. It was like coming home thirty, thirty-two years later. And, you know, we were all still alive. It was a very life-affirming experience. Everybody in that room had been through terrible turmoil. Life goes on. It's funny, the effect of being in the room, as that rehearsal started that afternoon, my whole life flashed before me. It was like the split second that I heard them play in Cork in 1972.

'Also it was something about going back to that original line-up, where they sat next to each other, the way that looked, the body language, the eye contact, it was like swimming, like riding a bike. It was a hugely emotional, powerful experience. At times of doubt in your life, about its value, about the work that you do, it was life affirming to see these four giant musicians sit together in that one room, with the gravity and the power that they had, but also with that ability to laugh at themselves and kick it all up in the air.'

For those who missed the Planxty concerts in Glór and Vicar Street and weren't content with just a DVD, there was more good news. Another round of concerts were announced for late 2004 and early 2005 in Galway, Belfast, Dublin and London. Never part of the original plan, this second round of concerts took in all-new venues and some set variations as well. It began with a three-night stand at the Radisson SAS Hotel in Galway on 6, 7 and 8 October. Johnny Divilly, Planxty's beloved road manager in the 1970s, was present in the audience and received the guest of honour treatment.

There were plenty of new additions to the set too. They played a variation of the *Cold Blow and the Rainy Night* polkas featuring Johnny Moynihan's '£42 Cheque', which was a personal highlight as I had begged them on several occasions to dust off this set. At the Vicar Street concerts, several people shouted for 'Sweet Thames Flow Softly' from *The Black Album*, but it wasn't ready at that point. Now, it sounded lovelier than ever. Christy brought his own song to the table too, 'St Brendan's Voyage' from his *Ordinary Man* album in 1985, a song with great singalong-ability. Andy had penned a brand-new song, which also fitted right into the Planxty mindset – 'O'Donoghue's Song', through which Andy relived the early days of Dublin's folk boom. It's a loving portrait full of witty detail, and it went down a bomb with the audiences.

Another new aspect of the Planxty concert introduced in Galway was the visual backdrop behind the musicians. Tastefully lit photographs were projected onto the back curtain by a music-visual specialist brought in from England. Although it did enhance the atmosphere of these concerts, it was agreed afterwards by the band that the pacing of these projections required a little more fine tuning.

The first three Dublin shows took place on the 28, 29 and 30 of December at The Point Theatre. It was certainly a challenge for an acoustic group to produce a live show in this big, empty space. 'We went to The Point, Christy and myself,' explains Paddy Doherty. 'There wasn't any seating in the venue and we were looking around thinking we've got our work cut out for us. We had to sit down and think and plan the best way this was going to work for the band and for the audience and make it as intimate as we possibly can.'

They employed a tiered-seating arrangement and found a lovely clarity for their music in The Point's vast acoustics. The visuals brought a nice focus to the stage, but really Planxty didn't need any enhancement. They were spellbinding on the big stage. The next two concerts happened on 3 and 4 January 2005. More famous names stopped by, from President Mary McAleese to soccer star Damien Duff, who was later approached backstage by a star-struck Andy Irvine!

Later in January, they revisited Belfast for the first time in many years and the three shows at the Waterfront Hall, on 19, 20 and 21 January, were emotionally charged and rapturously received. These concerts in Dublin and Belfast marked something significant for promoters Jim and his son, Peter Aiken. Peter was just fifteen years old when Planxty played the Carlton Cinema on O'Connell Street. 'I remember being in boarding school and every teacher in the school wanted tickets for it. It was a big thing at boarding school. It was either Planxty or Rory Gallagher. I was much more into Rory Gallagher. Planxty back then was something my teacher liked, which meant it was something I didn't like. But when I saw them in the Carlton Cinema with 2,000 people sitting on those big red seats, I thought they were fantastic.'

Those nights in Vicar Street, The Waterfront and The Point must have brought back many vivid memories for Jim Aiken,

who had booked numerous important concerts for Planxty
through the years. 'Everything was in segmented boxes in those
days – folk music, country, rock music, whatever,' explains the
Belfast-born promoter. 'People of one genre didn't go into
another. But Planxty were accepted by everyone. One of the first
concerts I put in the Carlton was Planxty. And it was such a
success we booked them in again three weeks later with another
concert. That was phenomenal in those days. Nobody had ever
done this before. I did well on them. The deals I had with them
then have stood to me now. The memory of how they were
treated and how they worked with me has stood to us. One of the
great nights in my life was standing in The Point, seeing it all
happening again and thinking about what had happened in
between, and what had happened to the members of the band.'

The final three Planxty concerts were booked by the well-
known music agent Paul Charles and staged at The Barbican in
London to 6,000 fans at the end of January. The concerts were
resounding successes. The audiences were made up of Irish
music lovers living abroad, people connected with the English
folk scene and, once again, a younger generation of curious
young listeners. As with the previous series of concerts in
Ireland, Christy's brother Luka Bloom travelled to London with
the band to play the opening set at the shows.

Luka played his first professional paid gig opening for Planxty
in Galway when he was sixteen years old. Back then, Planxty
were his saviours. 'I was born in 1955. I was too old to be a punk,
too young to be a hippie. What I got was Planxty, ample
compensation. Planxty were Ireland's Beatles. I was writing my
own songs, and Planxty gave me the sense that it was okay to
change things, to take chances with songs.'

It must have been like déjà vu to be back opening for them
again in 2005. 'Seeing them in Vicar Street was very emotional.

I thought they were better than when I heard them in the 1970s and I didn't expect that. Being their guest again was great.'

Some twenty-seven concerts took place from October 2003 to January 2005. For a band that had endured so many obstacles throughout their career, it was rewarding to see them treated like kings.

With these concerts, Planxty not only reconnected with their original audience, they sealed a bond with a whole new generation. If there was ever a danger of Planxty's music being forgotten, these concerts well and truly refreshed them for the twenty-first century.

'To this day,' says Liam O'Flynn, 'when I'm on tour people continually come up and say that it was through Planxty that they were first introduced to Irish traditional music. Or that their first contact with uilleann pipes was through Planxty and it changed their life. To me, that's fantastic. That's the greatest reward any musician can be given, to actually make that sort of impact on people and to hear the music is still alive and to know people are still going back to listen to those albums and finding inspiration.'

All four musicians remain in love with music today. Andy Irvine continues to roam the world for new adventures, performing solo or with his old friends in Patrick Street, or with Dónal Lunny in their international acoustic group, Mozaik. Dónal lives in Japan with his family. He continues to produce, score and arrange music and regularly returns to Ireland to work with our finest musicians.

Whether it's the Liverpool Philharmonic, the Hamburg Laeiszhalle, six nights in The Point Theatre or a one-off in DeBarra's folk club in Clonakilty, Christy Moore plays when the time is right and the feeling is good. His thriving collaboration with guitarist Declan Sinnott is captured in fine style on the recent *Burning Times* album. Liam O'Flynn holds proud his role as Ireland's master piper. He continues to explore his relationship with the mysterious instrument, whether it's in the company of presidents and nobility, in collaboration with Nobel Laureate Seamus Heaney, alongside symphony orchestras or amongst friends at a private session.

Whether these four musicians ever perform together again as Planxty will continue to be the perennial point of speculation. Yet, even if it doesn't happen, Planxty music will always exist and Planxty music will be passed on like the cultural bequest that it truly is.

Discography

Date	Title
1972	'The Drunken Maidens'
1972	'The Cliffs of Dooneen'/'Yarmouth Town'
1973	*Planxty Black Album* Ire/Eng/Ger/Fra
1973	*Planxty Black Album*
1973	*The Well Below the Valley* Ire/Eng/Ger/Fra
1973	*The Well Below the Valley*
1973	*The Well Below the Valley*
1973	*Planxty and JSD Band Festival Pop Celtique*
1973	Various artists: *Festival Pop Celtic Kerat France*
1974	*Cold Blow and the Rainy Night* Ire/Eng/Ger/Fra
1974	*Cold Blow and the Rainy Night*
1974	*Planxty Collection*
1976	*Planxty Black Album*
1976	Various artists: *The Best of Irish Folk*
1977	Various artists: *A Feast of Irish Folk*
1977	Various artists: 'A Feast of Irish Folk'
1977	Various artists: *A Feast of Irish Folk*
1977	Various artists: *Irish Traditional Favourites*
1978	Various artists: *The Irish Collection Vol 1*
1978	Various artists: *The Irish Collection Vol 2*

Company Reference	Format
Ruby 152	7" single
Polydor 2078-023	7" single
Polydor 2383-186	LP
Polydor 8-track cartridge 3820092	8-track tape
Polydor 2389232	LP
Polydor 2383232	LP
Polydor 8-track cartridge 3820093	8-track tape
Polydor 2488271	2 LPs
Barcay 920452753	2 LPs
Polydor 2383301	LP
Polydor 8-track cartridge 3820127	8-track tape
Polydor 2383392	LP
Can Amber ARB301	LP
EMI/STAL 1047	LP
AMC Release 197900	LP
Polydor Sampler Promo	7" single
Polydor 2475605	LP
EMI/STAL 1053	LP
Polydor 3188112	LP
Polydor 3188113	LP

Date	Title
1979	*After the Break*
1979	Various artists: *Nyon Folk Festival Switzerland*
1980	*The Woman I Loved So Well*
1980	*The Best of Planxty Live*
1980	Various artists: *The Best of Irish Folk*
1980	Various artists: *High Kings of Tara*
1980	Various artists: *Another Feast of Folk*
1980	Various artists: 'Another Feast of Folk'
1981	'Timedance/Nancy Spain'
1981	'Timedance/Nancy Spain'
1981	'Timedance/DJ version'
1981	Various artists: *Double Bill: All the Folk that Fits*
1981	*Christy Moore and Friends*
1983	*Words & Music*
1983	*Words & Music* – Canada
1983	'I Pity the Poor Immigrant/The Irish March'
1984	*ARIS*
1985	Various artists: *The Irish Collection*
1985	Various artists: *The Irish Folk Festival*
1987	Various artists: *Songs from the Emerald Isle*
1988	Various artists: *Easy Riding: A Feast of Irish Folk*
1988	Various artists: *Songs from the Emerald Isle*

Company Reference	Format
Tara 3001	LP
Paleo Gado 7910792	2 LPs
Tara 3005	LP
Planx 001	2 cassettes
Peters International PLD 20059	LP
Tara 3003	LP
Polydor 2904016	LP
Polydor Sampler Promo	7" single
WEA IR 28207	12" single
WEA IR 18711	7" single
WEA IR 18711	7" single
Polydor 2668026	2 LPs
RTE 59	LP
WEA 240101-1	LP
WEA Promo	LP
WEA Plan 001	7" single
Polydor 815229-1	LP
Tara 2014	Cassette
Sound 418137	2 LPs
EMI DL1104	2 LPs
Night Roc 11009	Cassette
EMI CDB7906562	CD

Date	Title
1989	*Planxty Black Album*
1989	*The Well Below the Valley*
1989	*Cold Blow and the Rainy Night*
1989	*The Planxty Collection*
1989	*Words & Music*
1994	Various artists: *Celtic Grace: The Best of Ireland*
1994	Various artists: *Planete Celtque*
1995	Various artists: *Guinness Celeba*
1997	Various artists: *Irish Ceile Reels and Jigs*
1997	Various artists: *Totally Irish: The Essential Irish Album*
1997	Various artists: *A Celtic Tapestry*
1997	Various artists: *Rare Oul Times*
1998	Various artists: *The Greatest Irish Pub Music*
1998	Various artists: *Celtic Evolution: Beyond the Tradition*
1998	Various artists: *Legends of Ireland*
1998	Various artists: *Celtic Love Songs*
1999	Various artists: *Thousands are Sailing*
2000	Various artists: *The Definitive Irish Folk Collection Vol 1*
2000	Various artists: *The Definitive Irish Folk Collection Vol 2*
2000	Various artists: *The Songs of Ireland Collection*
2000	Various artists: *Journey: The Best of Dónal Lunny*
2001	Various artists: *Artsta Mondo Celtic*
2001	Various artists: *The Greatest Irish Collection*

Company Reference	Format
Shanachic 79009	LP
Shanachic 79010	LP
Shanachic 79011	LP
Shanachic 79012	LP
Shanachic 79055	LP
EMI 8312162	CD
Actual 5050392	CD
GIN 5625	CD
EMI 85670329	CD
EMI 5668524	CD
Shanachic 78006	CD
RARE 1	CD
ARS Production 7404362	CD
SDVSOP 253	CD
RHINO R27202	CD
Shanachic 78016	CD
Shanachic 78025	CD
Promo 001	2 CDs
Sony Folk CD1	2 CDs
HMV 724352589524	CD
Hummingbird HBCD0024	2 CDs
Mondo Melodia 186850038 2	CD
HMV 724353541828	4 CDs

Date	Title
2002	Various artists: *The Definitive Irish Folk Collection Vol 2*
2002	Various artists: *The Definitive Irish Folk Collection Vol 2*
2003	Various artists: *The Gold of Ireland*
2003	Dónal Lunny: *Definitive Lisdoonvarna*
2004	*Christy Moore Box Set 1964–2004*
2004	*Planxty Live 2004*
2004	*Planxty Live 2004 DVD*
2004	Various artists: *The Very Best of Celtic*
2004	Various artists: *The Definitive Irish Collection Rare Aul Songs*
2005	Various artists: *BBC Radio 2 Folk Awards 2005*
2006	Various artists: *Come West Along the Road*

Company Reference	Format
Promo 002	2 CDs
Sony 5100932	2 CDs
RetroR2CD4248	2 CDs
Warner 505046671792	2 CDs
Sony 5148162	6 CDs
Sony 5173912	CD
Sony 210255349	DVD
NASCENTS NSCD2013	2 CDs
EMI CDROSI	2 CDs
ProPetFolk 01	2 CDs
RTÉ	DVD

Acknowledgements

Christy Moore, Andy Irvine, Liam O'Flynn and Dónal Lunny – thank you for the music, the insight, and the inspiration.

Thank you Leah Henry for your love and companionship and for reading this book over and over and over again.

Thank you Breda Purdue, Claire Rourke, Ciara Considine and all at Hodder Headline Ireland and UK for your patience and enthusiasm.

Special thanks to Paddy Doherty for his kind assistance.

For sharing their thoughts and memoirs, I would like to thank the extended Planxty players: Johnny Moynihan, Bill Whelan, Paul Brady, Johnny Divilly, Nollaig Casey, Noel Hill, Tony Linnane, Des Kelly and Kevin Flynn.

One of the highlights of writing of this book was experiencing first hand the goodwill so many people have for Planxty.

Kieran Kelly painstakingly compiled the Planxty discography and allowed so many precious artefacts to leave his secret treasure trove.

Marcus Connaughton didn't hesitate in handing over a bundle of memories. Kieron Seamons sent photos and best wishes direct from China. Kate Ackers filled some vital gaps.

John Coffey arrived early one morning at Athy train station with a disc full of gold. He saved the day.

For sharing their thoughts and experiences, I would like to express my gratitude to: Frank Lunny, Mick Hanly, Bren Berry, Peter Aiken, Jim Aiken, Luka Bloom, Brian Masterson, Clodagh Simmonds, Bill Leader, Grant Ryder, Pat Musick, Davoc and Anne Rynne, Dr Andrew Rynne, Mickey MacConnell, John Kelly, Philip King and all @ Hummingbird Productions, John Cook.

The genesis of this project was a TV documentary for the *No Disco* (RIP) series for RTÉ. Massive thanks to Rory Cobbe, Paul O'Flynn, Aoife O'Callaghan, Colm Crowley and all at RTÉ Cork and the RTÉ Library Archive. Love and thanks to Mary and Sadie.

For either practical or emotional support, I would like to thank the following people: Mick Devine, Cian Burke, Jim Carroll, Turlough Rynne, Niall Rynne, Barry Brophy, Colette O'Toole, Alan Kelly, John Cowhie, Gerry and Craig @ City Discs in Dublin, Tom Dunne, Ed Smith, Donal Dineen, Tom Hardy @ Today FM, *Foggy Notions* crew, the Henrys of Polranny, Eamon Sweeney, John Hennessy, Fachtna O'Kelly, Paul Murray, Brian Lynch, Stuart Slater, Con Collins, Albert Depetrillo, Brian O'Connell, Frank Gleeson and all @ Whelan's in Dublin, Gráinne Coffey, Pat Neary, Aine Carmody, Mac @ George's Street Arcade/Final Vinyl, Katie Verling and all @ Glór in Ennis, Gerry Quinn, Colin Harper, Sheila Reilly, Jane O'Flynn, Denis @ Cup O'Coin café in Blackrock Market, *The Clare People*, P.J. Curtis for writing *Notes from the Heart,* Terry Moylan @ Na Piobairí Uilleann, all @ Vicar Street in Dublin, Chris Doherty and all @ The Royal Spa Hotel in Lisdoonvarna, Julia Buethe, Richie Egan, David Kitt and all of Planxty's families.

Text from *The Vasectomy Doctor: A Memoir* by Andrew Rynne was reproduced with kind permission of the author.